Development and Taxation

Parthasarathi Shome is Chairman, International Tax Research and Analysis Foundation (ITRAF), Bengaluru. Prior to that he was Adviser (Minister of State) to the Indian Finance Minister, and Chief Economist, Her Majesty's Revenue and Customs (HMRC), United Kingdom. Earlier he was Chief of Tax Policy, International Monetary Fund (IMF), and Professor of Economics, The American University, Washington DC. He received the highest civilian honour of the Brazilian Government, *Commander of the Order of the Southern Cross*, and the Jeanne S. Mattersdorf Award of the National Tax Association of America as "an outstanding student in the field of taxation and public finance" for his Ph.D. thesis from Southern Methodist University.

Development and Taxation

60 Critical Commentaries

Parthasarathi Shome

ACADEMIC FOUNDATION
NEW DELHI

www.academicfoundation.org

First published in 2017
by

ACADEMIC FOUNDATION
4772-73 / 23 Bharat Ram Road, (23 Ansari Road),
Darya Ganj, New Delhi - 110 002 (India).
Phones : 23245001 / 02 / 03 / 04.
Fax : +91-11-23245005.
E-mail : books@academicfoundation.com
www.academicfoundation.org

Cataloging in Publication Data--DK
Courtesy: D.K. Agencies (P) Ltd. <docinfo@dkagencies.com>

Shome, Parthasarathi, 1950- **author.**
Development and taxation: 60 critical commentaries / Parthasarathi Shome.
pages cm
ISBN 9789332703889

1. Fiscal policy--India. 2. Taxation--India. 3. India--Foreign economic relations. 4. India--Economic policy--1991- 5. India--Social policy. 6. Macroeconomics. I. Title. II. Title: Sixty critical commentaries on development and taxation.

HJ1335.S56 2017 DDC 336.54 23

Typeset, printed and bound by The Book Mint, New Delhi.
www.thebookmint.in

In Loving Memory of Niharika Guha

Niharika Guha

Niharika Guha with grandson Parthasarathi Shome.

Niharika Guha with husband Pashupati Nath Guha and daughter Dipti Guha Shome.

CONTENTS

III
Taxation Matters

IV
Income Tax

V
Indirect Tax

VI
International Economic Relations

VII
Socio-economic Policy

VIII
Political Economy

IX
Newest Concerns

LIST OF TABLES AND FIGURES

TABLES

FIGURES

Preface

I have been writing in *Business Standard* for almost two decades. The first group of articles was written around 2000 and then resumed a decade later, a habit that has since endured mainly reflecting the unwavering encouragement of Mr Ashok Bhattacharya, prior editor. He also urged me to put the articles together in the form of a volume and Dr Uma Kapila of Academic Foundation readily agreed with its publication. Accordingly I gathered and brought together articles from the second period. This volume is the outcome of those efforts. As is my approach to analysis, I use a mix of verbal and graphical tools to make a point as and where needed.

The articles that I have attempted over time represent various thoughts that crossed my mind as economic, political economy and social challenges appeared on the domestic and international scene. They comprise reflection, analysis, conclusions, and recommendations on a wide variety of those issues. They pertain to international and domestic economic developments.

The articles address macroeconomic concerns including the estimation of GDP (gross domestic product), savings and growth, inflation and interest rates, financial markets, land acquisition, and others. They take up fiscal policy and India's Union budget experience over several budgets. They address taxation matters in some detail—both income tax and indirect tax—and, equally importantly, tax evasion and corruption. A topic that is considered on several occasions is the design and application of the GST (Goods and Services Tax). Corporate income tax rates, incentives and a minimum corporate tax and their interplay and impact on one another are also analysed in some detail. Finally, the low quality of tax statistics emanating from India's income tax department is critiqued through an analysis of those statistics.

The articles analyse and comment on emerging international economic relations across the globe. They consider issues from the United Kingdom's leaving the European Union and its ramifications on Indo-UK trade. They cover India's economic and strategic relations with Japan, China, Latin America, and, last but not least, with Pakistan. They touch upon the Euro Zone and journeying through parts of it such as traversing Italy, and also address issues emerging from global platforms such as the Group of 20 Nations (G20).

The articles also address India's deep challenges and failures in designing and implementing a range of socio-economic policies. Health and palliative care are taken up and an assessment made of their virtual lack of existence and failure of implementation. The matter of cleaning up India through the "Swachh Bharat" programme is critiqued by using statistical illustrations from the occurrence of open defecation in India contrasted to other even poorer countries, deterioration in the quality of the Indian Railways, and the stark reality of the failure to educate Indian youth thus vitiating the reaping of any demographic dividend, among other glaring gaps in the provision of socio-economic public services.

The volume concludes with a selection of essays with a political economy orientation including a socio-historical perspective on Brexit reflecting UK's domestic societal dynamics and the internal societal differences that could have led to sub-optimal outcomes for that society, how, more broadly, modern democracies suffer their own vicissitudes with few lessons to convey to younger democracies such as India, and how cities—London and Kolkata—or states—West Bengal and Tamil Nadu—tend to compare with one another when examined with fine toothcomb. Finally, the volume concludes on a philosophical note—that thoughts can comprise ideas, thus summing up, as it were, the overall stance in the narrative of the included articles.

However, new issues and concerns emerge every day and, even as this volume went to press, I added, and the publishers graciously included, two final essays on India's latest adventure on the demonitisation of its currency, and on India's failing struggle to improve on the ease of doing business in comparison to a cross-section of countries. Perhaps unsurprisingly, the constraints to the present Prime Minister's "Make in India" policy and in making it easier to conduct business in India get mentioned in both the first and the last commentaries featured in this volume.

Thus when considered together, the volume offers a variety of writings that should interest a wide readership. I appreciate the ready willingness of readers of my articles whom I requested to give their views for the cover of the book, to immediately respond. They represent a broad spectrum of professionals comprising economist, newspaper columnist, television anchor, tax administrator and academic, and are prolific authors themselves.

Among those I should mention with thanks are Ashok Bhattacharya, ex-Editor, and Shyamal Majumdar, present Editor, of *Business Standard*, for their support. Karan Singh, Rohitash Chaudhary, Tarique Khan and Kishore Parghaniya, assisted in configuring diagrams and tables whenever needed. Uma Kapila, Sanu Kapila, Rituraj Kapila and Sona Kapila of Academic Foundation made the publication possible together with its processing and design.

I dedicate the volume to Niharika Guha, my grandmother. Married at fourteen, widowed at twenty-five, she was dedicated to my education, taught me my first songs on her organ, and also fables and epics. She ensured my material and cerebral sustenance by providing not only top-notch tutors but also my first tennis racquet and guitar. I am proud to dedicate these writings to a classical Indian woman.

— Parthasarathi Shome

I

Macroeconomy

1

2016 Through a Looking Glass

A United Airlines Business First toilet bag brought in by a recent visitor amazingly lists the country of origin of every part of that little manufactured item: bag, socks, comb, eye mask, toothbrush, dental pick, tissue, earplugs, pen, mint, pouch, and lip balm made in China, toothpaste made in Thailand, B4 hand sanitiser made in the USA, Chamomile towelette and Cow Pat hand cream made in England and packaged in China. Five star hotels, cars and their interiors, electronic music systems and even compacted music are known to be built of assembled parts and materials from across the world. Obviously so are the minutest items. Thus, first, given the predominance of China on the list, who can confidently predict that China will be overtaken; rather, even with its slide, China should remain on top of trading nations and continue to deliver commensurate economic benefits to its citizenry.

India, by contrast, has just had one of the worst quarters in export earnings. A big year for state and local elections, 2016 will provide interesting applications of game theoretic strategy models while any role of ideology in the separation of political parties and their splinters recedes further. Thus, second, rising costs of Indian democracy will be in economic terms: direct financial cost of elections and non-functioning of parliament pre- and post-last parliamentary elections, the opportunity cost manifested in time lost in productive activity undermining the demographic dividend and capital investment, and decidedly arresting the likelihood of getting into that United Airlines source list. 'Make in India' will need concerted effort, well beyond prevailing signals.

Moving on from trade, monetary policy is likely to continue being merely exogenous rather than structurally sound or anchored.

One reason is the nature of components of measured inflation and a second is the long wait for robust modelling. Thus, third, the outcome will continue to be risk in taking investment decisions and a tough call for savers to select appropriate savings instruments with adverse impact on economic growth.

Fourth, trumpeting over improved ease of doing business ignores a glaring component that taxation related hurdles are perceived to have remained the same. The Income Tax Board has been issuing taxpayer supportive directives to field officers as never before. This is a commendable break from the past. Why then taxpayers by and large have been making similar complaints as before remains a question. The Board has to give incisive attention to this issue through taxpayer surveys so that meaningful conclusions could be drawn and appropriate action taken beyond circulars.

Fifth, while on taxation, the GST should be addressed. Remarkably, its structure has essentially not remained a taxpayer or tax administration concern. It has entered the political arena in a big way, begging the question whether it behooves professional assessment. Nevertheless, the chief economic advisor's (CEA) committee has made seemingly independent recommendations. The centre and states may ignore them though I hope I am wrong. If the CEA's recommendations are acceded to by political factions and levels of government, India may yet have an initially acceptable, though far from perfect, GST. Otherwise it would not assist economic growth or be globally recognised.

Sixth, regarding local governance, in an unexpected turn of events, Kolkata is turning out to be one of the cleaner cities and perhaps the cleanest metropolitan city. This magic has been wrought through installation and management of public toilets, garbage compactors after collection, disinfecting drains, cleaning up lakes, rejuvenating parks and constructing attractive walkways, completing flyovers and clearing away leftover concrete and rubble under them. By contrast, and contrary to anticipation, Bengaluru suffers deterioration. The collapsed condition of its roads has been rendered proverbial by the media. Excruciating impact on one's constitution is unavoidable while traversing them. On top, heaps of garbage at street corners, parks and ponds comprise a perennial sight. Where did the surveyors who recently declared it as the cleanest among capital cities go, to arrive at their conclusion? Varanasi too, by all counts, has remained as before despite the initiation of PM's Swachh Bharat campaign at Assi Ghat. There is little indication that compatriots are ready to embrace public cleanliness or social consciousness.

Seventh, cities are suffering from unsustainable levels of pollution, Delhi being the most polluted city. India just signed a global agreement on climate change that promises to limit temperature escalation. This is positive but it will hardly protect the average Indian's quality of life from free fall. The Delhi government's odd even license plate policy may seem draconian but the Supreme Court has reassuringly endorsed this swashbuckling step. More cities should follow it and more metro systems initiated. Banning new diesel vehicles should be supported.

Eighth, endorsement by United Nations General Assembly of India's inclusion in the Security Council is a significant step though its success can be assessed only when the Security Council accepts it, a burdensome obstacle to overcome. By the same token, India's role in the G20 nations was enhanced through active participation and contribution in OECD's formulation of recommendations to minimise tax avoidance by multinationals globally. Enhancement of that role in 2016 has to be forged. In addition, India has waited in the wings for an IMF quota increase while China has been fully successful just as with Security Council membership. Palpable IMF quota increase needs to be pushed forward.

Ninth, poverty reduction cannot be disassociated from non-performing loans by banks to big business while farmers end their lives, the former said to fuel the wheels of democracy. Without conscious recognition of this tripartite link and resolve to reset it, poverty is bound to remain the most convenient and used political agenda item. 2016 does not promise change.

Tenth, safety and security in the country have crumbled. It is immaterial whether it is wrought with abominable communication from the information super highway or inexplicable wrath of one community against another. Greater public resource allocation is crucial. 2016 may turn out to be a watershed for how all levels of government are perceived in containing it.

Business Standard, 23 December 2015.

2

Is there Economics in the 2015 Land Acquisition Bill?

"That is the question." And the answer is: little. We need to incorporate economic fundamentals in the legislation on land acquisition just as advanced economies tend to go through this process more methodically. Thus, the embedded economics deserves to be illustrated.

Figure 2.1 describes the agriculture land market in which government has entered with the objective of acquiring some land on behalf of industry public or private or in combination. S(L) is the supply curve of land which is a summation of distinct supply curves of individual farmers. While each farmer is likely to have a different valuation of his land asset and therefore possess a different price to supply relation, overall the market sums up to S(L). Note that S(L)

Figure 2.1

Supply-Demand of Land

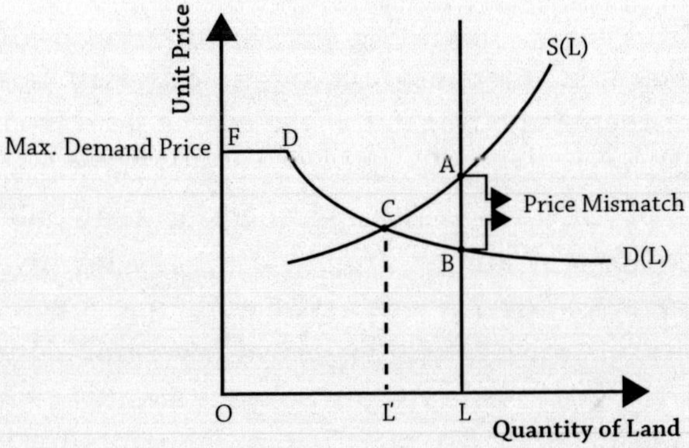

is upward sloping since more land will be offered in the market as a whole only as the price per unit of land increases.

On the other hand, the industrialist has a demand curve D(L) for land needed for his proposed project which reveals that he will tend to demand more land as its per unit price diminishes. However, he has a maximum per unit price, OF, above which he will not venture to offer a price for the land he requires. It is important to point this out since governments, in particular some state governments, run to offer land at prices above which they tend to believe industry would not be attracted to invest.

If government did not intervene, then equilibrium in the market would occur at C, the demand supply intersection, at a price of CL' and the land exchanged would be OL'. The problem is that this amount of land is insufficient for the project, the requirement being OL. At this point, AB emerges as the measurement of mismatched prices, the suppliers wanting a price of AL per unit and the buyer offering only to pay BL per unit. So government intervenes to find ways to acquire OL amount of land, and usually at a per unit price of less than AL.

The issue is where within the range AB, the government fixes the per unit price. Is it to be extracted from the supplier/farmer, the industrialist, or from the government budget. What is clear is that there is no economic justification in favour of government to subsidise industry by indirectly taxing the farmer. Government's role should only be facilitation of acquisition where this is not forthcoming due to the underlying intrafarmer variation in the composite S(L) curve. This the government could usefully achieve through variegated compensation among different farmers, while assuring that there is no transfer at the overall level from farmers to the industrialist.

The crux of the issue is the apprehension that public transfers do not work this way and invariably affect the farmer's or tribal's position adversely. Government's past economic practice is replete with examples, of which the 2006 Special Economic Zones (SEZ) Act or currently the 2015 Land Acquisition Act are just two. Figure 2.2 explains this using a box diagram. The initial points for industry and farmers are corner points A and B respectively. From here both would like to move, through a tatonnement process, towards the inside of the box where both would be better off. Thus, both would prefer to move as close to preference ranking 4 as possible through acquisition or sale of land. For example, at D, both would gain, though industry would gain more than farmers.

Instead, recent history has convincingly demonstrated that farmers have receded from B, their initial position, indeed appearing to move out of the box, to C, a worse-than-initial position. Figure 2.2 is drawn to show further that, instead of being a facilitator, government has bagged a benefit of BD through receipts from leakage or unfulfilled promises of 'rehabilitation and resettlement'.

Figure 2.2

Farmer-Industrialist Trade-off

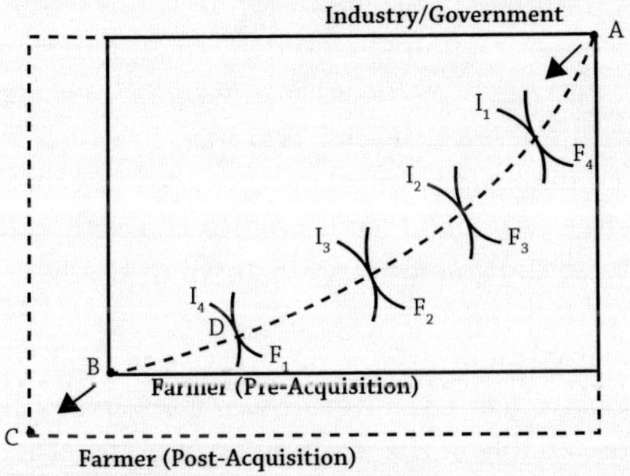

AD = Improvement for Industrialist	BC = Worsening of Farmers from Initial Position
DC = Government's Perceptible and Impervious Benefits	

The proposed 2015 Act fails to ensure that a movement from B to C will be averted since it has set aside the requirement of 70 per cent consent of communities affected by loss of land or associated livelihood as well as the requirement of a Social Impact Assessment (SIA) "in the public interest" related to projects pertaining to national security and defence; rural infrastructure including electrification; affordable housing and housing for the poor; industrial corridors;

and infrastructure projects including ones under private public partnership where ownership of land is with government.

Many advanced economies carry out SIA for major projects that India is proposing to eschew. SIA is terribly important so that, based on the SIA for each proposed project, a meaningful compensation plan would be necessarily drawn up and accomplished on a case by case basis. Under the current proposal, it appears that this government—like the previous one's SEZ Act—is giving itself and future governments immense discretion in major policy formulation and action without guaranteed discussion or adequate appraisal of their socioeconomic effects. The progressive direction of an advancing economy should be the opposite.

One cannot but ask why successive governments should be so keen to push ahead with projects that would proffer disproportionate benefits through increasing returns to the (upper class) owners of capital and (middle class) labour while (indirectly) taxing away those (lower economic groups) who own small parcels of land. This policy, combined with the recently emerging cascade of cases in urban areas irrespective of the political hue, in which certified, fully functioning, and taxpaying households, educational institutions, and other organisations are being subjected to the authorities' hammer, somehow hints at the role of land in fuelling the wheels of Indian democracy.

Thus, in the final analysis, one has to raise the following question. Has the political class considered whether prevailing political practices are sustainable in the medium term or, whether they should not be ready to chart a course that would not depend on, or result in, widely reported rent-seeking and, instead, bring to fruition the potential positive outcomes from transparency in the functioning of the largest and most vibrant democracy currently prevalent.

Business Standard, 14 July 2015.

3

GDP Estimation Methodology

Exasperating Improvements

Recently, the Central Statistical Office (CSO) revised India's GDP (gross domestic product) growth numbers scaling them up by some 1.5 percentage points for 2014-15. The world did not seem convinced. Even though earlier there was awareness of anomalies in the GDP series, in particular regarding the unorganised sector, there had been some confidence that the methodology had remained consistent so that comparisons across time were robust. Therefore, it was a jolt when CSO changed the basis altogether, and not just the base year from 2004-05 to 2011-12.

CSO decided to shift the basis of manufacturing estimates to businesses' balance sheets and income statements from exclusive use of indicators such as production and input use from the Index of Industrial Production (IIP) for first estimates and checked subsequently from the Annual Survey of Industries (ASI). The new numbers did not apparently pass consistency checks with production, inputs, or movements in the National Stock Exchange (NSE) index that should reflect the overall business and investment climate. Even if one ignored the NSE-listed companies, non-NSE firms could not account for the newfound spurt in manufacturing.

On the other hand, it would seem a safe principle to use what the productive sector itself reveals about their business outcomes. For one thing, CSO expanded its sample from ASI's coverage of 200,000 companies to the Ministry of Corporate Affairs' 500,000 accounts declared by companies themselves. Thus, not only should the confidence level for the new numbers be higher reflecting the much larger sample, but using the companies' own declarations to the government must bring the data closer to the true picture of the economy.

For example, to gauge tax evasion, advanced country tax administrations routinely check company accounts to gauge potential tax revenue and compare them with actual collection to estimate the tax gap. So why should CSO not adopt a similar approach? Indeed it has been found that what companies reveal in their balance sheets and profit-loss statements to shareholders differs from how they calculate them for the tax authorities where the numbers are less optimistic, thus yielding lower potential tax to be collected. No doubt there is some reason why tax administrations including India attempt to narrow the gap between the two sets of accounts.

Further, CSO's shift to using companies' income statements and away from production brings the estimation method closer to that of the services sector though, for the agricultural sector, a production method based on observed crop surveys, will continue to be used.

Analysing the old and new GDP reveals interesting differences in approach. First, CSO's new approach essentially implies that not only is value of production of a business included in its new manufacturing GDP, but also the cost of marketing and selling. In other words, distribution costs revealed in company accounts have been clubbed with manufacturing. Expectedly, GDP from manufacturing, mining and quarrying have gone from negative to significantly positive due to expanded scope of manufacturing. But this should have reduced the scope of corresponding services though, other than (1) real estate, financial and business services, and (2) electricity, gas and water, every other service has shot up including transport, storage and communication. The final outcome seems to indicate manufacturing gain has overwhelmed services loss.

Second, the new series uses the concept of value added or income or GDP directly rather than beginning with production and removing inputs. To explain, if the value of production of every economic activity is measured and aggregated, that yields gross "value" of the economy's production. Inputs that a sector has used from another sector's production have to be netted out across the economy to arrive at the economy's "value added" or GDP. Ideally, an economy's input use for each output can be represented in an input-output (I-O) table. It is challenging to produce one. I witnessed the tough process in Mexico in 1985-1987 which had a UN financed project to generate a new GDP series through an I-O method when I was attempting to measure potential tax revenue from Mexico's VAT (value added tax) using the I-O method. The intricacies of calculating sector by sector value added posed themselves on a daily basis in the deeper reaches of the tax office. I also recall Professor Sukhamoy Chakravarty expressing surprise that India did not possess an I-O table when he went to the Planning Commission in the early 1970s, resolving that he would generate one. In sum, the "production method" remains tough to adhere to even in the long run. CSO has opted to move from the production method to an "income method" of GDP derivation.

Third, after the derivation, indirect taxes need to be added in and production subsidies subtracted, so that only the exact value added generated by a producer in the production distribution chain is taken and nothing else. Fourth, perhaps CSO's inflation adjustment has had the highest impact on new GDP. By assuming lower inflation for 2014-15, when CSO divided nominal GDP by inflation, it obtained a higher real GDP growth rate. This imparted an immediate boost to the GDP number that seemed to comingle the issue of change in methodology with a ceteris paribus revision in estimation.

Looking forward, reform of the GDP series has to continue in particular in the services sector. Government salaries directly comprise services sector GDP whose any increase adds to GDP. Lamentably, GDP has little to do with productivity. Since GDP reflects any output of the economy without consideration of its morality or legality, output from illegal or immoral activities get included provided they can be measured. Thus, trafficking of bonded or child labour adds to the services sector GDP if their transportation is measured and reported. Incredulously, measured activities related to murder or suicide would also get reflected. Escalating up, activities from social conflict comprise GDP.

Given that such condemnable activities generate GDP, it is conceivable that as an economy gets riddled with social or political conflict, GDP might keep creeping up as long as such activities somehow are measured and documented. Is it any wonder that the value added or GDP of India's services sector is burgeoning in the backdrop of the rapidly deteriorating social environment, or that anthropologists and sociologists view economists with derision? Finally, reform of the GDP series should address how it can measure the correct extent of economic activity in the black, or non-tax paid, economy and then include it comprehensively in the series.

To conclude, while it may sometimes be useful to confuse oneself about an issue before trying to understand or solve it, in the case of GDP, the confusion doesn't seem to dissipate. How come the world depends on it as an exclusive tool to measure growth and development? I strongly recommend its thorough re-examination to reduce its irrationality and perceived inconsistency. In the present, more limited event, CSO should report the old with the new series for 5, if not 10, years so that their underlying differences are transparent on a continuing basis and they are able to serve the needs for research and statistical use. Otherwise, econometric work would have to continually use a dummy variable at the break point for analysis using GDP time series, certainly a potential source of frustration.

Business Standard, 14 April 2015.

4

Inflation and Interest Rates

What is the Reserve Bank's Policy?

The December 2 Fifth Bi-Monthly Monetary Policy Statement, 2014-15, from the Reserve Bank of India (RBI) declared, "On the basis of an assessment of the current and evolving macroeconomic situation, it has been decided to: keep the policy repo rate under the liquidity adjustment facility (LAF) unchanged at eight per cent ...," etc. Unfortunately, that "basis" remained unexplained: what is the background framework for the Indian economy based on which the RBI came to the conclusion as most central banks do?

That was followed by the RBI's assessment of the economy—comprising a lament of negatives clearly inconsistent with a continuation of its tightfisted interest rate policy. It admitted to a "slowdown" in rural wages, a "slump" in the growth of industrial production, a "persisting contraction" in capital and consumer goods production, "deceleration" in new business in the services sector, all leading to "weak" aggregate demand, a "critical" need for rise in investment, "still slow" pace in reviving stalled projects, a "deceleration" of exports since July, and a need to ease "stress" in the financial system since banks are "flush" with funds. What further consternation is needed to move the RBI into action? It is surprising that the Ministry of Finance made inaudible noises at this unfortunate development obviating wide-ranging anticipation. Unless the finance ministry initiates serious independent evaluation, the economic plot of the new government may soon be lost. Let me elaborate.

The RBI blamed the need to adhere to its conservative interest rate policy on weak tax revenue growth and slow pace of divestment. It does not take a trained economist to see that the economic morass the RBI itself described provides ample explanation for why there are no takers on the horizon for divested units and why tax revenue should be low in this ebb cycle unless the same extortion from taxpayers continues under the new government through stopping or delaying refunds and input tax credit, demanding unwarranted pre-deposits, and preponing tax payments through diktat in the last quarter, in other words, through pervading taxpayer harassment carried out through policy imposition on the tax administration. Indeed the RBI's observation, that "the government, however, appears determined to stay on course," seems somewhat supercilious. What about an optimal combination of monetary/fiscal/exchange rate policies, as well as bringing in real sector and trade policies into the matrix in an evidence based manner?

The RBI's justification for its inaction on the interest rate front despite "dissipating headline inflation" was, "the key uncertainty is the durability of this upturn". This gives rise to curiosity to examine recent data. Figure 4.1 fits a polynomial on the Consumer Price Index (CPI), the Wholesale Price Index (WPI) and CPI (Industrial Workers), or CPI (IW), observations between April 2011 and October 2014. CPI and CPI (IW) have declined from Q4 2013-14, and WPI has declined since Q1 2011-12 (beginning of the statistics depicted). This enables observation of real interest rate trends in Figure 4.2. The polynomials reveal that the real median base rate of scheduled commercial banks which has immediate relevance has been positive and rising from about Q3-Q4 of 2012-13 with respect to CPI and CPI (IW) and from Q1 2011-12 itself with respect to WPI. Given the uncontestable lengthy periods for which price indices have declined and interest rates have risen, what kind of "durability" is the RBI waiting for?

Fitting polynomials to other interest rate trends given their fickle movements was not found to be so revealing. Hence Figure 4.3 simply depicts the real base rate trends with respect to CPI, CPI (IW) and WPI. Reflecting the continuing decline in WPI (see Figure 4.1), it is not surprising that the real base rate has been throughout positive and rising with respect to the WPI since Q1 2011-12, with further sharp rises from Q3 2013-14, while, with respect to CPI and CPI (IW), the real base rate has been positive and sharply rising from

Q4 2013-14. Separating the rate into rural and urban yields similar trends (not shown). Further, the lower range of the real base rate follows the same trend just below the higher range rate (Figure 4.4), in fact, almost coinciding since Q4 2013-14.

Figure 4.1

Comparative Movement of CPI(IW), WPI and CPI (Y-O-Y)

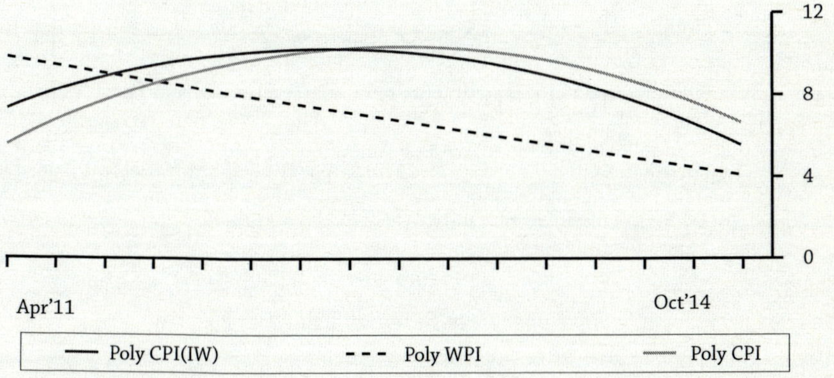

Note: Poly is polynomial.

Source: Reserve Bank of India, Central Statistical Office and Labour Bureau.

Figure 4.2

Real Median Base Rate of Scheduled Commercial Banks*

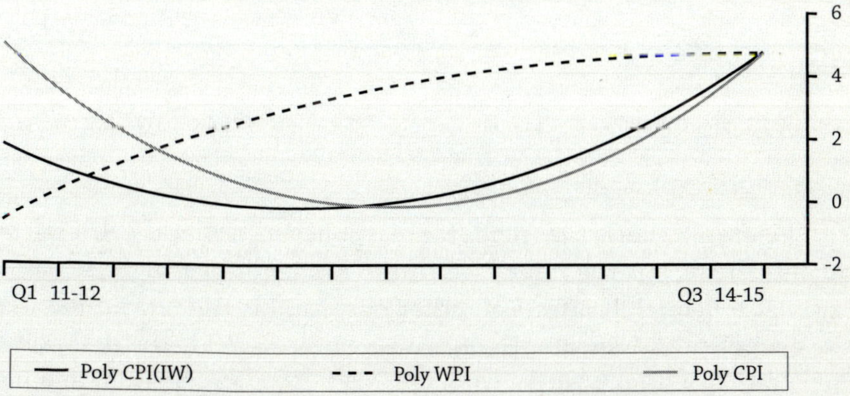

Note: * Median base rate is average of media in value of a range of base rates of Scheduled Commercial Banks (public sector banks, private sector banks and foreign banks).

Source: Reserve Bank of India, Central Statistical Office and Labour Bureau.

Figure 4.3

Real Base Rate Based on CPI(IW), WPI and CPI (Y-O-Y)

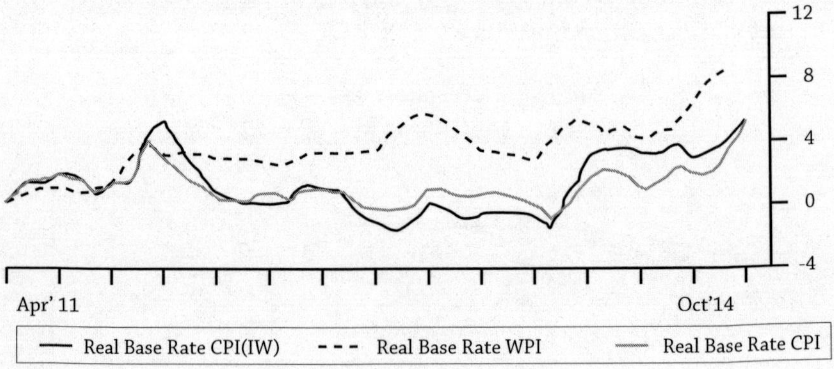

Source: Reserve Bank of India, Central Statistical Office and Labour Bureau.

Figure 4.4

Real Base Rate Based on CPI (Y-O-Y)

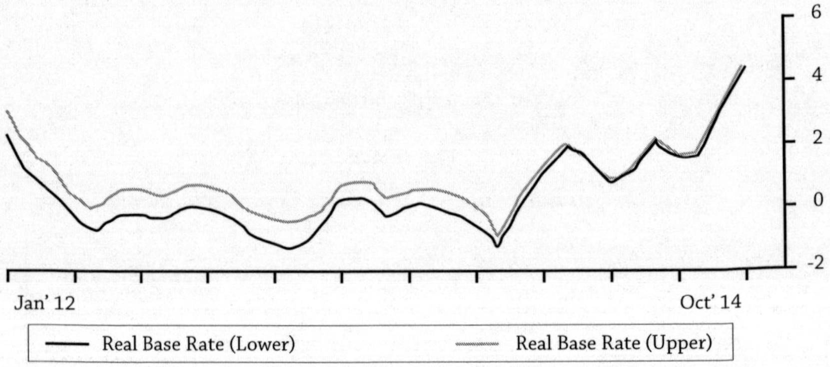

Source: Reserve Bank of India, Central Statistical Office and Labour Bureau.

Figure 4.5 shows the trends for real policy repo that the RBI talked about. The repo is the rate at which the RBI lends overnight to banks against collateral. It affects all other rates, and is the rate announced in the policy statements. Here, with respect to WPI, the real policy repo rate has been positive from Q3 2011-12, a long period, and has been rising significantly from Q3 2013-14. With respect to CPI (IW), it has been positive and rising since Q4 2013-14 and, with respect to the CPI, it has been positive and rising since close to Q2 2014-15. The latter is the rate that the RBI cited, but its position is easily countered by citing other relevant real rates illustrated above that have been positive for a significant period already.

Figure 4.5

Real Policy Repo Rate Based on CPI(IW), WPI and CPI (Y-O-Y)

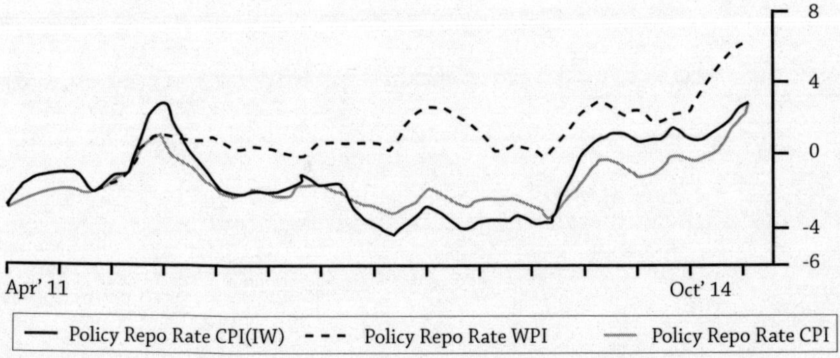

Source: Reserve Bank of India, Central Statistical Office and Labour Bureau.

Indeed most real interest rates have been rising reaching almost five per cent with respect to some indices and slightly less so with respect to other indices, all of which are of relevance to borrowers and during a significantly long downturn in economic activity. When all relevant borrower interest rates are considered together, the RBI's textbook interest rate policy demands immediate abandonment and substitution by a more accommodating policy. Indeed it is fallacy to call such improved policy "accommodating" since it is the only correct policy at this point.

One concluding suggestion for the RBI. Let its two-part inflation projection comprising base effects obtained from inflation momentum and time series for future momentum (*Monetary Policy Report*, RBI, September 2015) be supplemented by a comprehensive technical framework from which a more convincing interest rate policy could be demonstrated. India awaits conviction through appropriate analysis for the RBI's conclusions. Let the RBI change course.

Business Standard, 06 January 2015.

5

Is 25 per cent of GDP from Manufacturing Robust Policy?

The present government has, after the last, once again asked for manufacturing to reach 25 per cent of GDP (gross domestic product). This must be a genuine desire for preeminence as a manufacturing hub among emerging economies. Visuals cross section and time series are helpful in analysing this. To begin, it is essential to differentiate between manufacturing and industry. Figure 5.1(A) shows that in both Brazil and India, industry accounts for 25 per cent of GDP. Of this 13 per cent is manufacturing or about half (Figure 5.1(B)). In China by contrast, they are 44 per cent and 32 per cent respectively. It implies that, not only are China's industry and manufacturing in relation to GDP much higher, but manufacturing comprises a much higher proportion, 70 per cent, of industry. And, reflecting the vast difference in the GDPs of China and India (see Chapter 34 of this volume), the value difference in the size of manufacturing in the two countries is enormous.

Thus, unlike the growing difference in the size of their GDPs since the 1980s, note that the Figures also reveal that China's relative size of industry in GDP (around 45%) has always been far higher than India's (around 25%), and both have continued without much change. Brazil's industry, on the other hand, fell drastically, from 45 per cent to 25 per cent. Usually, as economies develop and grow, industry and manufacturing become increasingly specialised while services grow faster and become larger. This is what occurred in Brazil. But China steadfastly maintained its high octane grip on industry and manufacturing reflecting a deliberately designed policy even as its GDP was growing by leaps and bounds. Few countries including India can replicate this in reflection of their particular socio-economic attributes and administrative practices. Indeed, India's manufacturing sector has shown little sign of increased share of GDP as is amply evident from Figure 5.1(B).

Figure 5.1

Sector-wise Contribution to GDP

(A) Industry (%)

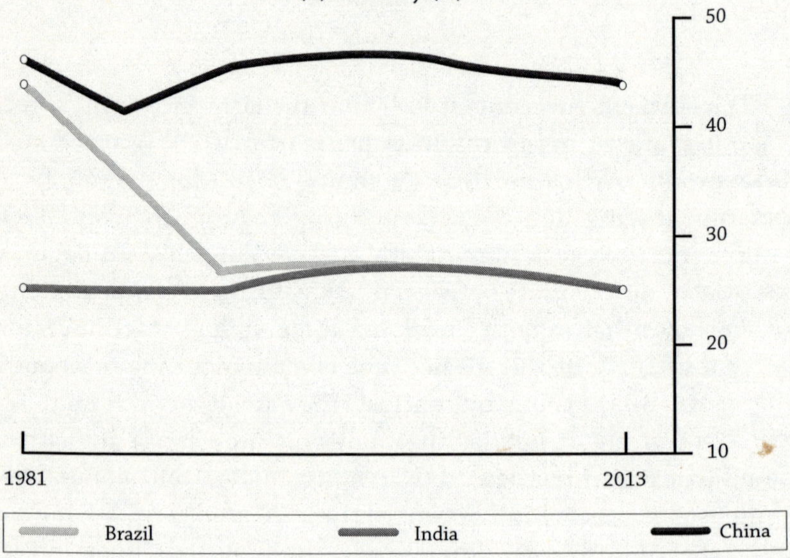

(B) Manufacturing (%)

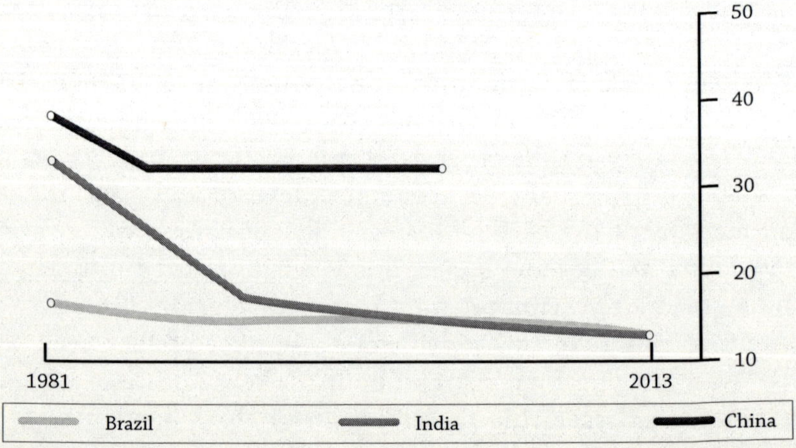

(C) Agriculture (%)

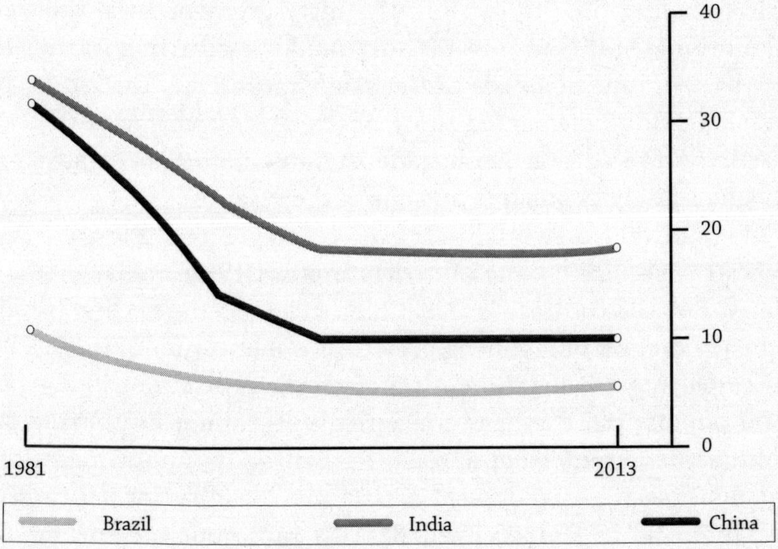

(D) Services (%)

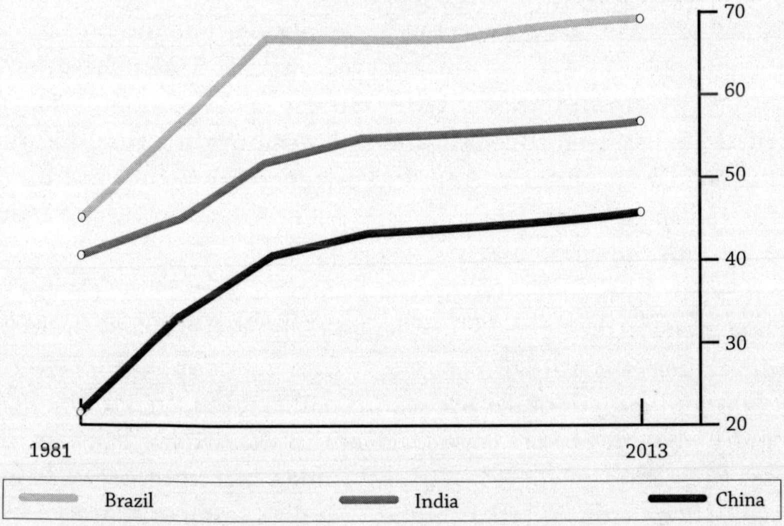

Note: GDP indicators are in the form of value added as % of GDP based on International Standard Industrial Classification (ISIC).

Source: World Bank.

It has been impossible for India to eradicate impediments—policy and administrative—at all levels of government to enable manufacturing growth. Is government resolute to defang obstacles? Is it spending time to get into the nitty gritty of laws, rules and regulations—tax and non-tax—by muddying its fingers and not leaving them in the hands of the same bureaucracy that so far has designed and implemented those obstructionist characteristics and practices? If rapidly reemerging industry discomfort is a signal, speed of removal of impediments remains of the essence.

Yet, other sectors should not be neglected. Figure 5.1(C) shows the secular decline of agriculture in GDP in India, similar to China. But the contrast is that China made up the decline through industry and manufacturing growth, a substitution quintessential for employment generation. Also, given the pressure of India's poor rural population, the need for agriculture cannot be sourced to a comparable extent from abroad. Returning to employment, only organised sector employment can assure social sector expenditure on labour as in China. Even Brazil's rapid decline in industry and manufacturing in GDP has been countered through social expenditure earmarked from additional taxes on companies' value added. India has failed miserably in its socio-economic services for the vulnerable since it has not achieved organised manufacturing or industry growth in terms of GDP. Yet, the socio-economic stability of rural life has been adversely affected, resulting in a rural-to-urban influx huddled in slums of A, B or C category cities. The government needs to design urgently a resurgent policy for two-thirds of India's population—our rural relatives.

If agriculture's relative status is not to worsen further, then raising manufacturing to 25 per cent would need services to decline by 10-12 per cent of GDP. Figure 5.1(D) indicates that, interestingly, the "rate" of growth of services in China has been no less than that of India, though China's services share in GDP is much lower. This is not surprising given, respectively, China's marathon towards high speed GDP growth, and that chunks of India's services share could be considered a residual. It has been demonstrated in *Oxford Review of Economic Policy* (Autumn 2012)[1] that India has comparative advantage

1. Shome, Parthasarathi (2012). "Rebalancing and Structural Policies: An Indian Perspective", *Oxford Review of Economic Policy* 28(3): 587-602.

in international trade in services together with the United States in contrast to say China or Germany which have comparative advantage in goods. This implies that India should open its services—retail, banking, insurance—to global markets as has the United States, and not protect it or subsidise it further. Tax incentives allowed segments of services such as information technology exports to grow while it brought some employment to the urban middle class. Setting the past aside, it is time for services to perform at potential in a global environment without the middle class and also without the crutches of domestic incentives.

Summing up, rather than pick out a number 25 per cent of GDP for manufacturing, if the government is seriously focused on generating employment for India's burgeoning labour force at the macroeconomic level, it has to identify those spots where the bulk of labour supply, and the need for economic infrastructure, match. This is in construction—highways, roads, dams, low cost and middle income housing, single to three star hotels—manufacturing not merely small scale, but all labour-intensive areas that require various skill levels including basic skills; agriculture through the construction of irrigation works and water resource management and power and electricity generation through nuclear plants and solar panels whose construction ensures labour utilisation. The objectives should be employment, socio-economic enhancement, and economic wellbeing. It is immaterial if 25 per cent of GDP in manufacturing remains wishful thinking.

Luckily, this is a propitious moment to begin the long march in light of favourable international oil prices, domestic prices reasonably under control, and India's cushion against any reemergence of global economic recession or commodity price volatility since India is less dependent than China on international demand. For success, Indian policymakers must put in place fresh processes with experts, not administrators, at the helm. Embedding expertise is not a new recipe, but would simply follow what China is doing for quite some time and what has always been the basis of Brazilian policy making.

Business Standard, 18 November 2014.

6

Having a Heart, Using the Head

The Union Budget is always expected to achieve multiple objectives. First, poverty alleviation and income redistribution through government's expenditure functions, while, second, garnering tax revenue in increasingly higher amounts, yet without causing disincentives for the taxpayer; third, providing guidance for forward-looking macroeconomic management; and fourth, a strategy for structural reform. Thus, if the exercise is carried out with care and due diligence, it has to be perspicacious, balancing the nation's heart and cerebrum. In real life this translates into structural as well as immediate matters that the forthcoming 2012-13 Union Budget needs to address.

Figure 6.1

GDP Growth (%)

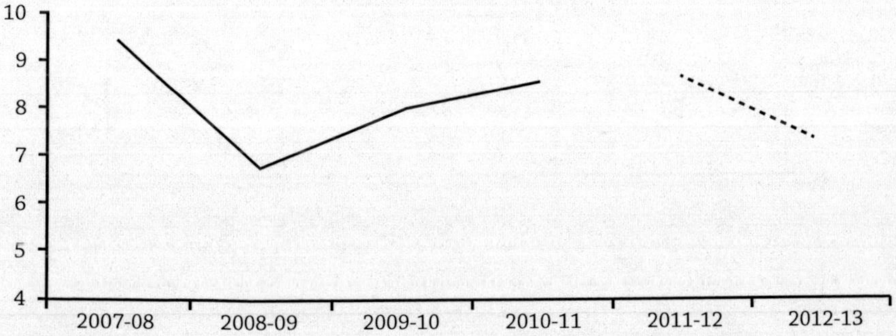

Source: CSO, India.

Let us take stock of recent economic developments that will be the springboard for the Budget. They reflect both lacklustre trends and some emerging challenges. While GDP growth suffered during the 2007-08 and 2008-09 global economic crisis, it began picking up thereafter. The sudden and unanticipated deterioration in GDP growth in the first half, or H1, of 2011-12 (Figure 6.1) (compared to H1 of 2010-11) was not anticipated. Though industry had been giving warnings, it almost became a matter of crying wolf too many times. Indeed, it is realistically a matter of jumps in costs and the near impossibility of planning business operations when facing rising and volatile commodity—in particular, oil—prices. Examining sectors, the numbers reflect negative growth for mining—and one wonders whether it is the southern wind or environment-related constraints that brought that piece of bad news. Whatever the causes, and there are more, it is imperative for investment to pick up from its lowered GDP share, and to reverse the declining investment growth of last two years (Figure 6.2). A major challenge in the Union Budget is how to address dampened investment and revive GDP growth.

Figure 6.2

Total Investment

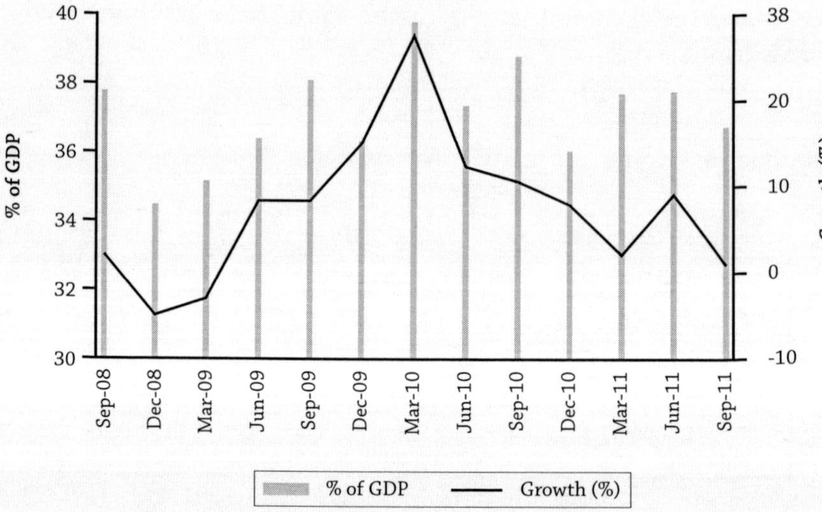

Source: CSO, India.

The uncertainty prevailing in the economy is taking its toll. Quarter to quarter, performances of both agriculture and industry have worsened and are volatile, while that of services has been both better and more stable (Figure 6.3). First, agriculture's share in GDP has been declining annually, even as recently as between 2009-10 and 2010-11—from 15 per cent to 14 per cent. Yet, 46 per cent of employment is provided by agriculture. The dips in agriculture at particular points in 2008-09 and 2009-10 were stark, crying out for policy redirection. Second, between the fourth quarter of 2006-07 and the third quarter of 2008-09, industry experienced declining growth rates, then picked up, but started declining again from the fourth quarter of 2009-10 (Figure 6.3). Policy needs to be directed to support industry in the light of a simmering global recession.

Figure 6.3

Sectoral GDP Growth (%)

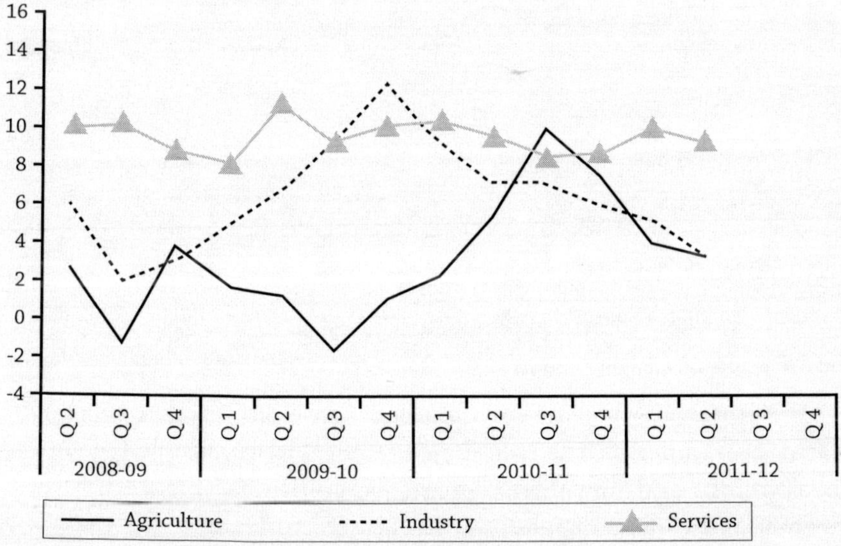

Source: CSO, India.

Given that there is little evidence that inflation can be reduced by serial monetary tightening at this point—since inflation has become highly structural in both domestic and international perspectives—the Reserve Bank of India's stance needs to be rationalised. Though real interest rates have not been high, due to inflation (Figure 6.4), industry should nevertheless be given a boost through monetary relaxation through interest rate policy. However, quantitative easing or tax incentives are not immediately essential. The year's continuing depreciation of the rupee by more than 10 per cent has provided a fillip to exporters, while posing higher import costs to industry for its raw materials and machinery. On balance, industry's experience seems to be not that positive as a result of the depreciation.

Figure 6.4

Real Interest Rate (%)

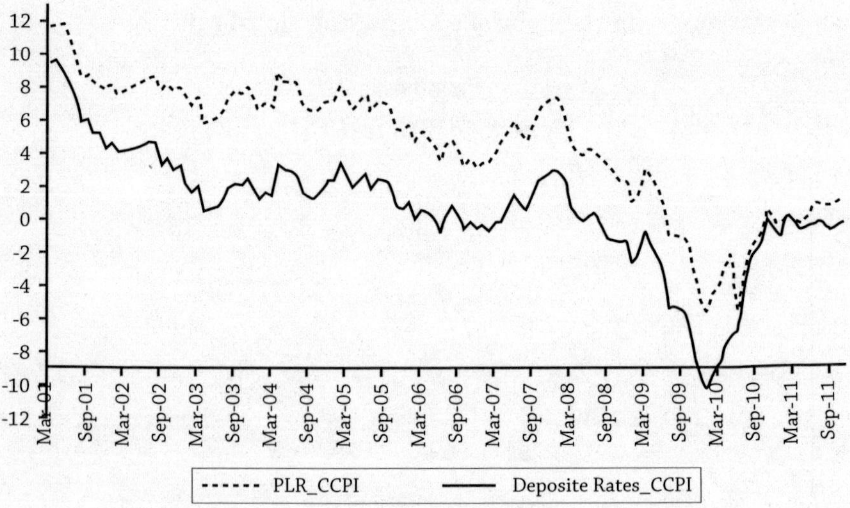

Source: Calculations using RBI database on Indian Economy.

Viewing the government's expenditure policies at a top-down macro level imparts little confidence either. Fitting simple trends for development and non-development expenditures (Figure 6.5) and revenue and capital expenditures (Figure 6.6) leads to an unhappy realisation: in terms of GDP, developmental and capital expenditures have decreased, while revenue/current consumption and non-development expenditure have increased. This implies that the investment support that industry and agriculture need has not been forthcoming as GDP grows; while direct subsidies rise despite landing up in unintended hands, government salaries grow irrespective of government productivity, and it has to pay out more in interest costs.

Figure 6.5

Developmental and Non-Developmental Expenditures of General Government (% of GDP)

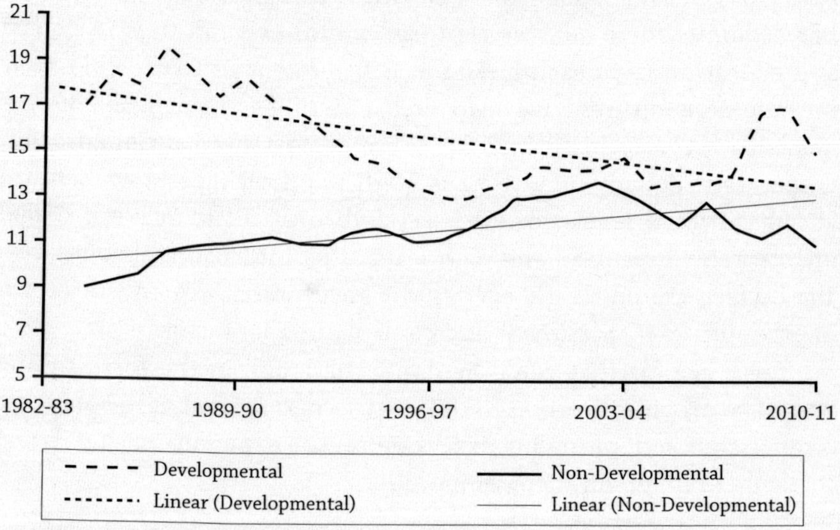

Source: *Handbook of Statistics on Indian Economy, 2010-11*, RBI.

Figure 6.6

Revenue and Capital Expenditures of General Government (% of GDP)

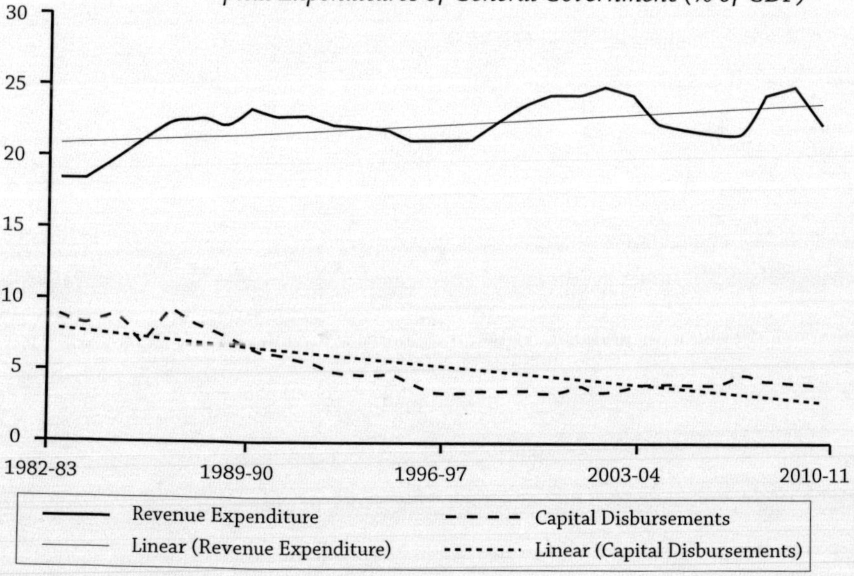

Source: *Handbook of Statistics on Indian Economy, 2010-11*, RBI.

Using the heart for the right reasons while keeping a steady head remains the Budget's challenge. Development expenditure policy has become suboptimal, lacking strategy, over the last years. For example, for a quarter century, capital expenditures in health and education have each lurked at 0.1 per cent of GDP, while their revenue expenditures have been almost 10 times as much. The Budget needs to reverse this trend, for these sectors need rationalisation desperately. Equally important is M&E (monitoring and evaluation) at sub-national levels for such expenditures. Field surveys reveal unacceptable execution and high leakage by international standards. The Budget should clearly specify the government's intended reform in expenditure management and control in social sectors.

There is a lot that could be done, therefore, in the forthcoming Budget to provide direction to the macroeconomy, and in re-balancing composition and improving execution on the expenditure side. Equal challenges remain on the revenue side.

Business Standard, 16 January 2012.

7

Financial Market Behaviour

A familiar issue is how to gain an edge over volatile international financial markets to obviate or minimise future global financial doldrums. Should capital controls be imposed by countries or under multilateral understandings or agreements? Should there be an international financial regulatory agency to initiate action under stipulated conditions? Should financial transactions be taxed? Some countries are making forward-looking suggestions; some are resisting; others are being Humpty Dumpties.

To address price volatility, price determination needs to be understood first. Traditional financial economics literature says the outcome of the market is a "random walk" in prices, or, all available information is already reflected in the current price, so that any future price movements would only result from random exogenous shocks. However, information has always been scarce. Thus, even quite early, such premises were already challenged. Ratti and Shome (1977) demonstrated that, in the presence of uncertainty, the usual solution for an auctioneer, to search and find a set of relative prices through a tatonnement process, at which there is no excess demand in any market, is no longer achievable. Thus, exchanges are not perfect Walrasian auctions. More recent evidence by Lo and Mackinlay (1999) showed that stock market prices do not follow a random walk; there is volatility that cannot be explained as an outcome of exogenous or uncontrollable factors alone.

Related questions arise on whether traders are rational; whether it matters that the marketplace does not determine a price through an equilibrating tatonnement process; and whether volatility is a market failure that needs to be addressed.

Figure 7.1

Stabilising and Destabilising Speculation

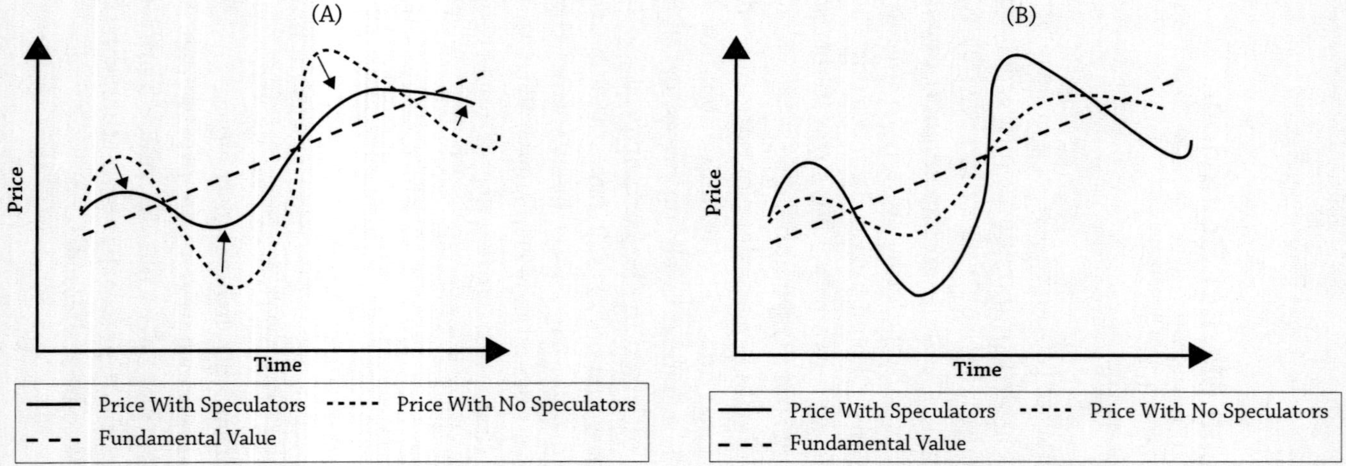

Are short-term speculators rational, "fundamental" traders that identify price discrepancies and push the market towards equilibrium?

Or, are short-term speculators rational, "Noise" traders that push the market away from fundamental values for private gain?

Therefore, to develop a coherent policy in an international framework, we need to first understand the behaviour of players in financial markets.

Consider Figure 7.1(A) and 7.1(B). The dotted straight lines indicate the line of "fundamental values" or the true underlying long-term trend values of a stock or share. The solid black lines (—) indicate price movements in the share market with speculators, while the dotted curved lines (-----) indicate the price trajectory with no speculators.

The question is: will speculation bring prices towards, or take them away from, the fundamental values? The old algorithm was that "stabilisation is stabilising". Thus, in Figure 7.1(A), when prices are high, speculators consider it a good opportunity to sell, and do that. Consequently, the prices decrease, which results in speculation bringing prices towards fundamentals. So, speculation becomes stabilising.

Figure 7.1(B) shows the opposite. When prices rise, operators buy in the hope that prices will rise even further. This type of "noise" trader is said to trade often, usually in a herd, who ignores market fundamentals. This is compounded by "technical or automated trading" that is software-driven and takes place on the basis of recent price and trade volume information rather than on any analysis of underlying economic data. The outcome is destabilising speculation—prices being pushed further away from fundamentals. The relative strengths of the two behaviours—stabilising and destabilising—determine the outcome of whether market activity leads prices towards or away from fundamental values.

Technical trading mimics destabilising speculation. This is because technical traders buy until a certain ceiling is reached when prices are rising, and sell when prices fall below a certain minimum level. Beinhocker (2007) has given an interesting example from Farmer et al. (2004), on the impact of a bid-ask spread. They studied one trade in AstraZeneca, a pharmaceutical company. AstraZeneca's "limit sell order"—offers to buy and sell that are conditional on a price—was set at £31.84. The next limit order was set at £32.30. When a small "buy order" of £16,000 came in, the asking price jumped from £31.84

to £32.30. This was an increase of 46 pence, which now represented the bid-ask spread; the share price moved up by 23 pence. This added £374 million to AstraZeneca's market value, though there was no policy or performance change of AstraZeneca on that day. Thus, a £16,000 buy order had generated a £374 million valuation jump for the company, reflecting solely the way market price recording and clearing take place in technical trading.

To curb volatility, those who recommend controlling financial transactions through capital controls or by taxing capital flows claim that such instruments would curtail technical intra-day trading or short-term transactions; and, in turn, the market would move more towards fundamentals or the underlying long-term trend. The opposite argument is that the reduction in transactions could mean that, when people do trade, they trade in larger amounts in a "thinner market" with fewer participants. This leads to bigger gaps between the limit orders in the market makers' order books. These gaps increase price volatility whenever a market order—an order to buy and sell with immediate fulfilment regardless of price—is placed.

Unfortunately, models of noise trading (De Long et al. 1990) are generally unable to adequately explain behaviours. They fall short of establishing one-to-one relationships between a trader and a behaviour or, for that matter, an "attitude to speculate". This is probably because of the multiple personalities of traders and investors. As a result, Grundfest et al. (1991) have even claimed that a tax on financial transactions would affect both (short-term) traders and (long-term) investors.

Thus, instead of modelling speculators' behaviour, would it not be more revealing to model financial markets themselves? One possibility is to model the chaos and complexity endemic in financial markets. The theory of chaos and complexity is best explained through an example of throwing a pebble in a pond. The ripples have no pattern and are, therefore, chaotic, as are financial markets. At the edge of chaos, where the ripples are dying out, however, complex patterns may be discerned. This is the Mandelbrot set, named after the scientist who programmed it.

Complexity theory is being used to explain biological cell growth and galactic formation, so why not financial markets? Global financial equilibrium has successfully escaped traditional analyses and prescriptions. We need new methodologies to take corrective action. If complex behaviour patterns are discerned in otherwise chaotic financial markets, we can observe those patterns and introduce policy to manipulate them. A new generation of economists could surely pioneer such methodologies and bring them to the policy table?

References

Beinhocker, E. (2007). *The Origin of Wealth: Evolution, Complexity and the Radical Remaking of Economics.* Random House Business Books.

De Long, J.B. and L. Summers (1991). "Equipment Investment and Economic Growth", *Quarterly Journal of Economics* CVI: 445-502.

Farmer, J., L. Gillemot, F. Lillo, M. Szabolc and A. Sen (2004). 'What Really Causes Large Price Changes?", *Quantitative Finance* 2: 383-97.

Grundfest, Joseph A. and John B. Shoven (1991). "Adverse Implications of a Securities Transactions Excise Tax", *Journal of Accounting Auditing and Finance* 6(4): 409-42.

Lo, A. and M. Mackinlay (1999). *A Non-Random Walk Down Wall Street.* Princeton, New Jersey: Princeton University Press.

Ratti, R. and P. Shome (1977). "On a General Equilibrium Model of the Incidence of the Corporation Tax under Uncertainity", *Journal of Public Economics* 8: 233-38.

Business Standard, 14 May 2011.

8

India's Savings and Growth

India's growth surge has been phenomenal. Growth reached 9.5 per cent in 2005-06 and 2006-07, and 9.2 per cent in 2007-08. Subsequently, the global financial crisis dampened growth to 6.7 per cent in 2008-09 and 7.4 per cent in 2009-10, but it is likely to pick up according to independent projectors. What lay behind growth of the Indian economy?

1. Was it neoclassical a la Robert M. Solow and T.W. Swan, who emphasised the role of savings—translated into investment—in economic growth?
2. Was it demand-driven a la John Maynard Keynes, where an x amount of expenditure, even if not backed by savings, would lead to a multiple yx of income?
3. Was it economic growth and rising incomes that triggered both savings and investment, in line with Arthur W. Lewis' capitalist surplus concept?
4. Or was it technological innovation that shifted up the growth path trajectory and endogenised technical change, as economists such as Paul Romer have hypothesised?

Link 1. What stands out most is India's savings trajectory (Figure 8.1). Gross domestic savings rose from 10.3 per cent of GDP in 1950-1955 to 36.4 per cent in 2006-07. This success is revealed even in international comparisons where India is shadowed only by China (at over 50%). Look at three components of savings. Specific policies facilitated growth in household savings. Population per bank branch fell from 90,000 in mid-1950s to 14,000 by early 1990s. Also reflecting active interest rate and anti-inflation policies, household financial savings rose from 1.6 per cent of GDP to 10.6 per cent during this period. Growth rate in corporate savings then became the forerunner; nevertheless the share of household savings in private savings comprised some 85 per cent since the mid-1990s. Public sector savings languished, however, declining from 1.7 per cent in 1950-1955 to -0.6 per cent in 2003-04. Dissavings first appeared in 1998-99 as the public sector failed to meet its own revenue expenditure. Subsequent discipline under the 2003 FRBM Act that enabled public savings to reach 5 per cent of GDP by 2007-08 was lost to fiscal relaxation. It fell to 1.4 per cent in 2008-09.

Figure 8.1

India: Savings (% of GDP)

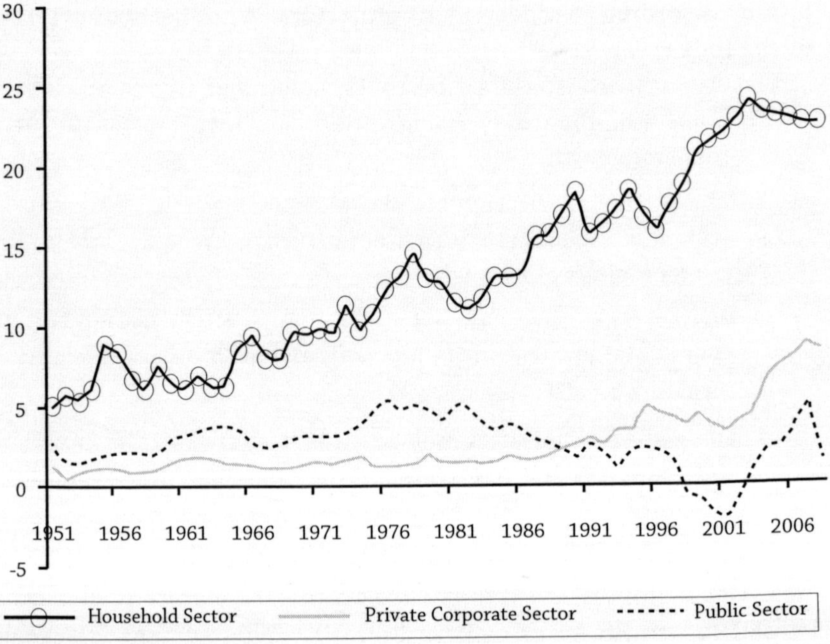

Source: CSO India.

Link 2. Expenditure (in the form of investment) played a significant role pari passu with savings right from the early Plans. In those years, government considered itself the engine of growth and assumed a leading role in investment in strategic, infrastructure and large industrial sectors. It confined private sector activity to only residual sectors. India made an economically costlier choice of self-reliance over the export-orientation of East Asia or Latin America. In hindsight, it did imbue India with a long-term advantage in today's international environment, by facilitating her global political and economic reach.

Figure 8.2

India: Investment (% of GDP)

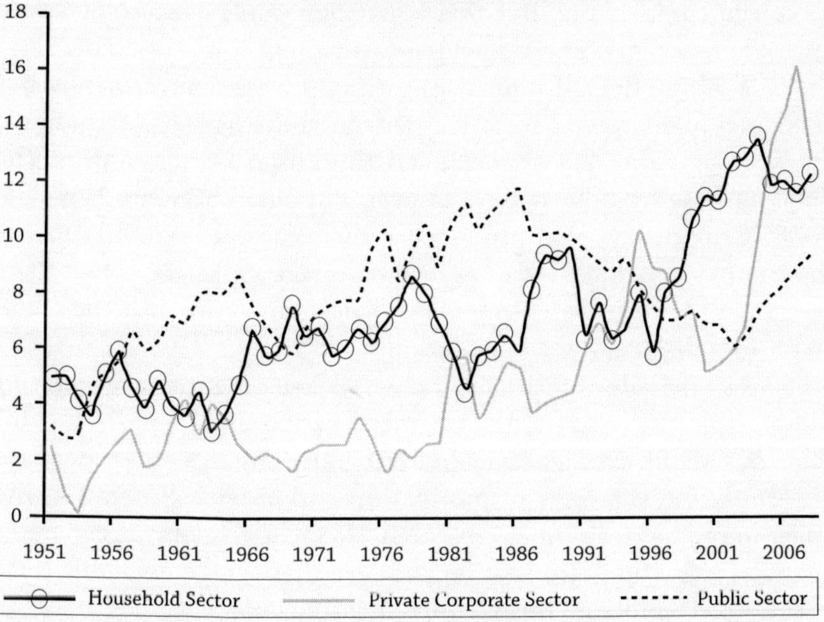

Source: CSO India.

That scenario changed with a setback in public sector productivity. From around the mid-1980s, public investment declined and private investment grew in terms of GDP (Figure 8.2). A resurgent phenomenon of the 2000s, however, is a reversal of that process with a rise in public investment at the cost of household and corporate segments. Given low public sector productivity, this manner of crowding out is not justifiable. When the private sector is capable of undertaking mega projects and is willing to do so, what is needed is an accommodative environment created by the government to enable private investment in infrastructure and large industry, protecting only the core strategic sector in its own brief. Accommodation is not tax incentives but removing non-tax barriers that comprise the real stumbling blocks for efficient allocation of resources between public and private sectors as well as for quantum of private sector resources that large businesses—foreign and domestic MNCs—are willing to invest. The private sector does vie for incentives not only on a large scale as reflected in both our income tax and indirect tax structures such as the SEZ Act but also for minuscule relative advantages over perceived competitors. But this behaviour would tend to dissipate once a non-tax level playing field begins to appear on the scene.

Link 3. The overall high savings-high investment economy has generated high growth. India has generated the largest international marketplace and has experienced the largest expansion in the taxpayer base from 15 million to over 30 million between 1995 and 2008. Growth has also produced robust capital accumulation as the country's middle classes as well as corporate sector activity and investment have grown. Economists[1] have found growth as the causal factor in India's capital accumulation.

Link 4. The role of technology seems below potential in generating India's growth. Apart from advanced economies, middle income countries are investing heavily in R&D. India's figures are inadequate. We emulate techniques of production and service generation but linger in productive primary research. No great economy is generated or sustained without innovation and invention, and embedding them in the growth process. This is India's missing link!

We are well poised for further savings generation. Our demographic projections reveal, up to 2045, the 25-59 age group of income earners will increase though our younger cohorts will diminish and retirees will increase (Figure 8.3). Thus, for the next 30-35 years, our savings and investment will increase further, have positive ramifications for economic growth, and vice versa. However, we need to innovate and take technology forward. The public sector has to step back once again and stop crowding out the private sector.

1. Chandra, R. and R.J. Sandilands (2001). "Does Investment Cause Growth? A Test of An Endogenous Demand-driven Theory of Growth Applied to India 1950-96", *University of Strathclyde Working Paper*, UK.

Figure 8.3

India: Age Structure

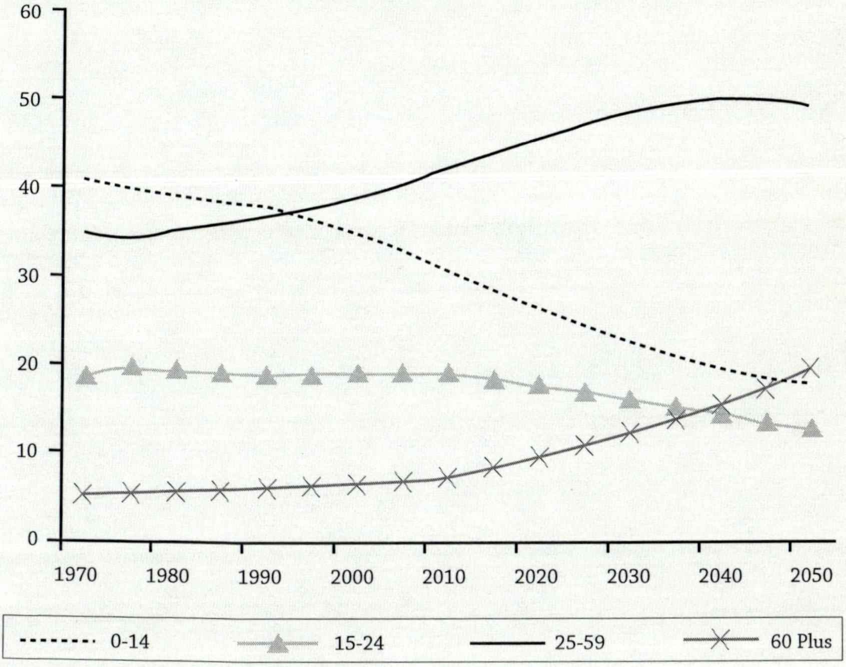

Source: United Nations Population Division.

We should eradicate custom-tailored tax incentives and create a level playing field for all productive activity. We will then surely witness a surge in economic growth and in tax revenue with which we might address our deep challenges in income distribution and poverty.

Business Standard, 8 January 2011.

II

Fiscal Policy

9

Ramifications of Budget 2016-17

TV discussions would lead one to view the Budget as having a shelf life of 48 to 72 hours. By that count, it is water under the bridge. Yet, listening to its delivery intently, I concluded that its ramifications would be long run, many adverse. Finance Minister Arun Jaitley started by saying we had crossed seven per cent real GDP growth. Juxtaposed on the quarter ending December with a crash in exports and zero growth in the non-financial non-oil sector, his assertion drew critical attention regarding how 2015-16 will turn out. Would it not have been safer to caution his fellow citizens of the impending Ides of March?

The FM's attention to the agricultural sector was direly needed following two seasons of drought for a community with a median income of less than ₹30,000 per annum (not month). But when it was declared that farmers' income would be doubled in five years, the necessity of an annual growth of 16-17 per cent tumbled out as against its current 6 to 7 per cent. So the question arose how this 10 per cent point per annum difference would be closed.

India is lucky to achieve agricultural real growth of two per cent. It has achieved four per cent as a windfall after it has had four consecutive years of above-average rainfall. Since the 1970s this has occurred five times or so. Yet if inflation is contained at six to seven per cent, then even four per cent real growth is insufficient for the next five years. Despite promises of rural infrastructure and irrigation, the fact is Indian agriculture remains so deeply rain-fed and irrigation has been so neglected or funds so pilfered that no government can achieve the needed output outcomes within a five-year frame. Would it not have been better for the FM to take

Indians into confidence and explain the choices he was facing and had considered?

What, for example, has he done about the promised MSP (minimum support price) of 50 per cent above cost? In fact, available information reveals that for wheat, cost has increased slightly less than MSP in the last three years but, for varieties of lentils, cost has risen faster than MSP, leave alone MSP being 50 per cent higher than cost. There can be little wonder at the spate of farmer suicides borne down as they are with unrepayable debt reflecting the vagaries of nature.

What is an amazing degree of irrationality is the bulk of the intelligentsia crying out for greater funding for recapitalisation of banks than Budget allocation. Given that much of the banks' woes are wayward capitalists and the public sector itself, government's first duty is to announce unconditional forgiveness of farm debt and, for unorganised sector lenders, pay those lenders directly on behalf of farmers. This duty precedes that of buttressing "the elephants that hide amidst the mice" as a Latin American finance minister confided in me once. The introduction of another tax amnesty scheme is another instance of rewarding the undeserving and reveals the government's underlying weakness in favour of short-term resources despite indications that amnesties don't change taxpayer behaviour permanently.

Regarding tax policy, the biggest disappointment was the compromise on the promised corporate tax reduction path. The FM could have reduced headline CIT rate by a half per cent or even a quarter per cent across the board and taken business into confidence why the reduction path would take longer reflecting the slowness in GST introduction. Instead of strongly reducing tax incentives, some of which was done, some were introduced including exemptions for certain SEZ's from MAT. Rather than fundamental reform, to make up for tax revenue loss, distortions were introduced: tripling STT on options, incentives for startups, new cesses, tinkering with Acts, rules and customs duties. Admittedly, the private sector's pre-Budget pushing for incentives even while rooting for CIT reduction revealed a continuation of past individualist behaviour rather than an emergence of maturity, clearly detrimental to the global good of a lower CIT. The discretionary tax measures would yield ₹23,000 crore in indirect taxes with a negative yield for direct taxes. This is not helpful for raising the direct tax to indirect tax ratio, often taken as a sign of a mature tax system and what had been accomplished by 2006-07. By now that ratio has reversed.

Reflecting low tax effort, the fallout was the heavy if not exaggerated dependence on non-tax revenue to finance and achieve a 3.5 per cent fiscal deficit target. Broad calculations show 45 per cent are from RBI transfers plus dividends, 20 per cent from telecom revenues, 10 per cent from disinvestment. Regarding the RBI, it already transfers all its surpluses to the exchequer; hence windfall transfers are now moot. Regarding dividends, pressure on PSUs and PSBs to cough up more money even as their valuations are dwindling seems fruitless. Instead, concrete plans to privatise both should have been put up-front. This was missing. The budgeted ₹56,000 crore from disinvestment has never been achieved earlier, even by this government. These expectations are not convincing.

Last but not least, looking at telecom, ₹99,000 crore are budgeted, of which ₹22,000 crore are from license and spectrum fees and perhaps achievable, ₹21,000 crore from arrears and deferred payments including disputed amounts languishing in courts, hence clearly not achievable in a single year, leaving ₹56,000 crore from spectrum auction of 700 MHz. This implies DoT will have to sell spectrum worth three times, that is, ₹2 lakh crore since companies only pay 30 per cent up-front. This will not occur within the time-frame even as large telecom operators have already indicated the price set is too high.

Summing up, the Budget has placed too little emphasis on tax reform or tax revenue sources of financing. The tax structure is worse today than on 28 February. Of the heavy emphasis on non-tax revenue, many have insufficient basis within the 2016-17 time-frame. The apparently benign objective of a shift towards the farmer does not stand on firm ground. The big question remains why government missed a genuine opportunity for working out a viable roadmap for fundamental reform, bring individuals and business into confidence by presenting a meaningful social contract, and then adhering to it.

Business Standard, 15 March 2016.

10

2015-16 Union Budget

The Must and the Must Not

The Union Budget a few days hence is sailing on the high seas of expectations. It is being perceived as the last chance for the new government to demonstrate its capability to act on the ground for, its previous Budget posthumously acquired a label of being far too simplistic, needlessly adhering to unachievable goals set by the previous government. Thus, it would not be too difficult for the forthcoming Budget to improve upon the last.

Yet, improvement is not what India is looking for. Bold, dynamic, growth orientation in taxation coupled with minutely targeted programmes for the truly vulnerable shorn of undeserving subsidies in consumption and production that have given subsidies such a bad name comprise every even minded person's expectation. This carries considerable challenges; yet this is the optimal moment, for people are ready for, and expect, cutting edge changes. If this opportunity is missed even in a non election year, government will not recapture it.

The expenditure side is where deep cuts are needed for, without it, the "tax terrorism" regime that the ruling party itself had coined when it was in the opposition would necessarily continue to be used and thus would get further entrenched under even its own government. That would be ironic indeed. It must be digested by the new policymakers that statements are believed only when well matched action follows; it is on the basis of those detailed policy corrections that business decisions are actually made. They must surely be made before the sunset of government's honeymoon with the productive sectors that elected it to represent them, appears on the horizon.

Once the government correctly perceives itself as having been elected to take action freely, it should be ready for going to war in correcting the morass of wrong economic policies that India is currently beset with. India is autarkic in its lack of interest in international policy experience, entrenched in its belief and conviction that 'we are different' than the rest of the world. In fact, even the smallest countries take for example Andorra, nestled between France and Spain with 400 sq km of space, nonetheless with 11 municipalities think likewise. The same could be said about India. But India is no different from the rest of the world in the fundamental economic principles that guide the well being or failure of an economy.

Research shows that vote bank politics erroneously thinks that false promises are better than promising truthful expected action. Voters will have more confidence in a government that is formed by those who did not make pre-election false promises and follows up fully with the limited promises—even the harsh choices—revealed before elections. This government should do the same before it reaches post election fatigue. The debacle of the recent Delhi elections could otherwise get exacerbated elsewhere.

The government can bury tax terrorism by curtailing expenditure. First, this should comprise penalties and incarceration following declared monitoring and evaluation procedures for its various expenditure programmes as all self monitoring countries do. The processes should not take asymptotically infinite time as in India. Second, subsidies should be targeted only for the extremely vulnerable and not for urbanites. The argument that middle class life is becoming intolerable may be acceptable in an absolute sense though it sounds unconvincing in the relative context of India's overall extreme poverty. Government should design subsidies only for the absolute poor. Third, production incentives for any named sector should be abandoned other than narrowly and clearly defined infrastructure. It should be confined only to investment. This will be government's biggest test. Fourth, government should announce a review and revision of the calculation of revenue loss from tax incentives that has been presented in every Budget since 2006. The methodology needs urgent re-examination. Fifth, government should create an Office of Expenditure Monitoring and Evaluation (M&E) that would be accountable for tracking efficiency of, and leakage from, expenditure programmes. One admits that the Centre cannot do the job alone. This is after all a federal state. The Centre cannot control many large states. And leakage there as has been, and continues to be, revealed, is mind-boggling. A Truth Commission is called for to address this national crisis.

On the tax side, first, fixed point revenue targets should be buried. Second, the Chief Economic Adviser (CEA) of the Ministry of Finance should be directed to develop a model of economic cycles with built in taxability of different productive sectors as has been developed in other emerging and advanced economies. This is the CEA's acid test. The model's continuing outcomes will enable the Finance Minister to give the tax administration meaningful moving revenue targets over the economic cycle so that, third, tax payers are spared illogical, if not illegal, tax collection. Otherwise, a second Salt Tax March could not be ruled out reflecting the lurking anger in the productive sectors. Fourth, to assuage good taxpayers, the Minister should announce the concrete framework he intends to put in place to enable good taxpayers to comply voluntarily. He should indicate how, fifth, he intends to clamp down on corruption and, sixth, raise accountability for resolving disputes by tax officers, the sum total of which has led to out-of-the-graph indicators for India's tax disputes and difficulty in conducting business. The Prime Minister's best intentions would otherwise continue to remain sullied. It must be admitted that the recent announcement that the stock of disputes would be examined comprises a step in the right direction though the Budget should announce a menu of comparable sensible measures.

This much is surely reasonable to expect as a start for, the reality in its details is far worse for the daily life of the economic agent and the good taxpayer. Tax laws and rules continue to be introduced without discussion. Tax revenue dissipates through rampant expenditure leakages. Is there much wonder that the taxpayer base has remained at 3.5 crore over the last decade despite GDP's impressive growth, so unsuccessful it has been to convince potential taxpayers—the so-called non-filers—to enter the tax net. Time is short. True and deep action is awaited in the much anticipated Union Budget. Let the government reveal that it can take serious action by introducing strong and meaningful measures that the country is expecting it to take.

Business Standard, 17 February 2015.

11

2015-16: A Union Budget with Sense and Sensibility

Reams have been written on the Union Budget extolling its proposals or damning them. As the discussion approaches an asymptotic termination, I find that something needs to be said in retrospect that balances the thrust of the debate that ensued soon after its presentation in Parliament.

The primary concern prior to the Budget was how to address the extremely negative aspects of taxation for business decisions that had driven domestic and foreign investment away from Indian shores. To elaborate, businesses face two obstacles when making a business decision. The first is risk. An investor has a perception of the risk he faces as a risk averter or a risk preferer. Reflecting his perception of risk in an investment, he decides to invest by taking risk insurance, or to stay away from the investment.

The second is uncertainty. The investor has a hard time assessing uncertainty, for it represents factors quite beyond his conceptualisation in the environment from where he should ideally be in a position to judge if a potential investment is worth it or not. Tax laws between 2009-2012 converted the investment environment quite uncertain. Worse, not only did uncertainty prevail for the future, but it was extended into the past through various retrospective amendments, some of which catapulted India to a global high as a poor place to invest.

To begin, the Budget has no doubt attempted to address uncertainty. First, it has postponed GAAR for another two years and has indicated its prospective application. However, this will not help unless tax officers are given intensive training as to how to use the instrument. Further, the income tax department has so far ignored the thirty plus examples provided by the 2012 GAAR committee for the use of GAAR. These examples should be vitalised. Otherwise, a mere postponement would be ineffective in removing uncertainty that would be caused by GAAR's application.

Second, Finance Minister announced that the taxation of indirect transfers will be addressed by CBDT through a clarificatory circular. That is welcome. However, there was no explanation why he did not prescribe primary legislation for it especially since such a circular can only address indirect transfers exclusively rather than remove or restrict retrospective taxation in a wider context. Yet, only the latter would remove uncertainty comprehensively. Further, the 2012 committee on taxation of indirect transfers had cautioned against (1) treaty override since India still is a capital importing country, and (2) taxing indirect transfers between companies registered and trading on the stock exchange. If these matters remain inadequately addressed, a Pandora's Box of issues will jump out to scuttle government's stated economic objective of enhancing ease of doing business.

Third, FM's mention that recommendations of the Tax Administration Reform Commission (TARC) that has just completed its work, will be implemented in 2015-16 was salutary though elaboration would have been useful for taxpayers to be reassured. TARC emphasised the importance of assigning accountability since, contrary to modernising tax administrations, India simply does not practice it, looking at the mass of tax disputes. It would not be surprising if the Indian total surpasses a combined rest-of-the-world. FM's mention of a Disputes Bill was salutary but details are awaited.

Fourth, following the announcement of GST introduction in 2016, it is time now to put any proposed structure up for discussion with stakeholders and to desist from introducing GST just on the basis of centre-state discussions at government level. Governments tend to discuss GST proposals in great detail with taxpayers and the Indian government should follow those modern principles. After all, a move from the current indirect tax structure would make sense only if GST is anchored on easing business and investment. Yet, so far there is no White Paper on GST structure leave alone deeper technical aspects that will undoubtedly affect taxpayers and fundamentally alter their interface with central and state tax administrations.

Fifth, FM's pre-announcement of government's intention to reduce the headline corporate tax rate to 25 per cent in consonance with GST dynamism was a daring step in the right direction. However, the super rich tax does impact corporations as well so that in the current year, they will be hit with a higher tax rate. This could have been explained through some justification in the government's view of a super rich tax that includes non-individuals.

Sixth, the abolition of the wealth tax that hardly yields revenue was a good idea but, in as poor a country as India, should government reject wealth taxation completely, or should it redesign it at a very small rate on a wide base as proposed in DTC 2013? This matter should be seriously reconsidered.

Indeed, seventh, FM's statement that the DTC was being dropped altogether on grounds that most DTC proposals had already been incorporated in the Income Tax Act reflected an erroneous view of the tax administration that the remaining tough nuts to crack could be safely set aside from the ITA. Even Yashwant Sinha expressed disappointment at this. FM should retract from this position not necessarily through another statement but through reexamination of DTC 2013 and incorporating the many reform features that remain to be included in ITA. This topic is worth revisiting at some point by tax experts.

Eighth, tax revenue has suffered due to the underground economy. While Switzerland has an announcement effect, the bulk of the problem resides in India. The Budget announcements to curb black money are the strongest ever made by any Indian government. It is to be seen how far government is able or willing to move on this. If it can, greater tax revenue will get rightfully captured in the exchequer and the administration would be more easily able to become customer friendly in its operations. The crux here would be to encourage and ensure voluntary compliance by not going after roving enquiries and thereby turning good taxpayers into non-filers.

Ninth, the small attempt by government to address environmental degradation by doubling the clean energy cess on coal from ₹100 to

₹200 per metric tonne was welcome though, certainly, this is not enough. Urban areas in India deplete life by three years on average; yet there is blindness in favour of pushing the concept of the small car hub. There has to be wider unilateral use of carbon tax in India without looking over our shoulders to see what other countries are doing. We owe this to ourselves.

Tenth, I would like to emphasise three salient features that added sense and sensibility to the Budget. First, it made sense to focus tax incentives on investment, primarily infrastructure where the widest gap exists. Second, it also made sense to extend the fiscal deficit target by one year for absolutely nothing was to be gained by strict adherence to a paper target when revival of the economy is of the direst importance. Third, there was a touch of sensibility by focusing expenditure subsidies on the absolute poor while cutting back on the ones fraught with leakage as field reports continue to reveal.

That the government bit the bullet to reveal its intentions and promises is a sign of apparent sincerity. However, its Budget did leave behind a veil over feasibility and a challenge of delivery.

Business Standard, 17 March 2015.

12

The Budget's Massive Tax Effort

Already, commentary on the Union Budget has been prolific. I propose to examine it from my concern over fiscal consolidation. The most striking aspect of India's fiscal stance since 2008-09 has been a slow erosion of the gains made in fiscal consolidation during the preceding four years. Indeed, many emerging economies may have made an error in going along with heterodox fiscal stimulus policies initiated by advanced economies most hit by the 2008-09 global recession. For example, there is scant analysis that India needed a stimulus following its successful conservative fiscal stance of 2005-2008 when, by global standards, record-high real tax revenue growth and containment of public debt were achieved (see Table 12.1). Subsequently, reversals from expansionary policies internationally appeared only in 2011-12 after further macroeconomic deterioration in advanced economies, and the concomitant realisation that expansionary policies cannot lead an economy out of deep breaches in economic fundamentals. Thus, the reversal was inevitable, since unfettered expansion failed finally to escape the judgement of global rating agencies.

India did not change its fiscal stance adequately even in 2011-12. Table 12.1 shows the deteriorated tax/GDP ratios, hovering around 7 per cent since 2009-10. Overall revenue receipts suffered the same experience. Total expenditure/GDP ranged between 15.5 and 16 per cent, though in 2011-12 it was constrained to below 15 per cent. In the toss-up, has there been any consolidation? The significant rise in the fiscal deficit indicates that indeed there was fiscal worsening, and what the 2012-13 Budget has proposed is to reverse direction and attempt fiscal consolidation by almost 1 per cent of GDP through a massive tax effort.

Table 12.1

Fiscal Performance

		2005-06/ 2007-08	2008-09/ 2009-10	2010-11	2011-12	2012-13 BE
		(% to GDP)				
1.	Revenue Receipts	10.1	9.3	10.3	8.6	9.2
2.	Tax Revenue (Net to Centre)	8.1	7.5	7.4	7.2	7.6
3.	Non-Tax Revenue	2.0	1.6	2.8	1.4	1.6
4.	Capital Receipts of which	3.7	6.6	5.3	6.2	5.5
5.	Borrowings and Other Liabilities	3.3	6.3	4.9	5.9	5.1
6.	Total Receipts	13.9	15.8	15.6	14.8	14.7
7.	Non-Plan Expenditure	9.9	11.0	10.7	10.0	9.5
8.	Plan Expenditure	4.0	4.8	4.9	4.8	5.1
9.	Total Expenditure	13.9	15.8	15.6	14.8	14.7
10.	Revenue Defict	1.8	4.9	3.3	4.4	3.4
11.	Fiscal Defict	3.3	6.3	4.9	5.9	5.1
12.	Primary Defict	-0.2	2.9	1.8	2.8	1.9
		Growth of GDP				
	Real (Constant Market Prices)	9.5	6.1	9.6	7.5	
	Nominal (Market Prices)	15.4	13.8	18.8	16.1	14.0*
	Ral (Constant Factor Cost)	9.5	7.6	8.4	6.9	7.6*

Note: * Budget projection.

Source: *Union Budget 2012-13.*

Fiscal consolidation is best examined through the annual changes in tax and expenditure. Positive numbers for both revenue and expenditure indicate desired fiscal tightening while negative numbers reveal fiscal worsening. It is apparent from Table 12.2 that, except for 2010-11, the high growth year, the tax side did not help fiscal tightening, though the expenditure side was more successful. Also, non-Plan expenditure was tightened more than Plan expenditure—a welcome feature.

Table 12.2

Fiscal Consolidation

	2008-09/ 2009-10	2010-11	2011-12	2012-13 BE
(% to GDP)				
1. Tax Revenue (Net to Centre)	-0.87	0.36	-0.22	0.38
2. Non-Tax Revenue	-0.13	1.05	-1.45	0.22
3. Capital Receipts**	-0.19	-0.05	-0.13	0.08
4. Total Consolidation of Revenue Side	-1.18	1.35	-1.79	0.68
(Δ% to GDP)× -1				
5. Non-Plan Expenditure	-0.50	0.50	0.65	0.46
6. Plan Expenditure	-0.30	-0.24	0.15	-0.34
7. Total Consolidation of Expenditure Side	-0.79	0.26	0.81	0.12
8. Fiscal Defict (7+4)	-1.97	1.61	-0.99	0.80
9. Primary Defict	-0.32	1.36	-0.95	0.86

Notes: 1) + Tighten / - Loosen.

** 2) Does not include receipts in respect of Market Stabilization Scheme and excludes Borrowings and other Liabilities.

Source: Union Budget 2012-13.

Table 12.3 elaborates on expenditure composition. For example, pension expenditure and defence have been on a tightening mode since 2010-11, and subsidies are budgeted to be significantly tightened in 2012-13, yielding an overall supportive outcome for non-Plan expenditure. Plan expenditure, on the other hand, has not, on average, been tightened and is budgeted to expand significantly in 2012-13. On the whole, therefore, within the complexity of a centrifugal coalition government, expenditure tightening and changes in its composition have been relatively successful.

Table 12.4 goes on to decompose subsidies. Interestingly, tightening has occurred, by and large, in fertiliser and food subsidies. This is to continue in 2012-13. On the other hand, petroleum subsidy has increased in recent years and has overwhelmed gains in other areas. It is no surprise that the Budget has proposed its most significant tightening for 2012-13. One can only speculate on its chance of success, however.

Table 12.3

Expenditure Consolidation

	2008-09/ 2009-10	2010-11	2011-12	2012-13 BE
	(Δ% to GDP)× -1			
	Non-Plan Expenditure			
1. Interest Payments and Debt Servicing	0.07	0.25	-0.04	-0.06
2. Defence Expenditure	-0.18	0.19	0.09	0.01
3. Subsidies	-0.38	-0.07	-0.17	0.56
4. Pensions	-0.19	0.12	0.12	0.01
5. Police	-0.06	0.05	-0.02	0.02
6. Other Non-Plan Expenditures	0.26	-0.03	0.67	-0.08
Total	-0.49	0.51	0.65	0.46
	Plan Expenditure			
On Revenue Account	-0.23	-0.16	0.21	-0.25
On Capital Account	-0.07	-0.08	-0.06	-0.09
Total	-0.30	-0.24	0.15	-0.34

Source: *Union Budget 2012-13.*

Table 12.4

Behaviour of Subsidies

	2008-09/2009-10	2010-11	2011-12	2012-13 BE
	(Δ% to GDP)× -1			
Fertiliser Subsidy	-0.17	0.14	0.06	0.15
Food Subsidy	-0.14	0.07	0.02	0.08
Petroleum Subsidy	-0.09	-0.27	-0.27	0.34
Interest Subsidies	0.01	-0.02	0.00	-0.01
Other Subsidies	-0.01	0.01	0.03	0.00
Total Subsidies	-0.40	-0.07	-0.16	0.56

Source: *Union Budget 2012-13.*

The effort made by the central government in tax revenue is the focus of Table 12.5. The overall tax effort is revealing in itself. It may be recalled that last year's net additional, discretionary tax effort—between direct and indirect tax measures—was some ₹3,000 crore only as I recall. That is reflected in the negative outcome in gross tax effort for 2011-12. In the light of this recent experience, it is as if the government has suddenly realised its folly and budgeted for discretionary tax measures of ₹41,000 crore for 2012-13, helping yield an additional 0.5 per cent of GDP tax revenue realisation for 2012-13. What is remarkable is that all of this, and more, comes out of indirect—customs, excise and service—taxes, since there is an actual discretionary loss from direct—income—taxes of ₹4,500 crore.

Table 12.5

Tax Effort

		2008-09/2009-10	*2010-11*	*2011-12*	*2012-13 BE*
		(Δ% to GDP)			
		Gross Tax Revenue			
1.	Corporation Tax	-0.04	0.10	-0.22	0.00
2.	Taxes on Income other Corporation Tax	-0.09	-0.09	0.06	0.00
3.	Customs	-0.40	0.48	-0.05	0.12
4.	Union Excise Duties	-0.44	0.20	-0.11	0.22
5.	Service Tax	-0.07	0.02	0.14	0.16
6.	Other Taxes	-0.09	-0.05	-0.04	0.00
	Total	-1.12	0.66	-0.22	0.50

Source: Union Budget 2012-13.

While a serious attempt at fiscal consolidation cannot be faulted, the impact of such a massive discretionary tax effort entirely from the indirect tax side on income distribution could be severe, as has been revealed time and again from economic literature.[1] It does not bode well that the government was able to design consolidation only through worsening income distribution. Of course there are a plethora of incremental income support measures, but they do not benefit the burgeoning lower middle classes who will certainly suffer from the indirect tax measures, and will damage the UPA's emphatic thrust. It is this type of policymaking that lacks any recognisable

1. Shome, P. (2011). "Consumption Taxes: Their Ramifications for Income Distribution", *ICRIER Policy Series* No. 8. New Delhi. *http://icrier.org/pdf/Policy_Series_No_8.pdf*

analytical framework or strategy that would cost the government precious votes in the near term.

Das ist the fiscal stance of the Budget. It promises a lot and comprises overall good intention; last year there was not even this promise based on a wake-up call. A caveat, however. The fiscal world and cross-country benchmarking will not be swayed by the effective revenue deficit concept as if the cost of creating capital assets by the government should just be ignored. The concept could conceivably provide a check in a tool box, but not anything more. In any event, if the private sector were appropriately encouraged, it would create and manage those assets more adequately and efficiently than bureaucrats and administrators ever could. Perhaps the Budget also deserves a fine-tooth comb examination of its tax and expenditure components—next month perhaps.

Business Standard, 19 March 2012.

13

Year of Fiscal Consolidation

The 2008-09 global financial crisis led to severe economic contraction—actual decline in GDP—in several advanced economies. In the UK, for example, the medium-term GDP trend shifted downwards for some years to come. This shift was accompanied by a decline in revenue/GDP and a rise in expenditure/GDP ratios reflecting unemployment benefits. The revival of economic activity was anchored on quantitative easing which did not work fast enough since the injected finance froze as the money multiplier collapsed. Focus turned to fiscal support through tax reductions and further current expenditure enhancements. The already rising fiscal deficit/GDP was further exacerbated. Public debt/GDP in some countries doubled. Stock market and rating agencies did not appreciate what the country indicators were showing and strategies had to be reformulated.

Strategies were refocused on fiscal consolidation and debates ensued on its pace and content. Elections were won and lost on this issue. Indeed, at Brookings, Alesina, Perotti and Tavares in 1998 had found fiscal rectitude to be rewarded by voters. The UK proved a case in point: Labour departed and a Conservative-Liberal coalition entered in May 2010. The latter's more austere fiscal positioning won the voters' confidence.

Later at NBER Harvard, Alesina and Ardagna[1] in 2009 also found that fiscal adjustments mostly on the spending side have a better chance of not creating large recessions on impact. Midyear, post-election UK opted for this route. The pre-election Labour Budget

1. Alesina, Alberto et al. (1998). "The Political Economy of Fiscal Adjustments." *Brookings Papers on Economic Activity* 29: 197-266.

(March) and post-election Conservative-Liberal Budget (June) viewed corrective policies quite differently. Figure 13.1 illustrates the additional tightening. The final calibration expressed in the coalition's Spending Review (October) that anchored a five-year austerity programme further recomposed expenditure in favour of investment over consumption. It cut back untargeted direct consumption subsidies and reduced the length and pattern of unemployment coverage.

Figure 13.1

UK Fiscal Consolidation Plans

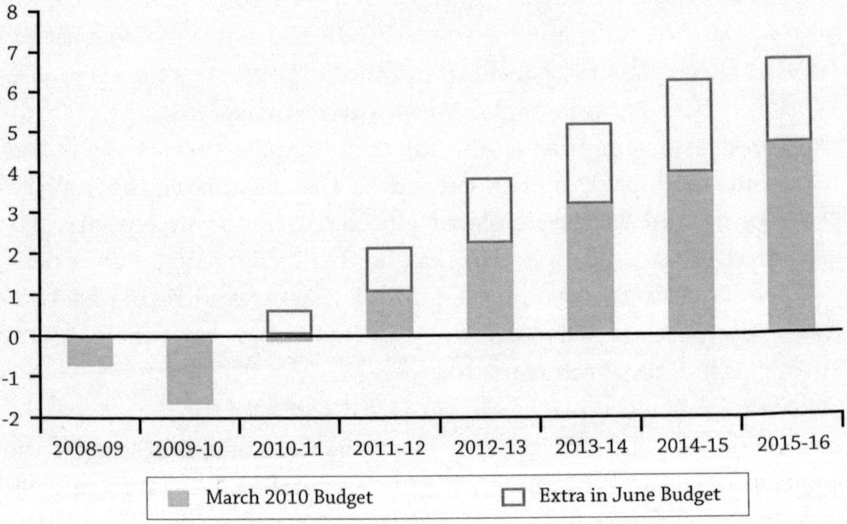

Source: Institute of Fiscal Studies (2010).

Table 13.1 presents published Figures on how the tightening—tax increase and expenditure reduction—was broken down in March, June and October. Only 2014-15, the last projection year, is selected for illustrative purposes, revealing a significantly tighter stance of the new government in nominal terms (row 8). The coalition, in two (June and October) steps: (1) increased taxes more; (2) maintained investment spending; (3) scaled back current spending considerably; and (4) within current spending, cut back benefits (direct subsidies) much more than public services (mainly National Health Service [NHS], the universal health coverage for which the UK is well known).

Thus, tax increase shot up between March and June Budgets (row 1) while expenditure reduction was more severe than tax increase (row 2). Cut in investment spending was a bit deeper in June than March but the cut was pulled back and investment spending was restored in October (row 3).

Table 13.1

UK Composition of Tightening: Projections for 2014-15

(in £ billion)

		March 2010 Budget	*June 2010 Budget*	*October 2010 Spending Review*
1.	Tax	21.5	29.8	29.8
2.	Spending	50.9	82.8	80.5
3.	Investment Spending	17.2	19.3	17.0
4.	Current Spending of which:	33.7	63.5	63.5
5.	Debt Interest	7.0	10.0	10.0
6.	Benefits	-0.3	10.7	17.7
7.	Public Services	27.0	42.8	35.7
8.	Total Tightening	72.4	112.6	110.3
9.	% Spending	70.0	74.0	73.0
10.	% Tax	30.0	26.0	27.0
11.	Forecast Net Public Debt as % GDP in 2013/14	74.5	70.3	69.7

Source: Institute of Fiscal Studies (2010).

The severe cutback instead came from current spending. The cutback almost doubled between the two governments (row 4). Interestingly, direct benefits (targeted and untargeted consumption subsidies and work incentives) had been protected in the March Budget; but they were reduced considerably in June by the incoming government—even more than their tax increase—and the benefits cutback was further increased in October (row 6). The reduction in expenditure on public services, the other major head of current spending—the significant component being the NHS—was also deeper between March and June. But in a reversal, the cutback was partially reduced between June and October. In sum, the new government reallocated the cuts within current spending between June and October, making them deeper for direct subsidies and less so for the NHS. Thus the right combination of cutbacks emerged between: (1) tax and expenditure, (2) between investment and current spending, and (3) between pure consumption and service-oriented current spending. The new mix relied more on spending cuts than tax increase (rows 9 and 10). Also, the deeper fiscal correction implied that public debt/GDP improved faster by almost 5 percentage points (row 11). Most importantly, the much deeper nominal fiscal correction will be achieved with a lower economic growth—and, therefore, income path—that is more realistic than the pre-election projections.

Table 13.2

UK Macro Indicators

	2010	*2012*	*2014*
*Real GDP Growth**			
March Budget 2010	1.25	3.5	3.25
June Budget 2010	1.2	2.8	2.7
October 2010 Spending Review[1]	1.8	2.6	2.8
*Public Sector Net Borrowing (as % GDP)**			
March Budget 2010	11.1	6.8	4
June Budget 2010	10.1	5.5	2.1
October 2010 Spending Review[1]	10	5.6	1.9
*Cyclically Adjusted Surplus on Current Borrowing (as % GDP)**			
March Budget 2010	-4.6	-2.5	-1.3
June Budget 2010	-4.8	-1.9	0.3
October 2010 Spending Review[1]	-4.7	-1.8	0.5
*Net Public Debt (as % GDP)**			
March Budget 2010	63.6	73	74.9
June Budget 2010	61.9	69.8	69.4
October 2010 Spending Review[1]	60.8	69.1	68.8

Note: * Figure given for tax years (i.e. 2009=2009/10).

1. Economic data taken from OBR's Autumn *Economic and Fiscal Outlook*.

Table 13.2 explains some basic macroeconomic projections between March, June and October. First is the considerable reduction in the trajectory of GDP growth between March and June Budgets, bringing the series closer to the average of independent projectors. The October Review made small differences to those projections. Second, projections of public sector net borrowing/GDP also declined from March to June through October. Third, a comparable change occurred in the cyclically adjusted current fiscal account surplus. The March figures had projected a deficit even for 2014. The subsequent tightening produced a small surplus in June figures for 2014, and a higher one in October. Fourth, translated into net public debt, the increase in the series in terms of GDP became less pronounced between March and June Budgets, and further so in October.

Thus, the incoming UK government undertook difficult fiscal measures in 2010 on both the revenue and expenditure fronts. These corrections were higher in nominal terms compared to the pre-election measures. And, since GDP projections were scaled down post-election, the measures represent tighter belt-tightening. This fiscal stance moved with academic empirical findings and won the regard of multilateral institutions. A challenge appeared much later when the inheritors of an almost doubled public debt/GDP were also informed that they would face an almost threefold increase in their university tuition fees. Clearly, the UK opted for a consolidated fiscal stance. India's forthcoming Budget should use fiscal policy to curb inflation. The components would be quite similar.

Business Standard, 12 February 2011.

14

The Evolving Fiscal Stance

The 2010-11 Economic Survey and 2011-12 Union Budget have come and gone. The immediate reactions sought by media have dissipated. Now is the moment to deconstruct and thus view the overall fiscal stance that is emerging over the last few years through, and post, global financial crisis.

First, India's fiscal developments reveal a relaxation in tax and expenditure efforts during the crisis followed by relative tightening after the crisis from 2010-11. Thus, consolidation is taking place during the current up-cycle. Overall, therefore, the stance has been countercyclical as it should be. And any overall fiscal strategy behind this has to be commended.

However, the total consolidation picture appears to be dependent somewhat on serendipity as non-tax revenue growth flip-flopped due to temporary gains from spectrum sales (Table 14.1, row 2) and disinvestment receipts. On the expenditure side too, though efforts towards countercyclical policy in non-Plan current expenditure have been successful, (row 5), Plan expenditure maintenance has been unstable over recent years. Of course, the finance minister expressed satisfaction in his Budget Speech that last year Plan expenditure was met.

The second good aspect is that post-crisis, in 2010-11 and 2011-2012, fiscal consolidation is coming mainly from the expenditure side rather than from revenue (excluding the spectrum windfall) (Table 14.1, rows 4 and 7). Academic research has shown that consolidation based on expenditure tightening is less recessionary than that based on tax revenue increases.

Table 14.1

India Fiscal Consolidation

		2008-09	2009-10	2010-11	2011-12 Budget
		(Δ % to GDP)			
1.	Tax Revenue (Net to Centre)	-0.87	-0.97	0.19	0.24
2.	Non-Tax Revenue	-0.32	0.04	1.02	-1.40
3.	Capital Receipts**	-0.76	0.39	-0.10	0.21
4.	Total Consolidation of Revenue Side	-1.95	-0.55	1.10	-0.94
		(Δ % to GDP)×-1			
5.	Non-Plan Expenditure	-0.72	-0.10	0.58	1.34
6.	Plan Expenditure	-0.82	0.30	-0.38	0.10
7.	Total Consolidation of Expenditure Side	-1.54	0.19	0.20	1.44
8.	Fiscal Deficit (7+4)	-3.5	-0.4	1.3	0.5
9.	Primary Deficit	-3.5	2.9	1.1	0.4

Notes: + Tighten / - Loosen; **: Does not include receipts in respect of Market Stabilisation Scheme and excludes Borrowings and other Liabilities; Δ: Change.

However, further scrutiny of the effort to reduce the fiscal deficit (row 8) as well as the primary deficit (row 9) indicates that, while fiscal deficit tightening, or reduction, turned out to be 1.3 per cent of GDP in 2010-11, it is budgeted to be only 0.5 per cent of GDP for 2011-12. One explanation for this tepid course of action is that there were no underlying discretionary tax effort or net revenue yielding tax measures in the Union Budget. Going deeper, since no net tax measures were taken, post-crisis, the tax revenue buoyancy is coming from economic growth rather than from tax effort. During the up-cycle, the lack of tax effort appears to be somewhat pro-cyclical and remains a challenge to be corrected in the 2012-13 Budget. A positive, and higher tax effort would enable a faster reduction in the deficit, and getting back on, and recharting the course of, FRBM quickly.

Further, whatever tax effort has been made in increasing indirect tax revenue has been given away through decreases in direct tax revenue. This is especially curious in an economy that should have been continuing to reduce its dependence on narrow production taxes while expanding the direct tax base even while reducing the headline income tax rates. And this would not have been a new direction since revenue reform had already made a solid start in this direction from 2005, tilting the revenue balance in favour of direct over indirect tax.

Table 14.2

India Tax Effort

		2008-09	2009-10	2010-11	2011-12 Budget
		(% to GDP)			
	Δ in Tax Revenue	-0.87	-0.97	0.19	0.24
	Composition of the Δ in Gross Tax Revenue				
1.	Corporation Tax	-4.4	-6.6	5.7	62.52
2.	Taxes on Income other than Corporation Tax	-15.1	-2.4	-15.7	8.9
3.	Customs	-28.4	-39.5	88.3	4.1
4.	Union Excise Duties	-50.7	-28.5	37.4	20.0
5.	Service Tax	6.0	-15.3	-2.4	8.1
6.	Wealth Tax	0.0	0.1	-0.1	0.0
7.	Other Taxes and Duties	-7.4	-7.5	-13.3	-3.0
8.	Taxes of Union Territories	0.0	-0.2	-0.1	-0.6
	Total	-100	-100	100	100

Note: + Tighten / - Loosen.

Indeed, the components of tax effort or buoyancy are widely different year by year (Table 14.2). Whatever the underlying explanations, overall it appears that varying tax policies have been employed through time, for example corporate income tax (row 1) in 2011-12 and customs duty (row 3) in 2010-11. The overall stance in the mix and sources of tax revenue change should ideally reflect a well-rounded strategy rather than a mere bottom-line. This should occur even if the DTC or GST is awaited since neither of them would represent an immediate solution to the right revenue balance between direct and indirect taxes. Indeed, no such calculation is known to have been conducted. Thus, the revenue mix and balance between direct and indirect taxes should be independently addressed and treated as another challenge for the 2012-13 Budget.

The third nice aspect in the 2011-12 Budget was the tightening of subsidies. This has been the case in all major subsidies and has taken place over recent years as revealed in the numbers (Table 14.3) for subsidies on fertiliser, food, and petroleum. This too is commendable.

Table 14.3

India Tightening of Subsidies

	2008-09	*2009-10*	*2010-11*	*2011-12 Budget*
	(% to GDP)×-1			
Δ in Fertiliser Subsidy	-0.76	0.44	0.24	0.14
Δ in Food Subsidy	-0.15	-0.11	0.12	0.09
Δ in Petroleum Subsidy	0.01	-0.18	-0.26	0.22
Δ in Interest Subsidies	-0.01	0.02	-0.03	-0.01
Δ in Other Subsidies	-0.01	-0.01	0.00	0.04
Δ in Total – Subsidies	-0.92	0.17	0.07	0.49

Note: + Tighten / - Loosen.

However, the Budget might have been cautious on its allocation of petroleum subsidy in the prevailing global environment of escalating oil prices that might not abate for some time. Instead, it has shown a tightening of 0.22 per cent of GDP in petroleum subsidy even after experiencing a loosening of 0.26 per cent of GDP in 2010-11 (row 3). It is this hue of optimism rather than judicious caution that is a bit worrisome in the Budget. It does detract from successfully garnering the confidence of analysts.

To sum up, India has been following countercyclical fiscal policy outcomes through, and post, crisis. This is a welcome overall policy stance. However, analysis reveals that some of it is chance. Also, discretionary tax effort is nil. It should be revived, and in such a way that direct tax revenue effort overcompensates indirect tax loss rather than the opposite way around as in the just introduced Budget. Subsidy policy is on the right track though realistic projections for petroleum subsidy are lacking in light of last year's experience and in anticipation of the international petroleum environment that is emerging. It would help if the derivation of important Budget numbers are presented to Parliament as in mature and many emerging economies. This indeed remains another challenge for the 2012-13 Budget.

Business Standard, 12 March 2011.

15

Dangers and Foibles of Tax Reform

Overall a sensible proposal, Graetz's CTP must also include subnational tax reform.

Of late the misappropriation of terms such as innovation and reform in the context of finance or taxation has become commonplace. Thus when the top tax practitioner in the UK passed me a book offering another tax reform plan for the US, I took it with some apprehension. Surprisingly, Yale professor Michael Graetz' *100 Million Unnecessary Returns* (Yale, 2008) is worth reading, with no algebraic skulduggery making it a rapid reader. A fortnight back, I reviewed in this page the main elements of his Competitive Tax Plan (CTP), pointing towards its sensible proposals, albeit with an important caveat that it is limited to federal or central government tax reform, essentially eschewing sub-national concerns. The book's other merits are what I touch upon today—its anecdotal historicity, with ramifications and anomalies of earlier US reforms and plans. And this is contextual and relevant for India.

For example, to keep track of tax incentives that become law, the US federal budget is required to contain a list of tax expenditures, defined as all tax credits, deductions, or exclusions that deviate from a "normal" income tax. The revenue loss is $700 billion per annum. In India too, a beginning was made in the Union Budget with a section on tax expenditures from 2005-06, though its rudimentary approach should now be sharpened. Reagan's 1986 tax reform reduced incentives just as Yashwant Sinha's budgets during India's 10th Plan. But base erosion has crept in: in the US, 66 items out of a total 146 (45%) have been added since then. In India, variegated regional incentives as well as the SEZ Act have sharply narrowed a reformed tax base.

Mr Graetz reminds us that, even though 1986 witnessed income tax reduction to 28 per cent, Reagan is not remembered for it. Indeed, the politicians associated with it never attained national prominence, suggesting that leadership in tax reform is not likely to reap political benefit. Soon after Mr Sinha's tax reforms, he was moved to South Block.

Graetz's accounts reveal that sensible ideas are shelved while populist ones have longer lives. For example, a panel rejected the replacement of the federal income tax with a populist flat rate tax or national sales tax. Instead, it sensibly supported income tax restructuring to: (1) reduce the top marginal rate; (2) replace personal exemptions and standard deduction with a tax credit; (3) rationalise tax credits for earned income and for children; (4) expand and simplify savings incentives; (5) extend deduction for mortgage interest to all taxpayers, but reduce its size; (6) eliminate the AMT (alternate minimum tax); (7) eliminate federal deductions for state and local taxes paid, and for charities; and (8) cap fringe benefit deduction for employer-provided health insurance. Yet, the proposal failed. It is well known that similar reforms are discussed regularly at India's Budget time but they remain discussion points.

Removing AMT would cost $1 trillion, implying that tax rates could not be reduced too much. Interest groups objected, including charities, the life insurance sector and pension professionals who would be adversely affected. Interestingly, Jeb Bush, Florida governor, wrote to his brother, the President, strongly objecting to the proposal. India's empowered committee of state finance ministers would also react to a Central proposal that would negatively impact the states' revenue!

In contrast, populist ideas have long lives. In the mid-1990s, in a "Scrap the Code" road show, two Republican Congressmen pushed for the replacement of income tax, corporate tax and estate tax with a national sales tax or flat rate tax on consumption. Graetz opines that the Flat Tax's survival reflects ill feeling towards the IRS under the belief that a Flat Tax could be administered by state tax administrations. Senate hearings took place at about this time over alleged IRS foibles—computer malfunction, liens, levies, audits, compounding interest and penalties—with the witnesses including employees, a priest, six anonymous IRS agents, and one seen IRS agent who indicated that the IRS wants to "stick it" to people who "can't fight back". The IRS did not fight back. Congress passed legislation revising IRS governance and operations and enhancing taxpayers' legal protection. The Indian tax administrations have not been scrutinised along comparable lines even though their computerisation has come under Parliament's magnifying glass.

The move to scrap the income tax was revived in 1997. A Tax Code Termination Act was introduced in Congress that would have ended the income tax at end-2001 without any revenue replacement solution. It passed the House though not the Senate. In the mid-2000s, Harris Polls revealed that almost 80 per cent of the public wanted overhauling of the federal tax system. Another Fair Tax proposal was introduced in May 2006, again to replace the income tax with a national sales tax.

Authors Boortz and Linder claimed that wages would go to workers tax-free and prices would not rise. Famed economist Jorgenson was cited for this double effect, though he took responsibility only for the no-price-increase claim. Separately, Kotlikoff had said that wages would not fall, assuming that prices would rise. Thus Graetz claims that populists selectively combine half-truths from different sources to arrive at a false, though convenient, result. Nevertheless, the Americans for Fair Tax movement continues. This is reminiscent of the arguments in favour of SEZs that did the rounds of Raisina Hill corridors and committee rooms before the SEZ Act's introduction.

Graetz claims that his CTP would avoid such problems since it would eliminate income tax for most Americans, lower income and corporate tax rates, and produce revenue from a federal consumption tax on goods and services. It proposes:

- A federal VAT: rate 10-14 per cent; preferably single rate; exempt turnover below $100,000 per year (leaving out 65% of the 25 million existing businesses); few exemptions to be allowed.
- Income tax: exempt incomes below an indexed $100,000 per family ($50,000 per individual). This will leave out 150

million taxpayers. Tax rate of 20-25 per cent. Allow limited deductions for charity, large medical expenses, (possibly) home mortgage interest, and state and local taxes. Allow employers to deduct retirement savings schemes and health insurance contributions until a national health insurance system emerges. Standard deduction, personal allowances, other tax credits to be eliminated.

- Alternative Minimum Tax: abolish it.
- Capital gains tax: raise it to income tax level of 20-25 per cent or retain at 15 per cent.
- Dividend tax: retain at 15 per cent.
- Corporate tax: reduce rate to 15 per cent, or a maximum of 20 per cent. Exempt small businesses with less than $100,000 turnover. Equalise book-tax accounts differences. Any difference—depreciation, R&D, foreign income and taxes—should be made explicit.
- Estate and Gift taxes: retain, while raising exemptions and protecting farmers and small businesses.
- Social Security tax: maintain structure until a new financing mechanism for national social insurance—retirement, Medicaid, Medicare—is in place.

I have already illuminated the reader as to why the CTP is essentially a sensible proposal, provided it also is able to propose concrete steps towards sub-national tax reform.

Business Standard, 02 May 2009.

III

Taxation Matters

16

Taxation Research

Emergence and Progress

Formulation of tax legislation and its subsequent administration have suffered persistent lack of analysis prior to implementation. Recently emerging in-depth research carried out by independent tax professionals may be about to break the mould. Three of seven papers[1] are highlighted here in a two-part series, today's focusing on tax policy and the next on tax implementation.

The first is reduction of CIT (corporate income tax) rate to 25 per cent pari passu with scaling back tax incentives. Mukesh Butani, Anuj Agarwal and Shivam Saigal point out that a high proportion of revenue forgone reflects export oriented units in the IT sector, SEZs, and infrastructure including power, bridges, highways, water treatment and industrial parks. The main question therefore is whether these sectors are willing to sacrifice incentives.

Butani points to dispersion of average effective tax rate of 23 per cent between 26.89 per cent for smaller companies (profit before tax up to ₹1 crore) and 20.68 per cent for companies at ₹500 crore or more. They blame this on phasing out profit linked deductions, as well as tax concessions being enjoyed disproportionately by larger companies. They clarify that companies that do not claim major tax incentives and pay taxes under normal provisions will benefit from CIT rate reduction with greater profits available for labour deployment and distribution to shareholders.

---

1. These papers are emanating from a corner in Bengaluru that is bringing tax experts to exchange ideas under the International Tax Research and Analysis Foundation (ITRAF). Its website *www.itraf.org* may be of interest to policy makers and researchers.

By contrast, companies claiming large tax incentives and consequently paying MAT (minimum alternate tax), may not enjoy immediate changes in tax liability since they would continue to pay MAT until tax incentives expire or phase out. During the four-year phased rate reduction, decrease in CIT tax rate would correspondingly increase MAT credit for such companies; consequently, they could accumulate more MAT credit, and more tax paid in advance. Eventually, such accumulated MAT credit could be used to mitigate future tax liability as incentives cease to exist.

Butani questions scaling back accelerated depreciation since he feels it is merely a timing issue for revenue receipt. He also points to challenges in removing socioeconomic or area based incentives including those related to bifurcation of Andhra Pradesh. However, as incentives decrease, he admits litigation over incentives should reduce. Butani recommends a more cautious approach, through more graduated phase out of incentives, differentiating sectors and locations, and initiating sunset clause from FY 2019-20. He cautions against adverse impact on capital formation; thus accelerated write off of capital investment for industrial and infrastructure activities should not be curtailed. He also asks for a review of the continuing need for MAT when headline CIT rate itself is 25 per cent. He remains in favour of continuing incentives for small and medium enterprises to reduce prevailing inequity.

Moving on to DDT (Dividend Distribution Tax), Indraneel Chaudhury, Saurav Bhattacharya and Gaurav Kumar Goyal recount the history of tax treatment of dividends internationally and in India. Prior to 1997, dividend was taxable in India in the hands of recipient at the normal individual income tax rate. The 1997 DDT exempted dividends in the hands of shareholders and began collecting it from companies, its current rate being 20 per cent. South Africa had a similar tax but removed it in 2012 as the perception grew that its CIT rate was higher than competitor countries.

Chaudhury posits that the economic burden of DDT ultimately falls on shareholders. They also bear an additional burden of disallowance of expenditure incurred in relation to dividend income (since such income is exempt in the hands of shareholders). On the other hand, if DDT is seen as tax payable by a company, then CIT rate (inclusive of DDT rate) is 45 per cent, too high internationally. He also points to deleterious cross-border effects. Since DDT is statutorily paid by a company (and not shareholders), beneficial tax rates for shareholders in any tax treaty cannot be availed either by shareholders or company, rendering those provisions of the treaty otiose. He also critiques DDT on grounds of cascading over multitiered corporate structures, and horizontal inequity since it falls on companies and not partnerships and others.

Hence, Chaudhury et al. recommends reverting to the classical system of taxing dividends at the hands of shareholders albeit at a reduced rate of 10 per cent. For early tax collection, a company may be required to withhold tax while paying dividends.

In a third paper, P.V. Srinivasan addresses remaining challenges of the proposed GST (goods and services tax). He points towards possible disputes over the event of taxation, classification, value, place of supply and applicable rates that would continue under GST. He also anticipates disputes in fiscal federal relations since GST Council decisions will not be binding leaving scope for non-harmonisation or divergence in the adoption of tax base and rates. He criticises the proposed one per cent tax on interstate trade whose revenue will be retained by exporting states.

Continuing to exclude petroleum will result in double cascading because petroleum industry cannot avail ITC (input tax credit) while neither can goods or services using petroleum get ITC for tax paid on petroleum. He calculates that prevailing contribution of petroleum and petroleum products is 20 per cent of indirect tax revenue which will stay outside the GST base and later consensus from states is not foreseen. Collectively, he calculates by listing and analysing all uncovered elements that 60 per cent of GDP will remain outside the scope of GST.

Srinivasan asserts that exempting part of the financial services sector will cause distortions as banks and financial institutions will be unable to achieve operational efficiency through outsourcing of their business process operations to service providers reflecting, once again, no allowable ITC. For construction industry, construction is likely to continue to be defined as work contract. This would require separation of goods from services vitiating a quintessential characteristic of a good GST. He also mentions distortions emanating from rental of residential housing if it is kept outside GST since ITC would not be allowed to the supplier. Srinivasan's level of aspectual detail surpasses most available treatises.

Business Standard, 19 January 2016.

17

Taxation Research

Interpretative and Administrative Issues

This article on new research in taxation is the second in a two-part series, the first having focused on tax policy (chapter 16). Though Central Board of Direct Taxes (CBDT) is issuing guidance notes to field officers to improve implementation, cynicism continues among taxpayers. Some reasons for this have been recently researched covering a spectrum of implementation issues. These are examined here.

The first issue is GAAR (General Anti-Avoidance Rules) that Mukesh Butani, Sumit Singhania, Anuj Agarwal and Shivam Saigal address. GAAR will equip officers to curb tax avoidance with wide and long reach. Effective implementation of the complex GAAR rests on adequate preparation and subordinate legislation which still suffer from lack of clarity on documentation standards and compliance requirements. CBDT should roll out rules and principles of best practices to guide officers to use GAAR only as a last resort. The authors insist that GAAR should not (1) be invoked in cases that are subject to SAAR (Specific Anti-Avoidance Rules); (2) override tax treaty provisions; (3) be invoked in intragroup transactions when there is no tax benefit at the group level; or (4) lead to penal action except very selectively.

The second issue considered by K.R. Sekar is termed PoEM (place of effective management) in taxing multinational enterprises (MNEs). A bone of contention between an MNE and tax officer is the jurisdiction where MNE management effectively resides for that is where tax should accrue. Sekar addresses lacunae in CBDT's recently proposed definition of PoEM. The explanation that PoEM is where key management and commercial decisions take place for conduct of business is insufficient. He uses a UK judicial case that distinguished PoM which determines residence, from PoEM to be used as a tie breaker in case of possible dual residence. Thus, PoM is not sufficient while PoEM remains the necessary criterion. He also identifies other areas that need clarification, for example, different or same corporate tax rate for parent and subsidiary, treatment of dividends for tax, application of minimum alternate tax (MAT), nature of withholding, and others.

Using Organisation for Economic Cooperation and Development (OECD) guidelines, Sekar recommends modifications. As in corporate law, tax law should also allow consolidation of accounts by an Indian MNE with a foreign subsidiary. Listing in the stock exchange should be a beginning criterion before applying the test to check if there is active business that is associated with PoEM. Shareholder control or participation should not be a sufficient condition for determining PoEM. If Board of Directors meetings occur outside India or decisions are not taken in India, then PoEM cannot exist. Mere existence of receivables from an Indian entity should not comprise assets. For determining passive income, definition of royalty and technical know how in a tax treaty should take precedence over domestic law. Capital gains should not comprise passive income. Modern technology enables accounts being maintained in third countries; therefore location of accounts maintenance cannot influence PoEM.

The third issue considered in a two-paper series by K.R. Girish is on Limitation of Benefits (LOB) that attempts to minimise treaty benefits going to unqualified MNEs but enabled through treaty shopping. He examines international experience, among others, the 1990 India-US Double Taxation Avoidance Agreement (DTAA) that was designed to prevent third countries from treaty shopping and explains how tests for ownership and main purpose of a business, tax base erosion, active business connection, and recognised stock exchange are determined by applying the US Model Convention. He discusses the controversial Indo-Mauritius Treaty that allows a residency certificate issued by Mauritian authorities to establish residence there which the Indian authorities are obliged to accept to their discomfiture.

Girish invokes the principle of *pacta sunt servanda* from the Vienna Convention on the Law of Treaties, 1969, whereby, in case of conflict between tax treaty and domestic law, treaty specification must prevail. Thus, domestic GAAR provisions should not override a treaty. While he concedes that tax abuse may amount to abuse of the Convention itself and thus may not deserve treaty benefits, after weighing the issue, he concludes that the proposed GAAR already led to outflow of funds; hence treaty override is not the correct solution.

The fourth issue considered is selection of tax returns for scrutiny. H.P. Khincha and S. Krishnan analyse whether Indian tax administration is using risk-based assessment that is the global norm. Routine assessment orders covering all taxpayers is to be eschewed. Conceptually, under Section 143 (1) of India's Income Tax Act, return-based refunds can be given without an assessment order. However, what is actual field practice is examined in this paper.

Even in making prima facie arithmetical adjustments, 20 per cent tax addition is made against making incorrect claims. Obviously this provides an incentive to spend time on routine assessments, leaving less time to undertake thorough investigation for selective, risk-based scrutiny. Computer assisted scrutiny selection (CASS) of two per cent of returns annually was introduced in 2003. CASS uses general criteria measuring quantum of specified taxpayer transactions and assigns a risk score to every return. Scrutiny selection is also possible on discretionary basis, say, foreign tax credit claims. Discretion is also used through manual scrutiny selection. For example, for Assessment Year 2015-16, one criterion was the addition to tax of ₹10 lakh or more in a previous year.

Khincha and Krishnan reveal both CASS and manual selection remain imperfect since they don't utilise industry data. The same taxpayer gets picked for same reason year after year while tax avoidance cases remain ignored for scrutiny. Judicial decisions overwhelmingly favour (70-80%) assessees. Pendency is phenomenal by global standards. In 2013-14, pendency in scrutiny disposal was 60 per cent and that in appeals 70 per cent. They recommend independent multimember settlement commissions to mitigate the problem. They also reveal that while corporate assessees increased by 8 per cent between 2012-13 and 2014-15, almost 30 per cent of working companies did not file tax returns in 2013-14.

They suggest a significant increase in monetary penalties as a deterrent after issuance of notice to both listed and unlisted companies. If they still do not file, prosecution under Section 276CC should follow. These papers are elaborated at International Tax Research and Analysis Foundation, Bengaluru, *www.itraf.org*.

Business Standard, 31 January 2016.

18

India's Effective Tax Ratio

The tax effort of a country is important since, ideally, only revenue collected should be spent on government expenditure whether current or capital expenditure. Tax effort is generally measured by the tax-GDP ratio. The "buoyancy" of a tax reflects its revenue generating capacity. The income tax is "buoyant" since it tends to be "progressive", that is, its rates escalate with income. Thus, when the economy is booming, so do incomes—and tax revenue rises more than proportionately compared to income. Of course, no intelligent government would legislate very high progressivity since that leads to tax evasion or reduced work effort. By contrast, taxes that have fixed rates suffer from a lack of buoyancy—though, if rates are set in ad valorem or percentage terms, rather than in "specific" or nominal terms, then revenue yield from such taxes would rise with inflation, if not as fast as if the rates were progressive. Such taxes are typically levied on domestic production such as excises, and on consumption such as VAT (value-added tax) or the GST (goods and services tax), as well as on imports in the form of customs duty.

Production taxes are easy to collect at the factory gate as is customs duty at importation points. Income taxes on individuals, corporations, firms, or capital gains, or taxes on wealth and gifts are not so easy to collect. First, collection points for production and imports are far fewer than points of income generation; so a nascent tax administration in the early stages of economic development has higher success rates collecting commodity taxes than income taxes. Consequently, the economy contends with lower revenue buoyancy until the tax administration is able to significantly expand the base of income taxpayers.

In India, the central government's tax/GDP ratio is around 10 per cent, with slightly higher collection from commodity taxes (5+%) than income taxes (5%). Interestingly, during 2004-2008, a golden age period for tax revenue growth in real terms—having crossed 20 per cent per annum in 2007-08—income tax collection surpassed commodity taxes. Major tax administration and tax structure reforms at the central level occurred, including the use of third party information on major transactions of taxpayers, enhanced computerised processing of tax returns, and scaling back the income tax rates while broadening its base—thus garnering a Laffer-type positive revenue effect. Revenue gains were achieved despite the lowering of excise and customs duty rates as a policy measure to reduce distortions in resource allocation caused by production taxes. However, the revenue gains were reversed subsequently during the global economic crisis with the central tax/GDP ratio declining considerably by about one per cent of GDP.

Adding states' tax revenue to the Centre's raises the 2005 tax/GDP to 16.5 per cent. It rose to almost 19 per cent in 2007 but fell back to 18 per cent during the global economic recession. Thus, it was not sustained. At the states' level, the revenue growth was achieved by introducing the VAT which was more broadly based than the earlier sales tax, as well as through administrative gains realised from the VAT's debit minus credit principle that facilitates a self-checking mechanism against tax evasion. This kind of tax revenue growth as experienced in India is no small feat for a developing emerging economy with all its constraints in generating revenue.

In international circles, a common theme is India's low tax effort. Is this true? We must consider India's subsistence population who cannot be taxed. Ideally, therefore, subsistence incomes should be removed from GDP when calculating tax/GDP. Doing that would yield the correct "effective" tax effort. A cross-country search revealed, however, that subsistence income data are difficult to obtain. A second best was to obtain poverty level income which, of course, is lower than subsistence income. Even if we use only the poverty-based concept—that is, non-poverty GDP (NPGDP) as in Table 18.1—India's effective tax/GDP ratio rises by more than 3 per cent, to almost 20 per cent from 16.5 per cent in 2005. Extrapolation would result in an effective tax/GDP ratio of approximately 22 per cent in 2007 and 21 per cent in 2009.

Table 18.1[1]

*Crosscountry Tax/GDP and Tax/NPGDP Ratios**

Country	*Ratio*	*2005*	*2006*	*2007*	*2008*	*2009*
Brazil	Tax/GDP	–	32.63	32.93	33.18	31.94
	Tax/NPGDP	–	32.72	33.01	33.24	31.99
Chile	Tax/GDP	41.42	43.99	45.56	42.16	34.42
	Tax/NPGDP	–	44.00	–	–	34.43
China	Tax/GDP	18.60	22.21	20.68	22.04	22.52
	Tax/NPGDP	18.92	–	–	22.22	–
India	Tax/GDP	16.55	17.92	18.79	17.52	18.01
	Tax/NPGDP	19.71		–	–	–
Sweden	Tax/GDP	49.05	48.43	47.61	46.72	46.75
	Tax/NPGDP	–	–	47.62	–	–

Note: * NPGDP is the GDP from the non-poor part of the population. States' revenue data for India for 2009 are from the *Handbook on Indian Economy*, Reserve Bank of India.

Sources: *IMF Government Financial Statistics* and World Bank Databank.

This exercise was carried out also for selected other countries where meaningful comparable data were available. The tax revenue data are from *IMF Government Financial Statistics*. They include cash and non-cash tax revenue and social contributions to central, state and local governments in units of local currency. The current GDP data are from the World Bank Databank in local currency. The poor population has been computed using the percentage of poverty head-count in total population at a $1.25 per day poverty line. Income of the poor is the product of the size of the poor population and their per annum income in local currency using the $1.25 poverty line. NPGDP is the difference between GDP, and GDP of the poor.

Because India is poorer than the compared countries, using NPGDP implies a higher increase in effective tax/GDP for India. For

1. Neetika Kaushal assisted with the Table.

Chile and Sweden, using NPGDP versus GDP makes little difference. For Brazil, it makes a small difference, and for China, slightly larger. For India, the difference is substantial. The difference would be larger with non-subsistence GDP. It is thus important not to blindly make cross-country comparisons of tax/GDP without recognising poor or subsistence populations. Indeed, India's effective tax/GDP is not as low as is usually made out to be when one considers from whom tax revenue can be realistically collected. This of course does not imply that the taxpayer population cannot be expanded since many under-report and some do not file tax returns, thereby failing to contribute their due share to the exchequer.

Business Standard, 17 December 2012.

19

A Time for Tax Reform

The central government's tax revenue has not been buoyant since the global economic crisis. Figure 19.1 shows that when direct and indirect tax revenues are added up, the total has declined in terms of GDP (gross domestic product) since 2008-09. The low performance becomes clearer in Table 19.1, which calculates the buoyancy of tax revenue, defined as the percentage of tax revenue change as a ratio of the percentage of change in GDP. Thus, it is a concept that adjusts for the decline (or increase) in GDP reflecting the crisis. It reports the buoyancies of various taxes in three segments: 2005-2008 before the crisis, 2008-2010 during the crisis, and 2010-11 post-crisis. What one observes is the decline in buoyancies of taxes during the crisis. The recovery thereafter reflects the low revenue base on which 2010-11 buoyancies are calculated.

The revenue setback has been officially explained in terms of the fiscal stimulus that was given during the crisis. It is doubtful that all that tax reduction was needed; instead, the strong base on which tax revenue had been anchored during 2004-2008 was lost. Table 19.2 shows that the revenue foregone due to tax incentives in terms of GDP—an exercise that we initiated in 2005-06—worsened in 2008-2009 and that, in broad terms, revenue loss from this source has not receded over the years. During the current fiscal year, the first three quarters expended 90 per cent of the fiscal deficit budgeted for 2011-12, and the GDP forecast has been scaled back. Hence, the fiscal deficit-to-GDP ratio will be decidedly larger than the forecast, with a higher numerator and a lower denominator than projected. Certainly not a good account to take to rating agencies.

Last month (see chapter 6 of this volume) I touched upon the expenditure side. Now let me consider what tax measures should be taken in the forthcoming Budget. These comprise short-run discretionary measures, forward steps in structural tax reform, and administrative reform.

Figure 19.1

Central Government Tax Revenue (% of GDP)

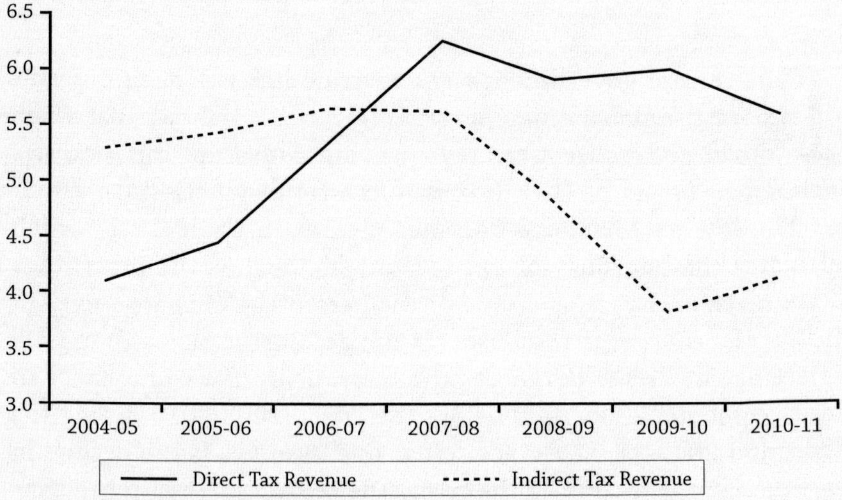

Source: *Handbook of Statistics 2010-11*, RBI.

Table 19.1

Central Government Tax Revenue (Average Annual Tax Buoyancy)

	2005-08	*2008-10*	*2010-11*
Gross Tax Revenue	1.6	0.2	1.4
Income Tax	1.7	0.7	0.8
Corporate Tax	2.1	0.9	1.1
Custom Duties	1.4	-0.7	3.1
Excise Duties	0.5	-0.6	1.8
Service Tax	4.1	0.6	1.0
Taxes of Union Territories	1.4	0.8	1.0
Other Taxes and Duties	11.4	-1.4	-1.2

Source: Union Budgets and CSO National Accounts Statistics.

Among the first, the excise duty or the central value-added tax (CENVAT) rate might be increased, reflecting the fact that its current base is just as far as the manufacturing stage while, under the forthcoming GST (goods and services tax), its base will be extended to include wholesale and retail value-added. If, under the GST, goods and services have the same tax rate—as indeed they should—then today's CENVAT rate should be set at a higher level than that of the service tax rate. The government can get a good amount of revenue from this measure.

Table 19.2

Revenue Foregone (% of GDP)

	2005-06	*2006-07*	*2007-08*	*2008-09*	*2009-10*	*2010-11P*
Corporate Income Tax	0.94	1.17	1.25	1.19	1.13	1.15
Personal Income Tax	0.37	0.36	0.76	0.67	0.70	0.66
Excise Duty	1.81	2.32	1.75	2.28	2.62	2.58
Custom Duty	3.46	2.88	3.08	4.01	3.02	2.27
Total	6.58	6.73	6.84	8.15	7.47	6.66

Source: Union Budgets and CSO National Accounts Statistics.

A second discretionary measure could be a generalised accelerated depreciation—and not selective ones—that would provide a fillip to industry as a whole. This would have an immediate adverse revenue impact but, with industry rejuvenated, revenue could pick up a bit later. Beyond such overarching measures, the government should ideally refrain from using too many micro discretionary measures to minimise tax-generated distortions in production and distribution.

The Budget should highlight structural tax reform. The government should indicate a realistic road map for the GST. It should also be transparent in indicating how it has had to deviate from international GST norms in order to clinch an agreement with states. It should say that it has not yet decided on a negative services list, that there is no finalisation on whether goods and services tax rates would be equal (which is a necessity in a GST framework), that it is being obliged to keep petroleum products and alcoholic beverages out of the GST base. What is happening on the IGST (inter-state goods and services tax) and the much-needed clearing house mechanism should be fully detailed and placed for public consultation, as every modernising finance ministry and tax administration do before introducing such major tax reforms.

Sometimes such consultation with the customer/client/stakeholder/taxpayer may take years. In India, only the central government, state governments and the bureaucracy consult; the role of stakeholders is minuscule. Even on as grave a matter as the direct taxes code, major changes have been proposed without taking even large taxpayers through a detailed consultative process. This should change if Indian administration is to become even slightly customer-friendly.

It is interesting that on 14 February 2012, the Press Information Bureau issued a bulletin titled "Government to provide citizen-centric governance in order to improve taxpayer services and redressal of public finances", citing the finance minister. Its coverage includes better taxpayer services, expansion of centralised processing of returns, and curbing black money. This is a welcome gesture and the tax departments have indeed initiated some customer-friendly measures, though the ministry and departments should test themselves by participating in a benchmarking exercise that compares them with Australia, South Africa and the UK, whose comparative results are already available.

There is space for only an additional point: the revival of LTUs (large taxpayer units), which were introduced with great effort in 2006 but now are by and large dormant. It is time to make them obligatory, as in the 50-plus countries across the globe and 20-plus in Asia that have them. The Budget should show firmness in taking this step. LTUs help large taxpayers come to one window to pay all central taxes and, at the same time, the two tax departments can receive and exchange useful data and crucial information between themselves, leading to a win-win outcome.

Many other administrative reforms have to follow, in championing technical analysis for formulating tax administration policy, structuring the organisation of the departments along functional lines that emphasise professional specialisation rather than geographical divisions, and combining the departments while making such a body autonomous. Some of these are achievable in the medium term, but such intentions might be put on the table for discussion reflecting international practice.

There is no space here to elaborate on these reforms but they are to be found in the just released *Tax Shastra: Administration Reform in India, UK and Brazil* (Business Standard Publishing, New Delhi). The real need is to make Indian tax administration comparable to modern tax administrations across the world, of which there are some in emerging economies such as Brazil, Chile, Korea, even Rwanda. It is time for India to run as fast as its bureaucracy can, in a leap to modernism.

Business Standard, 20 February 2012.

20

Tax Evasion as Corruption

India's social fabric has been dented in the past month over the issue of corruption. Corruption has many faces, one of the more important of which is tax evasion. Tax evasion can be unilateral, on account of taxpayers alone, or bilateral, through collusion between taxpayer and tax collector, thus robbing the state of its due revenue, or multilateral, where a society participates in it through resistance to remedial measures.

Tax evasion leads to inefficient and inequitable outcomes. Because tax evasion erodes tax revenue, the lost revenue is attempted to be made up through high tax rates. An example is real property tax rates in India that range around seven per cent, as opposed to developed countries where it approximates one to two per cent. Note, therefore, that paradoxically, an estimate of tax evasion based on this elevated or artificial or compensating tax rate would yield an exaggerated number. That is, if the tax rate were lower, tax evasion could also be lower. Thus, the consequence of those who get away with it is an extra burden of taxation on those who pay tax. This is an inequitable impact across taxpayers.

The sectors or activities that are amenable to tax evasion will fetch more investment, which would be redirected from other areas. And this reallocation of resources takes place often from more to less productive sectors. Thus, if investment in land is prone to evasion, more resources would go into construction than in the production of rail engines or food. Construction as an activity ends when a building or bridge is completed. Manufacturing and agriculture, by contrast, are more long-term and generate a longer time horizon of employment and supply of the product. Economists call this the outcome of inefficient allocation of resources.

Through time, scholars and governments have attempted to measure tax evasion. Estimation methods have used national accounts or expenditure survey information to assess the size of economic activity and compared it with reported activity. The difference between estimated and reported activity could then be related to the loss of tax revenue associated with it.

In India, tax evasion has not been directly estimated. In Latin America this was carried out widely in the 1980s and 1990s (Aguirre and Shome[1] for Mexico, Serra[2] for Chile, Shome[3] for Colombia, and others). In the case of individual income tax, the following method would apply. To personal income declared for tax purposes, adjustments should be made for those components of income that are included in the concept of income in the national accounts but are deductible for tax purposes, for example, personal exemptions, deductions, savings incentives. Adjustments need to be made for individual tax brackets if the tax structure is progressive. The resultant series of gross taxable declared income (by income class) should then be compared with gross taxable income from the national accounts to obtain an estimated undeclared income.

Similarly, for corporate income tax, adjustments to national accounts-based income for deductions for the array of tax incentives that are legally applicable, as well as for special conditions for small and medium industry, would have to be made, and then compared with declared taxable income from returns. To simplify the exercise, instead of national accounts, data by the Centre for Monitoring Indian Economy could be used to obtain more reliable conclusions, albeit from a more truncated information base.

For the VAT and CENVAT (or central excise), using an input-output table for the economy would be the ideal option. The widest theoretical VAT base is all purchasable goods and services,

1. Aguirre, Carlos and Partho Shome (1988). "Mexican VAT: Methodology for Calculating the Base", *National Tax Journal* 41
2. Serra, Pablo (1991). "Estimación de la Evasión Tributaria en el IVA", *Servicio de Impuestos Internos, Publicación* No. 91/05/C. Universidad de Chile
3. Shome, Partho (1995). "Colombia: Fundamental Tax Reform", *IMF Occasional Paper* No. 123

or GDP plus imports minus exports. However, given that the VAT base usually has a plethora of exemptions for not just the supply of outputs but also for the inputs of exempted outputs, it is not sufficient to use only GDP data. Instead, one has to go upstream and start with production data against which taxable inputs would have to be credited out since the VAT base is value added, or output minus input.

Tax evasion should be estimated in India. Another matter is how to limit tax dodging (Tanzi and Shome[4]). The first means should be to focus on those taxes that the tax administrator can monitor more cheaply or easily. For example, to begin, it may not be fruitful to spend a lot of administrative resources on monitoring small taxpayers. Thus, the service tax did away with 80 per cent of taxpayers from the bottom. The second is to design taxes intelligently. The VAT has a good design since input tax credit is matched between buyer and seller, and allowed only on the basis of physical invoices. The third is to use third-party information for individual income tax as has been introduced in India through Annual Information Returns (AIR) for third parties such as mutual funds, credit cards, property transactions and others who must report transactions they carry out with customers (using PAN numbers) above stipulated thresholds. However, it is crucial that such information is correctly used and interpreted by the tax administration so that a taxpayer does not suffer from erroneous matching of such information.

A final word. Tax evasion is not the only form of corruption. Corruption has more tentacles. According to Transparency International, India's Corruption Perception Index (CPI) ranking worsened from 72 in 2007 to 87 in 2010 amongst 180 countries. It is worse than Brazil at 69 and China at 78, but better than Mexico at 98 and Russia at 154. Though CPI does have flaws, it gives an indication of impediments to economic and social growth and equity. A worsening index is detrimental to attracting foreign investment and political stability. On a broader canvas, it is important to investigate

4. Tanzi, Vito, and Partho Shome (1993). "A Primer on Tax Evasion", *IMF Staff Papers*, Vol. 40.

what has been motivating and sustaining corruption before designing draconian measures to combat it. If the cart is put before the horse, the outcome may remain shy of success.

Business Standard, 10 September 2011.

IV

Income Tax

21

IT Department Statistics-I

The Income Tax Department's (ITD's) new tax statistics may be classified into two categories, macroeconomy and micro taxpayer levels. Accordingly I will analyse them in two parts, the present being macro, for 2000-01 to 2014-15. Reported 2015-16 numbers are provisional or incomplete. The GDP series used by ITD coincides with the Reserve Bank of India (RBI) series except for the initial four years.

Conclusions from the statistics are a mix of bad and good: (1) growth in tax buoyancy (percentage response in tax revenue to one per cent increase in GDP) is not too impressive; (2) initial gain in direct tax collection has been challenged by indirect tax and the difference is closing; (3) pendency in completing assessment of taxpayers by the tax administration has relatively improved; (4) ITD has suffered severe relative decline in its own budget; and (5) the number of assessees has grown.

First, Figure 21.1 plots annual buoyancy of the tax system and shows its changes (arrows). Buoyancy crashed in 2008-09 and 2009-2010 reflecting the loosening of taxation after the 2008 global crisis. I have maintained it was not needed to the extent loosened since India was not severely exposed to the crisis. Now looking forward, what policy mix would move the buoyancy upward from the steady state at which it appears to be languishing? Obviously more tax incentives will not help while base broadening would. Accordingly, the Finance Minister's last Budget thrust would need to be redirected in the next.

Second, Figure 21.2 demonstrates a scissors pattern with direct tax steadily gaining and then overtaking indirect tax in share of total revenue from 2007-08 but, after achieving the highest difference in 2009-10, the gap has been narrowing. An indicator of development is higher dependence on direct tax over time reflecting less dependence on distortionary customs duties and domestic excise taxes. That gain has been eroding in the case of India. Some explanations may be given.

(i) Rate of growth of private final consumption has been higher than rate of GDP growth so that tax collection rate from the consumption base may be expected to be higher than from the income base.

(ii) Service tax rate has been increasing.

(iii) Robust petroleum revenue is protected if its revenue per litre is maintained even as its international price per litre declines.

Figure 21.1

Buoyancy Tax Revenue

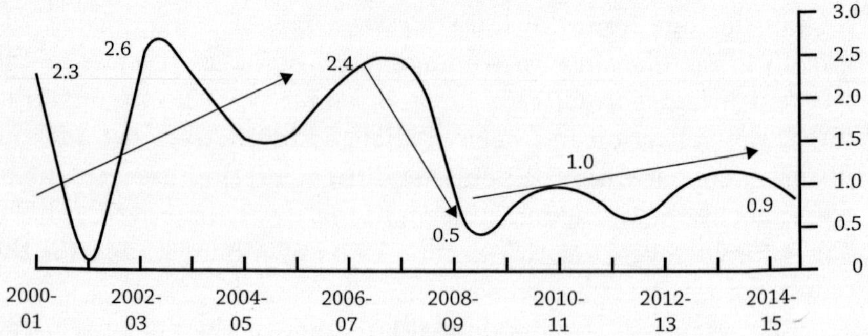

Figure 21.2

Direct and Indirect Tax as Per cent of Tax Revenue

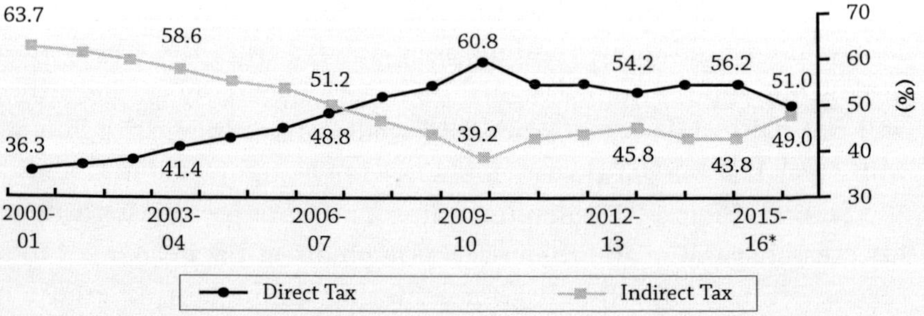

Note: * Provisional.

Third is the issue of assessing officers' workload. This is the sum of last year's undisposed assessment cases plus current year's new cases. ITD's Table 1.8 (not reproduced here) reports data on: (1) year-beginning workload or "total" cases; and (2) year-end disposed cases. We converted this to: (3) undisposed cases; and (4) year-beginning "new" cases, as follows. For 2013-14, (1) is 30,456,681 and (2) is 19,924,496. Thus, the difference, (3) 10,532,185, is undisposed cases which are carried forward to 2014-15. Thus, the new cases for 2014-15 must be (4) 21,254,217, which is the difference between carried forward cases (3) for 2013-14 and total cases (1) for 2014-15 (reported in Table 1.8 as 31,786,402). We repeated the exercise for all years.

Table 21.1

Number of Effective Assessees (in million)

PAN Category	*AY 2011-12*	*AY 2012-13*	*AY 2013-14*	*AY 2014-15*
Company	0.59	0.65	0.70	0.71
Firm	0.95	0.99	1.03	1.03
Hindu Undivided Family (HUF)	0.89	0.93	0.95	0.90
Individual	40.88	44.347	49.03	48.66
Total	43.63	47.26	52.09	51.67*

Note: Only the categories mentioned have been considered; * Returns for Assessment Year (AY) 2014-2015 can be filed till 31.03.2016.

Figure 21.3

Workload Indicators of Assessing Officers

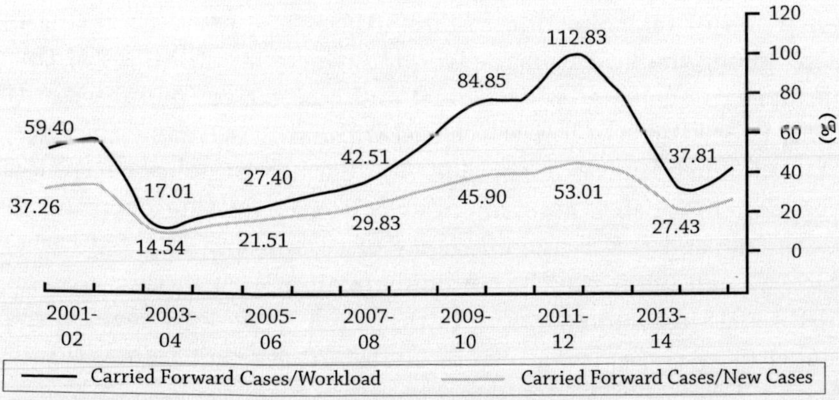

Figure 21.4

*Cost of Collection of Direct Taxes**

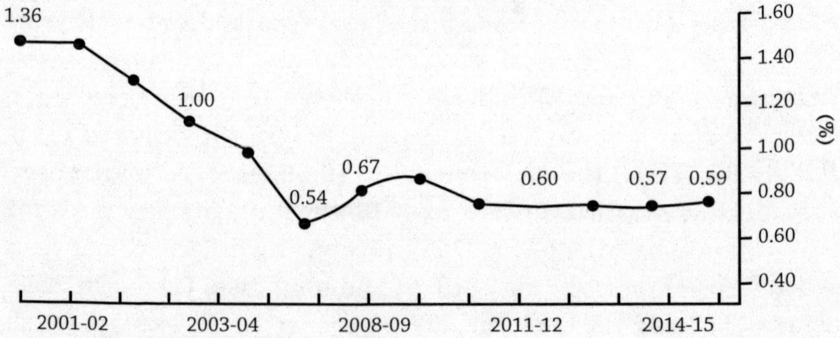

Note: * Department Expenditure over tax collection.

These calculations enabled Figure 21.3 which plots: (i) carried forward cases over total workload, and (ii) carried forward cases over new cases. From 2011-12, both trends have declined i.e. indicators have improved, revealing relatively less cases remain incomplete. Further, from ITD's Table 1.8, it is obvious that workload had increased in 2008-09 to 2010-11 and, correspondingly, disposal had also shown improvement. This was possible through the new Computerised Processing Centre (CPC) in Bengaluru. It is hoped that the positive trend is not reversed from 2014-15; and it is also true that pendency in nominal terms needs to be brought down even further.

Fourth, is it fair to expect too much improvement given the cutback in resources given to ITD, declining from 1.36 per cent in proportion of tax collection in 2000-01 to 0.59 per cent in 2014-2015, among the lowest in the world? Adverse ramifications of this continues in quantitative (revenue) and qualitative (moral hazard) terms. Policy correction is warranted without which modernisation of tax administration is impossible. Another urgent policy correction is needed: rationalise assessment selection by cutting out routine assessment and enhancing efficiency of completing selected cases, which was an important Tax Administration Reform Commission (TARC) 2015 recommendation. Fifth, as our Table 21.1 reveals, the number of assessees has grown by almost 20 per cent from 2011-12 to 2013-14. ITD's "effective assessees" concept includes income tax returns plus those subject to TDS (tax deduction at source) but have not filed returns. It is a useful indicator, but it does not necessarily mean all of them actually paid tax. The effort to increase the numerical base needs to be intensified so that the burden on those who are already paying tax is alleviated, is another recommendation of TARC. Hopefully ITD will continue publication and researchers will respond by using it intensively.

Business Standard, 05 June 2016.

22

I-T Department Statistics–II

In the second of two articles, I examine patterns across ranges in taxpayer returns for FY13 that have just been reported by the income tax (I-T) department. No doubt the information is dated. Nevertheless, an examination should pave the way for comparisons with the next, hopefully more up-to-date data, to observe worsening or improvement, and thus design future tax administration policy reform. Note that (1) taxpayer returns fall short of the number of effective assessees as was explained in my June 5 article (chapter 21). For example, there were more than 44 million effective individual assessees in AY13 with 29 million returns filed by individuals. (2) These numbers were 0.65 million and 0.63 million, respectively, for companies. (3) Individuals comprise 92-94 per cent of total taxpayers (see Table 22.1).

Table 22.1

Effective Assessees and Number of Tax Returns (AY 2012-13)

	Effective Assessees		*Number of Returns*	
	Number	*Per cent*	*Number*	*Per cent*
All Taxpayers, of which*	472,67,582		311,88,609	
Individuals	443,46,852	93.82	287,66,258	92.23
Firms	9,95,648	2.11	8,62,408	2.77
Companies	6,54,766	1.39	6,35,034	2.04

Note: * Other categories also include.

On 16 June the prime minister at the Rajasva Gyan Sangam asked I-T department to double taxpayers from the current 50 million. By taxpayers, PM was referring to I-T department's "effective taxpayers", a concept I had endorsed in my June 5 article. At the same time, in 2015 the Tax Administration Reform Commission (TARC) recommended that taxpayers filing returns be increased to 50-60 million and detailed the means to do so. That benchmark remains robust and achievable. In that context, it is crucial to see what the tax payable in each income range is, for, as will become obvious below, tax payable declines phenomenally as income range increases.

Focussing on returns, for individuals (and a third category, firms), 55-56 per cent of the total number of returns reflect an income range of less than ₹2 lakh while, for companies, that share is 46 per cent. Nevertheless, as Figure 22.1 shows, overall, there is significant clustering at lower taxable incomes for all taxpayers filing returns; and, after that, the share of number of returns falls off significantly for all taxpayer categories.

Figure 22.1

*Per cent Share of Number of Tax Returns***

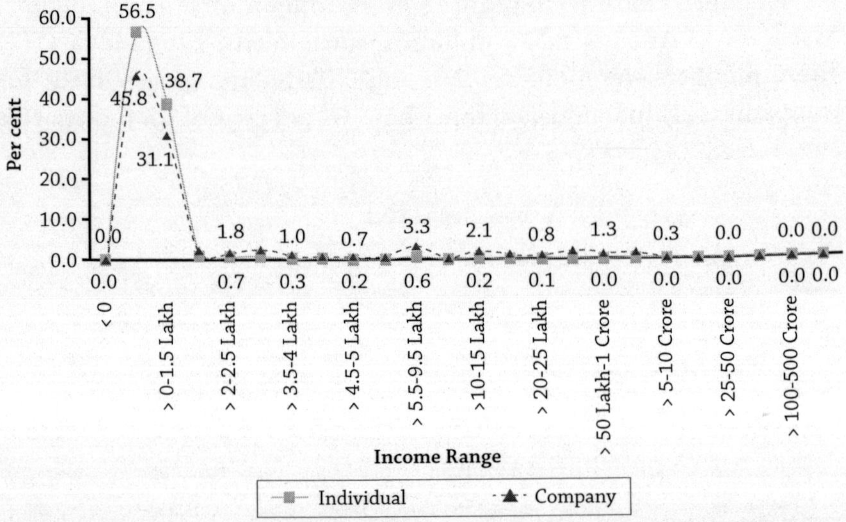

Note: ** Per cent Share = (No. of return/ Total return).

Moving from returns to incomes, however, I-T department tables appear to need further clarification or modification. "Average Tax Payable" for individuals (I-T department Table 2.9) and companies (I-T department Table 6.9) appears too high even though Note 1 of I-T department Table 6.9 explains, “Tax Payable is the aggregate tax liability as computed in the computation of tax liability on total income schedule of return of income. Tax, surcharge, cess & interest after giving credit under section 115JAA and relief under sections 89/90/90A/91 but before giving credit for taxes paid (advance tax/ TDS/TCS/self-assessment tax) constitute Tax Payable”.

Figure 22.2

*Per cent Share of Tax Payable**

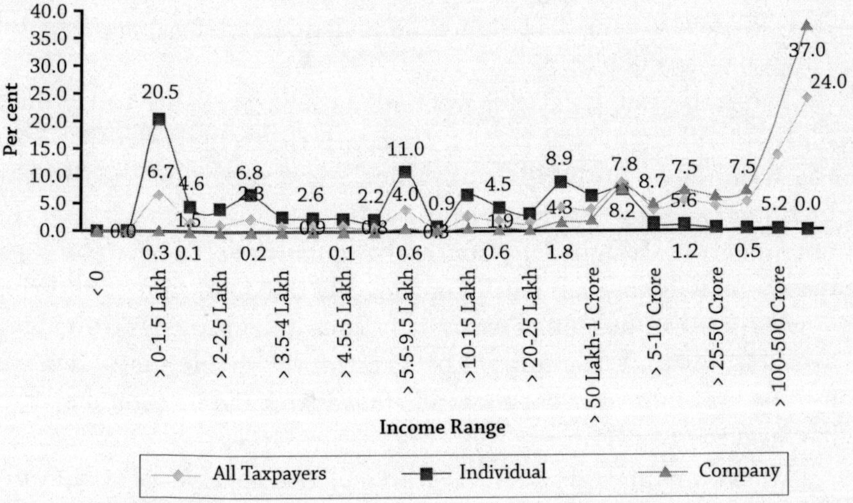

Note: * Income Tax Department (ITD)-Table 1.10, 2.10, 6.9. Per cent Share = (Sum of Tax Payable/Total Tax Payable).

Data on “Sum of Returned Income” (I-T department Table 6.8) appear to be more plausible. However, since Tax Payable (I-T department Table 6.9) is too high, when the ratio of “Sum of Tax Payable” over “Sum of Returned Income” is calculated for companies or individuals, the series is too high (hence not shown). This part of the data thus needs to be revisited or explained. I then excluded loss-making companies (income range less than zero) but again, for remaining companies in many income ranges, the ratio remains too high (hence not shown).

I-T department data on Average Tax Payable i.e. total tax payable over the number of returns by income range, also needs correction (hence not shown).

Despite data corrections needed, one broad observation that could perhaps be made is that the lowest income range could account for some 20 per cent of tax payable for individual returns, 5 per cent or so for firms, and insignificant for companies (Figure 22.2). For companies it continues to remain low and appears to increase steeply only after ₹50 crore. By contrast, middle class individuals falling between ₹5 lakh and ₹50 lakh represent an observable rise in their tax payable while, somewhat alarmingly, the share of tax payable by individuals declines rapidly after ₹5 crore income. Note, however, that I-T department data should be revisited by I-T department for removal of any doubt.

Nevertheless, if I-T department data as available today does represent likely overall trends, then it reflects India's reality that the number of individuals who declare taxable incomes in the high income ranges is close to insignificant. This is enabled by the tax structure designed by successive governments whereby high income individuals can legally opt for the dividend route and bring down their tax burden. Clearly it is time that the DDT (dividend distribution tax) be replaced by taxation of dividends under the income tax. The argument that India needs to build its capital market has weakened with time.

For companies, as indicated above, tax payable is steep only at high corporate incomes. It is possible that high tax falls on the financial sector and MNEs which face a higher corporate tax rate (but no DDT). What is also possible is that domestic capital owners are able to divert individual income not only to lower-taxed dividends but also to corporate incomes whose effective rates remain low except for MNEs. Admittedly, this is not yet tested as a hypothesis; it is thus imperative for I-T department to provide correct data such that analysis may be successfully conducted.

Tax distortions continue to represent production constraints. In a 2013-14 World Bank survey of 9,281 private sector Indian enterprises, corruption, tax rates, and tax administration were cited as the first, third and eighth of 15 business environment obstacles (the second was electricity). Further, corruption was on the top for all—small, medium and large—enterprises. Regarding tax rates, obviously as the number of government cesses increases, as the service tax rate has inevitably increased, and as excises and customs duties have been resistant to being brought down to global levels, businesses are suffering from increasing tax rates.

Individual tax returns currently pass through the CPC (centralised processing centre) faster than before but slowdowns occur; besides, selection of scrutiny cases through CASS (computer assisted scrutiny selection) continues to be erroneous and cases get unnecessarily extended longer than needed. These are matters of grave concern since such practices stand out in contrast to benchmarks achieved in comparable emerging economies. Due to the production constraints they pose, until and unless the I-T department takes serious corrective measures, national goals of Make-in-India cannot be achieved.

Business Standard, 18 July 2016.

23

MNEs' Tax Avoidance and Overdealt Response

The Group of 20 Nations (G20) asked the Organisation of Economic Cooperation and Development (OECD) based in Paris to suggest comprehensive measures to address egregious tax avoidance by MNEs (multinational enterprises) that the latter typically structure through a process of tax base erosion by shifting profits (BEPS) among their parent companies, branches and subsidiaries across national boundaries. Essentially they locate profits in low tax jurisdictions and successfully minimise their total tax contribution in terms of their global profits. Though their operations were legal, advanced country tax administrations began to perceive such practices as unreflective of the intention of the law.

Despite comprising a cluster of advanced economies, the OECD invited Brazil and India to participate in the BEPS steering group. Even a decade back India looked askance from the OECD as a rich country club and it required considerable effort to get India to participate in selected OECD deliberations. Subsequently, India's posture on international taxation was strongly and publicly criticised by tax authorities of advanced economies, compelling India to modify its position. In the end, India's role in BEPS has been commendable and it has made useful contributions to the 15 BEPS reports that were released by the OECD in Peru at a G20 Summit last month.

First, there is the matter of vindication. India steadfastly argued well before BEPS that tax revenue must justly accrue in source jurisdictions where value added is created in the international supply chain of a commodity or service. Advanced economies by and large ignored this stance, their position being, revenue should accrue where risk taking and management decisions are made and where capital resides. However, with the collapse in advanced economy revenue with the onset of the 2008 global crisis, they began to realise the potential revenue benefits of applying the source principle as India did. Recognising the validity of India's position, advanced economies pointed out, their disagreement lay less in India's philosophical positions than in the unpredictable implementation of Indian tax laws pertaining to international taxation as well as its practice of retrospective legislation that changed risk parameters of businesses ex-post.

Second, upon examination of the array of BEPS recommendations, one may assess that there are good possibilities they will be of benefit to India and other emerging economies. For example, Action 5 of BEPS highlights the so-called substance test, linking the accrual of IP (intellectual property) rights and associated income and the right of taxation thereof to where R&D (research and development) take place, making jurisdictional tax-ability a more transparent phenomenon than before. This supports India's viewpoint to the extent that India is host to R&D of MNEs. To achieve transparency, BEPS raises exchange of information among tax administrations to a high pedestal, a matter that has also been pushed for by India while advanced economies have been historically reticent about it. At the same time, the OECD tends to neutralise its position inasmuch as BEPS Actions 8 to 10 go deeper into the relationship between risk taking and intangibles such as IP to ensure that they are not dissociated from revenue rewards, thus tilting towards a position in favour of advanced economies.

Another area of clarity where the Indian view has been vindicated is BEPS Action 6 on limiting treaty abuse and controlling treaty shopping by specifying the principal purpose of an MNE operation in a taxing jurisdiction. This should assist India and emerging economies to receive a more rightful share of global MNE revenue.

Nevertheless there were limits to what India and similar emerging economies could achieve. BEPS Action 1 could be safely viewed as not having fully achieved adequacy in the taxation of the digital economy, a matter that has been of some concern to India where the digital economy has made a strong presence while escaping taxation and leading to intractable disputes. The BEPS' superficial assertion that already agreed upon taxation arrangements specified in the DTAAs (double taxation avoidance arrangements) should be adhered to, limits the ability to tax the digital economy since most DTAAs did not anticipate and do not address this issue. It also reveals the continuation of strong influences of advanced economies in what position the OECD may be finally able to take.

One area where India should have taken a different stand is Action 14 on dispute resolution. The quantum—generation, accumulation, management, resolution—of tax disputes in India far exceeds the rest of the world. India decided not to be a part of the mandatory arbitration process on sovereignty grounds, and missed an opportunity to rationalise disputes. What improvement will it bring in the Mutual Agreement Process (MAP) that addresses double taxation—a sore point with India's treaty partners? India's position would also continue to affect investment adversely. The Indian tax administration needs to rise above being a mere revenue collection agency shorn of and supra the growth context.

More fundamental than how the revenue pie is shared among tax administrations is how accountability and compliance cost would be dealt with between global tax authorities and MNEs. MNEs have been productive in technology, in supply, and in raising living standards globally. Their tax performance should be segmented into good and bad performers. There are likely to be good taxpayers even among those who fall above the high threshold that BEPS Action 13 has stipulated for the detailed 3-step—master file, country-by-country (CbC), local—reporting of their global operations. The authorities' expectation is that CbC coupled with information exchange would reduce disputes. Nevertheless, the importance of Advance Pricing Arrangements (APAs) whose speed is slow, cannot be minimised.

A heavy handed reporting system applied to all MNEs indiscriminately is detrimental to global productivity and growth. It is expectable that Action 13 would be scaled back in future deliberations reflecting that collapse in global growth was the motivator for the G20's BEPS initiative while revenue decline was only its outcome. Ultimately, revenue at the cost of growth is unlikely to receive sympathetic ears from global policymakers.

Business Standard, 17 November 2015.

24

Corporate Tax Rate and Links to Incentives

A sensible tax policy announcement by the finance minister in the last Union Budget was his intention to reduce the headline corporate tax (CIT) rate to 25 per cent. It would be decreased in phases pari passu with identification of alternate revenue sources. Subsequently on 1 July, the government reassured that a linked policy package would follow within 45 days. It is awaited. Soon a new Budget exercise will begin. There is urgency in the matter.

India's CIT rate including surcharge and education cess stands at 30.9 per cent for taxable profit less than ₹1 crore, rising to 34.61 per cent above ₹10 crore. For foreign companies, rates are 41.2 per cent and 43.26 per cent, respectively, though they do not pay the 15 per cent DDT (dividend distribution tax) (plus surcharge and education cess on DDT) that domestic companies pay. This rate structure is among the highest in the world, comparing only with the United States (40%), Argentina (35%) and Brazil (34% effective). The US frequently discusses corporate tax reform though it can essentially set it at will reflecting its economic might, while Argentina collects relatively little from individual income tax and Brazil from consumption or production taxes at the central level, their revenue dependence shifting disproportionately to CIT.

A selection of countries from where India attracts investment or where India's own capital is going reveals that they generally offer better CIT rates including Australia (30), Germany (29.65), South Africa (28), Bangladesh (27.5), China, Colombia and Malaysia (25), Chile (22.5), Russia, Turkey and the United Kingdom (20), and Singapore (17). Thus, India's announcement of achieving 25 per cent is apt and timely.

Despite best intentions, there are real challenges in achieving 25 per cent. The prevailing effective CIT rate—how much tax is collected in proportion to corporate income—is 23 per cent. Thus, (1) the difference between 30.9/34.61 per cent and 23 per cent is substantial and mainly represents tax incentives (or tax "expenditures" quantified in every Union Budget). And (2) after the CIT rate reduction, there will remain very little revenue space between 25 per cent and 23 per cent to accommodate tax incentives (on a revenue neutral basis). Yet, absence of tax incentives will be tough for industry to swallow, used as it is to special tax regimes. Hence, the challenge is to convince productive sectors that a lower general rate would benefit all and remove the prevalent system of favours targeted towards narrow industry and service sector groups.

It is thus important to identify existing tax incentives and take a view of the landscape. To begin, they include agricultural income (Section 10(1)), new units in SEZs (Section 10AA), new 100 per cent export-oriented units (Section 10B), and charitable/non-profit organisations (Section 11). The next are infrastructure development in industrial undertakings (Section 80IA) including projects of highway, bridge and rail, water supply, water treatment, irrigation, sanitation, sewerage, solid waste, port, airport, inland waterway and others. This is followed by non-infrastructure (Section 80IB) such as cold chain facility (Subsection 11), processing, preserving and packaging fruits, vegetables and meat (Subsection 11A), biodegradable waste (Section 80JJA), rural hospitals (subsection 11B), and hospitals in non-excluded areas (Subsection 11C). Some of these are being phased out while others not.

Others excluded from tax are offshore banking units (Section 80LA) and cooperative societies (Section 80P) engaged in most categories of economic activity. Another kind of incentives is regional, for special category states (Section 80IC) and North Eastern states (Section 80IE).

If prevailing conditions of infrastructure—be they highways, bridges, railways, hospitals, irrigation, sanitation or sewerage—or growth in the targeted states are considered, one immediately notices their sorry state. Incentives have not worked and continuing them would not help the sectors develop. Experience also reveals that even high profile NPOs (non-profit organisations) may be prone to tax avoidance or even tax evasion despite the overall legitimacy of the sector. Certainly it is time for them to contribute to the exchequer in a regularised manner. Exclusion of export oriented profits from taxation made little sense in the past and even less at this point when India is flushed with foreign exchange. There can be little justification for continuing windfall profits generated by income- or profit-oriented tax incentives.

In the past, eradication of tax incentives has remained well-nigh impossible. In the 2001 Tenth Five Year Plan Committee Report that I chaired, tax incentives were listed in detail that Yashwant Sinha, then finance minister, promised to remove in his 2002 Union Budget. He barely began his task before he became external affairs minister. The 2009 Direct Tax Code on which we toiled from 2007, recommended a 25 per cent CIT rate and streamlined tax incentives but it was unsuccessful, for the 2010 DTC reinstated many (though DTC 2010 did correct some poor DTC 2009 features that were later reinstalled in DTC 2013 ostensibly to protect powerful interests). I intensively managed the 2013 DTC as assigned by Finance Minister P. Chidambaram, mainly to recoup lost reform areas and to carefully consider recommendations of Chairman Yashwant Sinha's parliamentary finance committee. DTC 2013 did not go to Cabinet despite completing the rounds of line ministries. Detractors of fundamental tax reform and seekers of tax incentives remain in powerful places inside and outside government. Whether the present government can bite the bullet and finally eradicate incentives remains the crucial question.

Unless a slash and burn policy against tax incentives is unleashed, a 25 per cent headline CIT rate is infeasible. Government could afford to leave intact only a handful of investment incentives, while eschewing profit based incentives altogether. Help could have appeared from revenue productivity of a new GST but GST is unlikely to lead immediately to GDP growth or bountiful revenue reflecting its structural distortions from continuation of cascading. Thus a severe cut back of tax incentives is imperative, matched with a lower and more equitable CIT. This will impulse economic growth and, in turn, generate additional revenue. If the finance minister undertakes deep cuts in tax incentives through a pre-announced sequence comprising a three-year process, he could simultaneously achieve his stated policy of a 25 per cent headline CIT rate successfully.

Business Standard, 11 October 2015.

25

Minimum Alternate Tax on Foreign Companies

The government has given clear and rational signals by avoiding taking aggressive litigatory positions and attempting to stay or resolve contentious matters with respect to selected international taxation issues. A case in point was the decision not to appeal against the judgement of Bombay High Court in the Vodafone transfer pricing case that related to a dispute between the income tax department and the multinational corporation over a ₹3,200 crore tax liability arising out of differences in share valuation. It is, therefore, surprising why the matter of imposition of MAT (minimum alternate tax) on FIIs (foreign institutional investors) was allowed to reemerge. In particular, as I shall explain, the matter was at the cusp of resolution a year back. In a few cases, such unanticipated income tax action seems to be followed by a retreat by the policy-makers. Such actions tend to blemish the friendly assurances of top leadership.

A public stakeholder consultation window was created by the last government, called the Tax Forum, that addressed 47 indirect tax and 29 direct tax issues and resolved most of them through meetings that were held in a two-month period during August-September 2013. Industry and tax authorities participated in incisive dialogue on individual issues in a template framework. The FII-MAT issue under consideration was one of them. That meeting was held on 26 September 2013. Industry chambers Federation of Indian Chambers of Commerce and Industry (FICCI) and Confederation of Indian Industry (CII) represented.

On that day, a memorandum from industry raised the issue, to the Tax Forum, of applicability of MAT to foreign companies in the financial services sector. The genesis of the issue lay in the context of particular observations and conclusions of the Authority for Advance Rulings (AAR). It pertained to the case of Castleton Investment Ltd (AAR No 999 of 2010). In its decision, the AAR departed from the view expressed in a previous ruling in the case of Timken Company 2010 (326 ITR 193) (AAR). In the Timken case, it had been held that the MAT provisions—Section 115JB of the Income Tax Act—would not apply to a foreign company that had no presence in the form of a PE (permanent establishment) in India. This was obviated in the Castleton case by the AAR.

Industry represented that the AAR had failed to appreciate the fact that, in case of non-PEs, or foreign companies having no presence in India, there was no requirement under law to prepare profit and loss accounts (which in other cases had to be prepared in accordance with the provisions of Parts II and III of Schedule VI of the Companies Act, 1956). Accordingly, it would not be possible for a foreign company having no presence in India, that is, a non-PE, to comply with the requirements of Section 115JB(2) of the Income Tax Act.

Industry also represented that the AAR failed to appreciate the beneficial provisions of Article 13 of the India-Mauritius Tax Treaty. Under Section 90 of the Income Tax Act, foreign companies were entitled to enjoy beneficial tax treatment under applicable tax treaties. If the proposition that MAT applied to every foreign company was accepted, then in every case, despite treaty protection, income tax in the form of MAT would be payable. Such an interpretation would give MAT an overriding effect over the tax treaty, or, an unintended and certainly unexpected, treaty override. Such a consequence was contrary to the intention of the Income Tax Act and would render tax treaties ineffective and otiose.

Finally, industry asserted that the context and the legislative history of MAT provisions had to be interpreted to read as limiting the applicability of Section 115JB to Indian companies, that is, companies formed and registered under the Companies Act, and foreign companies that had established a place of business within India, as enunciated in Section 591 of the same Act.

Reflecting the industry position described above and the income tax department's indication that non-PEs were indeed not supposed to prepare India-specific accounts, the Tax Forum concluded that non-PE FIIs were not liable to pay MAT. The conclusion was the outcome of understanding and agreement between industry and the tax department in a consultative environment. Accordingly, the Tax Forum suggested to the then finance minister that the ministry of finance should clarify the matter to avoid unwarranted litigation on this issue, and that instructions should be given to the tax authorities to the effect that MAT should apply only to foreign companies that had a PE in India in case of a treaty country, or established a place of business in India within the meaning of Section 591 of the Companies Act and where the foreign company was required to maintain accounts in India.

Accordingly, in the last days of the previous government, on 12 May 2014, the then finance minister took a decision that an amendment to 115-JB be drafted for the Finance Bill to be introduced by any forthcoming government. This could have been done even through an explanation in the law in a way that would avoid any legacy issue that could be detrimental to past investment.

Following international practice between outgoing and incoming administrations, as well as taking into account the positive ramifications for industry in line with the new government's intentions, a list of already considered issues was conveyed to the new authorities prior to their 2014 Budget itself. They included the FII-MAT issue as well as several Tax Forum and other pending issues that could be relatively easily addressed since they were essentially awaiting drafting. In particular, in the instance of FII-MAT, it was clear that the two governments were on the same wavelength; hence, action was anticipated to be quick and decisive in the 2014 Budget itself and, if that was too soon, then at least in the 2015 Budget.

If the information so provided fell through the cracks, the question still remains if and how the matter was flagged to the new policy-makers reflecting what had already been debated and decided through the Tax Forum by the outgoing administration with planned action for the 2014 Budget. The appearance of demands on FIIs citing the AAR ruling was, therefore, surprising. Using the AAR to issue tax demands was not only not imperative for the department, but it went against already arrived-upon understandings. One must ask, can a non-adversarial approach from tax officials be expected, leave alone assured, by the new regime despite its multiple assertions to investors. Reflecting the joint work concept and approach of the Tax Forum, it may be time for FICCI, the CII, the Associated Chambers of Commerce of India and others to initiate active re-engagement, rather than immediately jump into the litigation route (as has just been reported with respect to AFISMA). Cooperation must continue in order to contain disputes and avoid litigation. As for the department, a well-drafted circular should be quickly issued, followed by legislation as necessary.

In particular, where the Central Board of Direct Taxation (CBDT) and the Central Board of Excise and Customs (CBEC) had already agreed to take action at the Tax Forum deliberations, those matters should be methodically brought to the attention of the current policy-makers. Otherwise, confidence of industry would erode in the face of government statements that appear unmatched with policy application that follows. Wrong signals that move in contradiction to prevailing policy intentions escalate the already high opportunity costs for doing business. After all, the Tax Administration Reform Commission (TARC)'s final Feedback volume that also listed all its recommendations highlighted deep reforms needed in customer focus, stakeholder consultation and dispute management. The finance minister had indicated in his 2015 Budget speech that the TARC recommendations were in their final stage of consideration and that they would be implemented in 2015-16.

Business Standard, 19 May 2015.

26

Are Corporations an Enigma?

Corporations, in particular MNCs, are viewed as messengers of deceit by a majority of people worldwide. They are believed to destroy the environment while making sky-high profits for themselves; it is perceived that top corporate managers look out for themselves rather than for shareholders; and it is thought that corporations behaviourally avoid tax by provisioning for losses that they themselves cause—not only for themselves, but for their entire economy, if not the global economy in the case of MNCs. Recently, cases of fraud in various forms—Ponzi loan schemes, insider trading and other forms of information-peddling and illegal interest rate-setting—have rubbed their reputation in the dust. But do all corporations behave in this detrimental manner? It is crucial to divide the corporate world in two—financial and real. The former's behaviour at the level of international finance has been reprehensible. The latter, by and large, has driven economic growth through innovation and investment, though some have indeed strayed.

In an early study, the Boston Consulting Group demonstrated how corporations expanded through eliminating inefficient competition and gave lower product prices back to consumers that, in turn, reflected reinvested corporate profits in research and technology. The aluminium industry provided a case study. The automobile industry would be another example. The corporate legal form itself emerged as a shelter that protected the corporation from unlimited liability so that production and supply could continue with a reasonable degree of assurance that productive activity would continue without looking over one's shoulder to cover for unreasonable claims of compensation from aggrieved parties.

With the emergence of large corporations as identifiable entities, it became convenient to tax the incomes of corporations. Often a point is missed out on the philosophical basis of corporate income taxation. Recall that a VAT (value-added tax) is exactly the same in its effects as a retail sales tax. The worldwide popularity of the VAT is because it is a better tax collector. Instead of focusing only on the retail stage and thereby incurring the possibility of not being able to target and collect sales tax from small retailers, the VAT collects the same tax in small amounts as the full retail value builds up in the process of production and distribution. Thus, missing out the final retail stage would still ensure revenue from earlier stages. Further, if one stage is missed, it is made up in subsequent stages. The corporation income tax is to be viewed in a similar light.

The corporation is a legal entity that conveniently acts as a conduit for the individual income tax. Ultimately, it is the individual who bears the burden of income taxation since he is the economic agent who earns income—salary, interest, dividends/profits, capital gains—though quite a bit of it is channelled through corporations. There are far less corporations than individuals. Hence, it is simply easier to collect tax from the former than from the latter. Otherwise, income tax would be collected entirely from individuals. I will elaborate conceptually below.

Given the reality that the corporation income tax does exist and possesses a significant stature in country tax systems, a big question that has been debated is who really bears the tax. Is it consumers or producers? Many economists believe it is incorrect to view the problem in this manner, since the tax is a tax on capital, which is an input or factor of production. Hence, the right question is whether the tax is borne by capital owners or shifted to labour (who are both, in the final analysis, individuals).

Note further that the corporate income tax is a tax on capital in the corporate sector alone. Thus it is a "partial" tax. As a result of this tax, capital moves out of the corporate sector. It has to be absorbed into the non-corporate sector. But the latter sector is generally more labour-intensive. If it is forced to absorb capital, it will do so only at a price of capital lower than its price when the tax was imposed.

Hence, the return to capital will have to fall relative to wages. Thus, conservative tax economists claimed that the tax is borne entirely by capital.

But, given that the non-corporate sectors—including agriculture and real estate—are the major land-intensive sectors, some economists viewed land as a specific input used mainly in the non-corporate sector. Its use in the corporate sector was small by comparison. For the sake of analysis, then it is not just labour and capital but also land that should be considered as a factor of production. And, because land is fixed and cannot move like labour or capital, it is obliged to absorb some of the burden of the tax, sharing it with capital. Thus, both capital and landowners share the burden of the corporation income tax. To the extent that labour cannot flee, labour too might bear some of the burden. The actual division of corporate tax burden depends on whether, post-tax, they are easily absorbed in the non-corporate sector. If they are easily absorbed, they will not bear much of the tax; if they are not easily absorbed, they will bear a high burden.

Thus, corporations tend to bear at least some or most of the tax burden in their role as capital owners. It is not surprising that they go out of their way to devise structures that enable them to minimise tax. They use the term "tax efficiency" which implies that they should not pay more tax than they need to. To counter such excessive behaviour, tax authorities design rules to minimise corporate tax avoidance. But there is need to consult. These rules are important and necessary, and the challenge is to design them in a way that they eliminate abusive taxpayer behaviour while not inadvertently introducing barriers to investment or inducing capital flight.

Again, this type of corporate behaviour must reflect that they at least believe that they have to bear the burden of corporate tax unless they form complex structures to avoid it. Of course they claim that such structures emerge due to market-driven business reasons. Interestingly, the evolution of extremely complex transnational corporate structures is leading corporations themselves to increasingly attempt to control and minimise the spread of their organisational structures. This takes the form of corporate simplification that comprises consolidation, reduction of costs, and enhancement of cash flow. Simply put, it combines the benefits of legal entity reduction and business transformation, and a general preference for converting subsidiaries into branches of a single entity.

Typical corporations work to produce, supply and innovate, with innovation resulting in keeping prices in check, and they do pay tax while, like individuals, they also minimise their taxes. If abusive, institutions should be set up to monitor and counter such behaviour through regulation, imposing appropriate penalties, and taking even stronger action where needed. The mix of good and bad behaviour makes the corporation an enigma—though, as a legal form and function, they should not be automatically considered to be so.

Business Standard, 16 July 2012.

27

The Vodafone Affair

The Layout

The Supreme Court's ruling asserting the non-taxability of an acquisition by Vodafone, and the reaction of Indian revenue authorities in introducing an amendment to the Income Tax Act in the 2012 Finance Bill enabling retrospective taxation, have brought up a string of questions on the interpretation and subsequent treatment for tax purposes of businesses. The particular context has been with respect to businesses operating in one country while dealing amongst themselves in another. Analysing this from a taxation point of view is challenging, especially when the minister of state for finance has asserted that the revenue implication of the amendment could be ₹35,000 to ₹40,000 crore.

The amendment's overall economic impact is also a matter to be reckoned with. For instance, another minister of state for finance is reported to have indicated that foreign investors make their decisions taking into account all relevant factors, and that the investments are admitted into the country within the framework of the applicable laws and regulations formulated to promote the country's interest. The question remains if this was meant as an ex-post statement; if so, it would imply that a business would have to anticipate all relevant changes that might come in the life-cycle of the proposed business venture. That is not possible. If, therefore, it is to be taken as an ex-ante statement, then one would have to ask how such investors will react when the relevant factors and prevailing framework of applicable laws on the basis of which investment decisions were made are suddenly changed in an unanticipated way—that is, without consultation with stakeholders.

Figure 27.1

Pre-Acquisition

Hutchinson

↑

Hutchinson Telecom International (Hong Kong)

↑

CGP Cayman
(CGP held entire share capital of the below Mauritius company)

↑

Mauritius company
(owned by different, including Indian, entities)

↑

Mauritius held company ($\frac{2}{3}^{rd}$) (foreign)

__________ India __________

Hutchinson Essar (HE) ---------------- Essar ($\frac{1}{3}^{rd}$) (not foreign)

Figure 27.2

Post-Acquisition

Vimbu (Dutch group entity of Vodafone)

↑

CGP Cayman
(Vimbu acquired entire capital of CGP of $11 billion)

↑

Mauritius company

↑

Entity 1, the company held 52 per cent, Entities 2, 3 and 4 (IDFC) held 15 per cent to make a total 67 per cent foreign held. Thus, in a sense, HE created this Mauritius entity that held $\frac{2}{3}^{rd}$, thus complying with Indian law.

__________ India __________

Hutchinson Essar (HE) ---------------- Essar ($\frac{1}{3}^{rd}$) (not foreign)

Indian law limits foreign investment in telecom infrastructure to 74 per cent of total capital. Figure 27.1 shows, to this author's understanding, how the business was organised prior to the acquisition while Figure 27.2 shows the post-acquisition situation.

The issues to address are: first, though the economic activity took place in India, the transaction that enabled the changing of hands took place outside India; second, given the manner in which the transaction took place, and however dexterously we interpret it or which side we take, there is a general question of international tax minimisation if not avoidance, so that the expectation of making globally operating MNCs (multinational companies) pay their fair tax share continues to jar and frustrate; third, that Hutchison was the seller and Vodafone the buyer but, apparently since Hutchison was out of the picture, the revenue authorities pursued the buyer regarding the tax payments while, conceptually, it should be the seller who should pay the tax; and fourth, the interpretation of the gains as income or capital gains determines taxability—since, if it is income, India can tax it but, if it is capital gains, the foreign government does so as per tax treaty (which does not matter in the Caymans or Mauritius since there is no capital gains there).

First, referring to Figures 27.1 and 27.2, all transactions took place above the India dividing line. Indeed, entities in Hong Kong, Netherlands, Cayman Islands and Mauritius, not just India, were involved, revealing the well-known prevalence of mind-boggling global corporate structures. Yet, Hutchison Essar, the entity under consideration, continues to operate and generate income and profits in India before and after its acquisition by Vodafone. Second, given the prominence of tax havens Mauritius and Caymans, and adherents of international tax competition in short headline tax rates Hong Kong and Netherlands, it does not take much intelligence to realise the overwhelming role of tax avoidance in the transaction.

Now come the difficult parts. Third, given that it was Hutchison the seller that must have made income or capital gains from the transaction, does not the onus lie on Hutchison to pay whatever tax they owed to the revenue authorities? What prompted the latter to go after the buyer and could this be justified? Reversing the onus of tax payment is called withholding tax or reverse charge in common taxation parlance. Take an example from the VAT or GST. If a construction industry contractor subcontracts out to small operators, then the former is asked to collect VAT from the latter before making payments to them. Then he has to pass the collection to the revenue authorities. Thus it works well typically when a large entity (on one side) and many small entities (on the opposite side) are transacting together. For the authorities to operate this principle between two large operating entities as a withholding tax is unusual and, in any event, the tax withholding provision (Section 195) does not apply extra-territorially.

Fourth, the question to examine is whether what technically took place was a transfer of shares of a non-resident entirely outside India, or a transfer of a capital asset situated in India. The *mere* transfer of shares abroad can be restricted from being interpreted as buying interest in the property in India. If so, it is not a transfer of a capital asset and, in turn, would not give rise to income chargeable to tax in India. I have used mere in italics since in reality it is of course not a small transaction. But small or large, unfortunately, it does not legally make it a transfer of a capital asset, and remains a transfer of shares. The revenue authorities, however, chose to interpret the proceeds as income rather than as capital gains from a sale of shares. While they won in the Mumbai High Court, resulting in Vodafone facing a tax bill of $2 billion, the Supreme Court subsequently reversed the judgement of the High Court.

Business Standard, 10 May 2012.

28

The Vodafone Affair

The Deconstruction

To deconstruct the Vodafone affair in continuation of my previous presentation ("The Vodafone Affair: The Layout", May 10), let us hypothesise a publicly listed Indian hotel conglomerate. It builds a hotel in Bogota, Buenos Aires or Caracas. It is publicly listed on NASDAQ where continuous share transactions take place. Would we want Colombian, Argentinian or Venezuelan revenue authorities to come after the Indian shareholders every time they buy or sell shares and insist that they have transferred property—a capital asset—and that they should pay tax on it to them? That would be onerous for them to collect and impossible for the Indian shareholders to sequentially keep paying. Just because the revenue authorities could identify Vodafone as the sole buyer, it does not hopefully weaken the thrust of the argument.

To conclude, we may feel some vicarious pleasure in seeing an MNC in distress and increasing its global tax outgo—for, after all, which country does not lament the low tax liability that they are deemed to conjure?—or some empathy for the Indian revenue authorities for pursuing the right, or a moral, objective and taking a bold step, but their conceptual and legal interpretation has to be seamless and rational, not unconsulted and tied in knots.

The Supreme Court has given its judgement against the High Court, absolving Vodafone from paying additional tax. The subsequent reactive proposition in Parliament through the 2012 Finance Bill that would allow retrospective application of a new law is in contraposition of that judgement. It carries with it the potential of unbalancing the fine balance of powers among the different branches of government. This is because, if the legislature can pass a retroactive change in an existing law after the judiciary has made a ruling based on the prevailing law, then there exists the potential that a judgement of the judiciary—that has already been made in time t—can be nullified by a subsequent law in time t-1. This implies a subsumption that the legislature can actually go back and change an already passed judgment—based on existing law—of the judiciary. The resultant anomaly in the balance of powers certainly could not have been the intention of our Constitutional fathers.

India increasingly compares itself with its BRICS partners. As in India, Brazil's Constitution gives different levels of government the competence to impose taxes. They have to adhere to three important principles, however:

- Legality: No tax can be imposed or increased, when it is not established by law. To introduce a tax (i.e. a tax base), a two-thirds majority of both Houses of Parliament (not just of those present) is required. To change a tax rate, 50 per cent+1 majority of those present in both Houses of Parliament is needed. Parliament also specifies the rate band for municipal taxes through "complementary law". A municipality fixes the actual rate through "ordinary law".
- Prospectivity: Tax cannot be collected in the year when the law is published; and
- No retrospective legislation: Prohibition to collect taxes related to facts or events that occurred before law came into force.

On the other hand, the UK Treasury has accepted a "wholly exceptional" criterion for retrospective legislation, though any retrospective measure involves public consultation. While there is no recourse to the UK Supreme Court in such cases, the European Court provides final recourse. Charles Sampford's 2006 book, *Retrospectivity and the Rule of Law* (OUP), and Daniel Sandler's 1993 article, "Retrospective Tax Decisions", in the *Cambridge Law Journal* point amply towards the fallacy of retrospectivity.

The Indian finance minister has reassured the public that there is little to worry with retrospectivity. He has maintained his position with Mr Geithner, his US counterpart. Indeed, there is probably little doubt that he would break his promise. But the new provision may be expected to last, with windfall powers falling in the hands of the authorities, uncertainty in international and domestic business decisions, and an intrinsic inconsistency in the balance of powers envisaged among the three branches of government.

The correct step would have been to revise those DTAAs (double taxation avoidance agreements) that countered original intentions and objectives and whose deleterious impacts on revenue or the economy could not have been foreseen. This has been done by some countries when their direct interests were jeopardised. It is therefore understandable that the revenue authorities have indicated that the DTAA with Mauritius would be revisited, a matter that, if earlier corrected, would probably have minimised the current hiatus over the Vodafone affair.

To conclude, what detrimental ramifications might there be with retrospective taxation? To answer this, one should consider double aspects. On the one hand, large MNCs, including Indian ones, make a beeline every year to compete evermore for tax incentives. Yet there is little doubt that economists view tax incentives as distortions in optimal resource allocation in the form of costs to economic activity. (1) They distort relative prices, thus affecting the equilibrium allocation of resources, i.e. causing "inefficiency" in resource allocation. (2) They treat selected sectors preferentially, which can be inequitable since it implies a heavier burden on non-preferred sectors for raising the same revenue. (3) This means the allocation of resources gets more distorted since non-preferred sectors pay more taxes. (4) Monitoring costs increase, implying tax administration becomes less simple. (5) Tax incentives could increase tax evasion in the resultant system that becomes more complex, with high selectivity, and administrative discretion and control.

On the other hand, retrospective taxation could be perceived not only to worsen the economic climate and deepen uncertainty in business decisions and result in a truncated willingness to invest, but also to exacerbate the inequity in tax treatment similar to the effects of tax incentives. To conclude, neither do policy makers have to hand out tax incentives selectively—instead, focusing only on how to make it feasible to continually bring down headline tax rates—nor do they have to resort to retrospective taxation except under the most exceptional circumstances and that too after open, transparent, and long, as necessary, consultations with the stakeholders.

Business Standard, 22 May 2012.

V

Indirect Tax

29

Pushing Forward on GST

Two events took place in June that should mean something in terms of moving the GST (good and services tax) forward from the back burner. The first was a frank speech by Sushil Modi, Chairman of the Empowered Committee (EC) of states' finance ministers that oversees their preparations for GST. The second was the set of hearings on GST at the Standing Committee on Finance of Parliament chaired by Yashwant Sinha.

Mr Modi rightly pointed to why a GST is needed, among them: (1) to correct for existing limitations of the CENVAT-VAT structure, the Centre being truncated to taxing up to the manufacturing point and the states being excluded from taxing services, (2) to absorb many existing small taxes, and (3) to make India a common market such as the European Union (EU). In the process he conceded that there has been a misunderstanding that states would lose autonomy since even the Centre would have to function through the proposed GST Council (henceforth Council) and thus lose autonomy in the same vein.

Then he mentioned what more states would specifically like. The first is compensation for revenue loss of the already reduced—and eventual abolition—of the CST (central sales tax) on interstate trade. They want a five-year compensation package of ₹50,000 crore built into the Constitution Amendment Bill (henceforth Bill).

Second, they want flexibility in the rate structure. Citing the EU, they eschew the single rate concept and prefer a floor rate and a narrow band on top, while allowing only two—standard and lower–rates within the band. Third, they want flexibility on rates during emergencies such as floods or droughts when they should be allowed to put rates of ordinary times in abeyance.

Fourth, on dispute resolution between the Centre and states, the Bill proposes a dispute resolution authority to ameliorate any action by a state or Centre that adversely affects the harmonised GST structure. States, Mr Modi asserted, are unanimous against the formation of a supra body that would have the power to dictate to states on matters of dispute resolution. The EC prefers the Council to devise an appropriate mechanism to resolve disputes rather than another body with "legislative supremacy". The EC has been asking the Centre to incorporate this aspect in the Bill. It feels that, in the worst case, if a dispute cannot be resolved at the Council level, then the judiciary could be approached as needed.

Fifth, the Council itself will take decisions on the basis of a consensus—but how many of the states would have to be present? The EC would like the presence to be raised to two-thirds, and that this should be in the Bill. Mr Modi said that the fourth draft has been sent to the Standing Committee on Finance and wondered aloud why the states' concerns are still not reflected in the current version. He expressed the hope that their concerns would be met and that the Standing Committee would submit its report before the Monsoon session of Parliament. Yet he was pragmatic enough to admit that, given that the constitutional amendment would need a two-thirds majority in Parliament and ratification by 50 per cent of the states, many obstacles would have to be removed "before the GST sees the light of day". He noted that the Union finance minister had not mentioned any deadline during his 2012 Budget Speech. He concluded that the process was "inching towards a GST".

In summing up, Mr Modi was nevertheless optimistic for no state had challenged the idea of a GST and that it was never a matter of politics, but one of genuine concern among states regarding revenue loss. Thus, unless the Centre was "flexible" on this count, it would be difficult to implement GST. At the same time, he recalled that there was the same fear with respect to the VAT, but that there had been high revenue gain from its introduction. He was optimistic the same would occur with GST.

So where does the GST process stand at this point? The most obvious conclusion is the existence of a "trust deficit", a phrase Mr

Modi did not desist from using, between the Centre and states. It appears that this is the reason why the states want selective administrative and structural matters to be included in the Bill. CST compensation could be viewed in the administrative category. Their demand, and the Centre's acceptance, of the exclusion of petroleum products—petroleum crude, high-speed diesel, petrol, ATF and natural gas—from GST through the Bill itself, could be viewed in the structural category. Unfortunately both are fallacious in principle and should be avoided.

Many appropriate design elements are yet to be assured and incorporated. First, the singularity of treatment of goods and services in terms of tax rates is not yet concluded. Not having the same tax rate for goods and services—even allowing for floor rates and a band—would comprise a major lacuna since classification problems would continue and are likely to multiply, in contrast to global practice in an ideal GST in which goods and services are not separated. By the way, it is worth pointing out here that a 12 per cent manufacturing level excise tax is not equivalent to a 12 per cent retail level service tax, as has been claimed in the 2012 Union Budget.

Second, the information-technology support needed to appropriately operate interstate trade remains nascent. A high-level task force has indeed been set up, though its outcome is yet to emerge into view. TINXSYS as a system was in development for almost a decade to manage interstate trade processes and cross-state reimbursements; where is it now? Without an appropriate clearing house mechanism in place, dealers will naturally overstate their interstate trade, knowing full well that it will be difficult for state tax administrations in the importing state to check all imports. Hence cross-state input tax credit might soar.

Third, if both petroleum products and alcoholic beverages are to be excluded from GST for reasons of revenue protection, almost half of the potential value-added or consumption base of GST would be excluded. The cost to the information chain could be insurmountable. Also, input tax credit would not be available to either product, raising their tax burden. As in the rest of the world, both should be within the GST base so that the debit minus credit framework would work through the supply chain. On top of that, selective turnover based excises could be imposed on these products to protect revenue.

In the ultimate analysis, the GST that will be introduced will be judged internationally and by business as to whether business costs and compliance costs have been reduced. It must be understood that such a major tax reform such as moving to a good GST should, by itself, improve revenue performance through enhanced economic growth just as the VAT enabled, by Mr Modi's own admission. Mr Sinha and his Standing Committee had their first GST hearing and indicated that they would like to complete their work before the Monsoon session. It can be hoped that, while the design of GST should keep implementability in mind, they will also recognise the most important economic elements of a good GST and make their recommendations accordingly. Reflecting his salient moves in his Union Budgets against tax incentives when he was finance minister, one remains hopeful.

Business Standard, 18 June 2012.

30

GST: Remains of a Decade

India is rushing towards a so-termed GST replacing service tax and excises (or CENVAT) at the Centre and VAT and small consumption taxes of the states. In a decade-long process of replacement, major successes were occurring to meaningfully consolidate the nation's domestic consumption tax structure. But in the last mile, many essential elements of a robust GST have been shaved off, so the current version of GST is neither sufficiently aligned to easing the way of doing business nor internationally benchmarked.

I write today because I care about this tax, having assisted some 30 countries in its reform or introduction, becoming involved in India since 1995. Neither will I be shy in revealing that as chairman of the task force on tax policy and administration for India's Tenth Five-Year Plan, in 2001 that report recommended a seamless tax on goods and services with parallel channels for the Centre and states. I made presentations to K.C. Pant, the stalwart Deputy Chairman, Planning Commission. After an early presentation, I confessed that some of the recommendations might seem idealistic but asserted, albeit apologetically, that they nevertheless were optimal. Addressing me as professor, Pant replied solemnly that I should present the best and not think of downsizing for which others would be readily available. Technocratic Yashwant Sinha, then finance minister, mentioned the report in his 2002 Union Budget speech, indicating he would streamline tax incentives following the report's recommendations. Today that seems long ago. A decade later, Mr Sinha, then chairman, Parliamentary Finance Committee, invited me to provide views on GST which are on record. The 2015 Parliamentary Select Committee on GST also invited me for my views.

If constructed appropriately, GST makes transparent the tax administration and is revenue productive. It removes distortions in businesses' production decisions by effectively taxing only consumption (not production). It does not differentiate goods from services, or within goods or services streams. Following his GST announcement in Union Budget 2006, a comprehensive report was convened by P. Chidambaram, then finance minister. As permanent invitee to the Empowered Committee (EC) of state-level finance ministers, I co-authored that first report and submitted GST's best achievable structure on 31 December 2007. It hopefully occupies a place in the annals of EC.

The current GST proposals fail essential tests including Mr Sinha's Parliamentary Committee recommendations. The shedding occurred reflecting individual states' interests. They bypassed national concerns while the Centre, appearing to be in a hurry, accommodated this watering down process. I wonder what Pant would have to say were he to witness these developments.

First, presuming that GST will occur on 1 April 2016, India is the first country I have experienced with considerably less clarity regarding the intricacies in its proposed structure, transitional arrangements, administration and procedures, and framework to contain inflationary ramifications. In other countries, consultation on the actual proposals would have taken place in an open manner.

Second, one major characteristic of GST is that it should not distinguish between a good and a service. Yet, in its GST, India is likely to continue with a distinction. The argument put forward is that services are currently being taxed at only 14 per cent at the level of the Centre; hence any equality of rates between goods and services would raise the tax rate on services too much. But the solution is not to keep a separate lower rate for services, rather to consult, educate and arrive at understandings with business chambers and traders.

Third, states have been allowed to have bands in their GST rates. This debate started with states initially pleading they should be given some flexibility with rates in periods of emergency for temporary extra revenue. That then snowballed into full-fledged bands that even their prevailing VAT does not allow. Theoretically a band being a continuous line, the SGST could have infinite rates. I cannot imagine the impending impossible life of an interstate dealer. Thus GST could potentially go back to the future, reinventing the sales taxes era that prevailed prior to VAT.

Fourth, excluding petroleum products will rob GST of comprehensive ITC (input tax credit). Relatedly, capital goods would continue to be given ITC only over two years and not in one year. Both these would result in considerable cascading or 'tax on tax' for businesses and, since they will certainly attempt to pass this downstream to consumers, the latter will face an array of prices that would not reflect market demands accurately. Instead, the relative prices among all goods and services will reflect different cascading elements in them, reducing GST to a hybrid production/consumption tax. (Exemption of alcohol for domestic consumption will also suffer from, and contribute to, similar limitations.) Given that one state that would considerably enjoy protection of revenue from petroleum production is the Prime Minister's own, this is the moment to rise above state specific interests and, in the national interest, include petroleum fully in GST, just as he displayed acumen by retracting from his 2015 Land Acquisition Bill to reincorporate social impact analysis and states' views (see my 14.07.15 Opinion in this paper).

Fifth, a one per cent interstate trade tax will be retained and later reviewed by GST Council. This tax will cascade since exporting states will retain its revenue without allowing ITC. Again, this will favour exporting states that are richer. Fiscal federalism comprises not just Centre-state but also interstate equity. The finance minister could boldly remove this tax from GST framework, declaring it will not only be inefficient due to cascading but inequitable among rich versus poor states, just as he has accepted not to impose MAT on FIIs (my 19.05.15 Opinion).

In sum, there remains much work to design a good GST. Otherwise, it can be called GST but neither will price distortions reduce, nor business decisions or consumption reflect demand-driven prices, nor administration or compliance be simplified, nor GDP be impacted positively, nor revenue excel, nor the world accept it in a global pantheon of GSTs.

Business Standard, 15 September 2015.

31

Tax Policy and Administration—A Conversation

If Petroleum is Out, It's Not GST[1]

If you were to make an action plan for the next Government, what would be your suggestions?

I think the primary focus has to be on tax administration. First, remove uncertainty for taxpayers. Ensure there are no retrospective amendments, like in Brazil and Sweden. Second, make tax administration accountable for its actions and decisions and ensure timeliness. Third, accountability must be linked to minimising infructuous demands and tracking recovery. Fourth, tax evasion should be appropriately identified and followed, rather than basing your premise on taxpayers as tax evaders. Fifth, and perhaps the most important, move away from a static revenue target principle of revenue collection. Finally, regarding structural reform, of course, I hope the DTC (Direct Taxes Code) and GST (Goods & Services Tax) would be picked up. But, as I said, the first thing they should take up is a balanced approach to tax administration.

Both the Congress and the Bharatiya Janata Party (BJP) have voiced support to GST. Do you think a consensus is possible after formation of the new Government?

The intention of policymakers is clear, that they want GST. The issue is the Centre's disagreement with some states over technical aspects, though the technical work on GST is complete. For example, inclusion or exclusion of petroleum products. There are certain states

1. Parthasarathi Shome tells Indivjal Dhasmana and Vrishti Beniwal in an interview that the next government's priority should be removing tax uncertainty, while avoiding retrospective amendments. Edited excerpts of the interview are reproduced in this article.

that led the disagreement over inclusion of petroleum products in GST. But, if you keep petroleum products out, no tax policy designer could call it GST. Another issue was compensation for CST (Central Sales Tax). For how long the Centre has to give the compensation was also a point of contention. In my view, there should be quick cutoff for CST compensation. That was not worked out fully. Flexibility to states was also given in terms of differential rates, which means states will have floor rates and can move the rates up or down. This would cause a high compliance burden on taxpayers. For the same products, he will have to deal with two different rates in two states. Interpretation of which commodities belong to which rate would also add to GST's complications. The concern among policymakers about compliance cost seems rather little, because the major focus seems to be on how much revenue can be obtained. Unless we move away from an exclusive revenue objective, and towards revenue collection based on increased production of goods and services, I don't think we are getting the concept of GST right. When GST is taken up again, I hope this fundamental concern will become the quintessential focus of the GST design, even if it requires a rethink on issues.

BJP said GST could not be rolled out because the Centre did not address the concerns of states and the IT (Information Technology) infrastructure was not ready. Do you agree?

I wouldn't like to isolate particular groups. You cannot agree with every point states make, for two reasons. One, states' views keep changing. Two, if you agree with all the changing views, you are not getting to GST. Yes, you may have to make some modifications to accommodate political realities or even for field conveniences, but you can't move too far away from the crux of GST. On IT preparedness, I agree, but I don't think the Centre is to blame for that. For example, the Centre has its own IT framework for the Central GST. The other part it can play is a clearing house role for interstate trade. These can be done easily. It's states where IT-preparedness varies a lot; so, as a whole, they have to pick up.

Do you think it was a good idea to propose the superrich tax of 35 per cent on those earning over ₹10 crore a year in the revised DTC draft?

At the level of above ₹10 crore, you look at the UK, Germany, Chile, China, South Africa... the rates are even higher, between 40 per cent and 50 per cent. So, raising it to 35 per cent in India is not high. The US has 35 per cent. An Indian consumer commands much more at ₹10 crore in terms of purchasing-power parity. I think it was justified and essential, given our overall economic status and income distribution and where the government is spending huge amounts to reach out to the poor.

The Vodafone case has seen too many twists and turns. What could be a possible solution to the row?

Retrospective amendments can be made for correcting errors or for making clarifications in favour of taxpayers. In any event, you can't have retrospective amendments to specifically counter the Supreme Court rulings. If the government insists on retroactivity in certain cases at the moment, there should not be application of interest or penalty. The committee's draft report was given, a final report followed but the final report is not yet on the net. The department has not come out with any position. Its acceptance would have reassured investors. If you make international comparisons, the number of disputes that we have in India far exceeds other countries. That shows policies simply need an in-depth revisit and rationalisation. Investors view all this, and they become ever cautious about investing in India.

Many accuse the Finance Ministry of scaring away investors. Do you think by reviewing the General Anti-Avoidance Rules (GAAR) and other initiatives, the Ministry has removed that perception?

Here I speak as chairman of the committee to review GAAR. The introduction of GAAR was not questioned; it was the way components of GAAR were formulated in the Budget of 2012 that was in question. It was rather extreme in terms of prevailing global practices. So, the committee examined it and made it rational and more applicable. The reaction was good. But I don't think it is sufficient to expect a change in approach overnight. The fact that a tax administration, nascent in the field application of GAAR, did not recognise the dozens of examples the committee provided in its report where GAAR should, or should not, be applied is deeply revealing to me on the approach being adopted by them. I keep hoping that new generations will bravely alter that stance for their own benefit. To continue, whether GAAR is implemented with revenue in mind, or with anti-avoidance as the goal, whether officers are sufficiently trained to use this kind of instrument or not all of these will have to be experienced. That would eventually prove how investors take the GAAR matter with respect to their decision to invest in India. The continuing variations in the application of transfer pricing with a revenue objective is sufficient evidence of my apprehension, but I remain hopeful things will change.

Have you Given a Thought what would you do after your term in the Finance Ministry expires?

The work of TARC is supposed to continue for another year. Beyond that, my plans are set. I have to complete three books I have agreed to. I have to bring out the pictures I have taken for decades across the globe. I have to read the collection of my books and listen to my music, each selected over the years with care. I want to learn Sanskrit. I want to travel to the nook and corner of the world I have missed but, importantly, to discover India in her deep recesses.

How do you look at your two stints at the Finance Ministry?

It has been an excellent, challenging and chastening experience. In the first stint, I was operating on the basis of my earlier experience in India, as well as in several emerging economies. After the first stint, I was in the UK for three years, which is an advanced tax administration. So, during my first term, I could bring in emerging-country experiences wherever they were relevant. For example, regarding AIR (annual information returns), Brazil uses information from 40 third-party sources. We introduced 6. We could use other country experiences for fringe benefits tax or bank cash transaction tax, too. We could take out the surcharge for smaller firms, since we found corporate tax incidence was very downward sloping, or, tax burden went down as a firm's size increased. Or, we introduced calculation of revenue foregone due to tax incentives in the Union Budget. These were straightforward exercises in the first stint.

Then, I went to the UK. That experience gave me the realisation of how to trust taxpayers. That would need a sea change in the thinking here, and continues to challenge and chasten my efforts. I saw what happened in the context of GAAR and retrospective amendments to IT rules. I became more convinced that we had to give a partnership role to our taxpayer stakeholders. In the UK, they don't use the term taxpayer any more. It is customers for individuals, and stakeholders for businesses. I thought we should experiment with that approach. Some people doubt whether it will work in India, but I think it will certainly work here if administration takes the first step forward.

The first term, I worked hard on DTC 2009 and GST. In the second, I worked very hard on DTC 2013. I found it was a very different tax code from 2009. The one I had worked on in 2007, whose modified form came out as 2009, had completely changed. Working on the new 2013 version was very challenging. In my assessment, DTC 2009 comprised a deeply fundamental tax reform. DTC 2010 returned close to the current IT Act, but had been already commented on by the Parliamentary standing committee on finance. First, I had to digest the fact that we had retreated so much between the 2009 and the 2010 versions. But we did the best to improve DTC 2010 and achieved DTC 2013.

On GST, I had worked from the VAT and wrote, with the EC (VAT), the first GST report at the end of 2007. I thought states accepted it by and large.

When I returned from the UK, I found GST was being deconstructed. Currently there does exist a draft Constitutional amendment, but big breaches in Centre-state relations remain; these have to be bridged if we are to have a globally recognised GST. And, the design certainly needs to be revisited if we want a GST with low compliance cost. So, the challenges have not ended.

Business Standard, 28 April 2014.

32

An American VAT?

Graetz promotes a tax-mix on income, wages and wealth to ensure progressivity, and a VAT for revenue.

The principles of tax reform emphasise its effects on equity, efficiency of resource allocation and revenue productivity. Michael Graetz, in his recent book, *100 Million Unnecessary Returns*, proposes for the US a Competitive Tax Plan (CTP) to ensure these objectives. He reveals widening income and wealth gaps. Between 1979 and 2006, the incomes of the richest 1 per cent nearly doubled, while that of the middle class grew 11.5 per cent. Wages of the lowest decile increased 4 per cent, while at the top they grew 34 per cent. Regarding wealth, the wealthiest 1 per cent owns a third of all wealth. The bottom 50 per cent holds 2.25 per cent. The average net worth of the top 10 per cent of families is 30 times that of the middle 50 per cent. Graetz rightly cautions that any tax reform should not worsen distribution.

The prevailing tax burden is not regressive, however. More than two-thirds of income tax is paid by the top 10 per cent of earners; more than a third by the top 1 per cent. An exclusive consumption tax, as proposed by the Flat Tax and Fair Tax, would not retain progressivity. Yet the income tax alone would offer an inadequate revenue base, given increasing international factor mobility and flight. A mix of taxes on income, wages and wealth, with high thresholds, is needed to ensure progressivity while a consumption VAT would provide revenue.

The US is not a high tax country. Federal, state and local taxes represent 25 per cent of GDP in contrast to 40 per cent for the EU (before accession) and 36 per cent for the OECD. The US relies on income and payroll taxes to contribute 92 per cent of federal revenues. US income tax is comparable to Europe—13 per cent of GDP, as opposed to 14 per cent for the EU. The difference reflects consumption taxes.

A VAT of 10-14 per cent could finance the cost of exempting income-tax payers with family income of $100,000, and reduce the income (IT) and corporate tax (CT) rates. The US goods would become more competitive by enabling a low CT rate, and prevailing negative household savings should improve.

On income tax, until 1932, the top 5.6 per cent of the population filed tax returns. In 1940-41, new legislation quadrupled the number of returns to 28 million, and by 1943 (reflecting the War effort) to 50 million—70 per cent of the population. Compliance costs are high. Two-thirds of returns are completed by paid preparers. By excluding those earning less than $100,000 from the income tax, CTP would help diminish administrative burdens of IT on IRS, the tax authority.

Only 4 per cent of taxpayers paid the Alternative Minimum Tax (AMT) in 2002, while 20 per cent are expected in 2010 as lower tax rates on income, capital gains and dividends trigger AMT calculations. In India, MAT applies only to businesses. Graetz wants AMT to go. India cannot afford to let MAT go, reflecting a finance ministry analysis that reveals an inequitable CT burden across businesses.

Reagan dropped the top IT rate from 70 per cent to 50 per cent in 1981 and 28 per cent in 1986. Bush Sr agreed to raise it to 31 per cent, and Clinton raised it further to 39.6 per cent in 1993. It was reduced to 35 per cent in 2001 by Bush Jr. Capital gains tax rates have also reduced to 15 per cent. Graetz recommends 25 per cent. The dividend tax rate was also reduced to 15 per cent in 2003 to reduce "double" tax on income. Graetz is critical since these reductions did not safeguard revenue from previous taxation of these incomes at the corporate level. He finds that dividend payout consequently increased, while reinvestment suffered.

The overall rate reduction affected income distribution adversely. For the top 0.1 per cent, it grew from 3.3 per cent to 10.5 per cent. And the amount needed to join this group grew from $234,000 to $1,278,000; i.e. it quintupled. Interestingly, the shift in income distribution has resulted in a higher proportion (two-thirds) of income tax being collected from the top 10 per cent of earners despite lower tax rates. In contrast, Graetz's CTP proposes to return IT to its pre-World War status: low rate falling on a thin top slice of high income earners—above $100,000. This would eliminate the standard deduction, personal exemption, and child credits, and eliminate special income tax credits and allowances.

Graetz's sole justification for having a CT is that its absence encourages spurious corporations. High CT rates favour debt to equity financing; and the burden is likely to be passed to labour. The 1986 reform reduced CT from 46 per cent to 34 per cent while scaling back deductions, thereby improving revenue and enabling the lower IT rate of 28 per cent. Clinton in 1993 got a 1 per cent increase, to 35 per cent. Graetz favours a low 15 per cent—or a maximum 20 per cent—reflecting global competition, with matching capital gains and dividend tax rates. He also proposes simplification—yet sharpening—of disclosure rules to combat complex tax avoidance schemes for international business income. He eschews increasing penalties. These are also burning CT issues in India today.

Graetz says that the Social Security Tax (SST) has to stay. The payroll tax has grown from 10 per cent of the total budget in 1953 to 40 per cent today. The 1935 SST Act fixed the rate at 1 per cent of wages. Today it is 15.3 per cent up to a maximum wage income. For most families, the payroll tax is higher than income tax. Although SST is regressive, the social security benefit system is progressive.

SST's problems have reemerged. As the US becomes older, its fastest growing cohorts are those above 85. 16.5 workers supported a retiree in 1950, 3.3 workers do it currently, and 2.1 will do so by 2040. Only a 5.5 per cent SST rate hike would cover the gap 50 years hence. Therefore Graetz recommends retention of SST, while increasing the retirement age (though he does not specify how the elderly will find jobs).

Graetz guarantees progressivity through wealth taxation. He recommends increasing estate tax, which yielded 11 per cent of revenue in 1946 but only 1 per cent today. He also recommends an inheritance tax.

In sum, Graetz's CTP package meets the three objectives of tax reform. Nevertheless, CTP is essentially federal and excludes sub-national concerns. His chapter, "Bring the States Along", alludes to states piggybacking the federal VAT using its advanced information technology. Today US state and local governments use retail sales taxes (RST), with 7,579 RST jurisdictions. Large multistate companies file more than 200 RST forms every month, with high compliance costs. Thus Graetz feels states should naturally adopt a VAT, but provides no framework. A national US VAT design is needed, specifying federal and state VAT chains, minimising cascading, removing distortions from interstate trade, and ensuring predictable federal-state revenue effects. India consolidated central VAT and introduced service tax in 1995, introduced state VAT in 2005, and has a road-map for a national—central plus state—GST in 2010. Hopefully, a sound indirect tax structure will be finally put in place.

Business Standard, 22 April 2009.

VI

International Economic Relations

33

Indo-UK Economic Relations After Brexit

Last month I offered (chapter 54) a socio-historical background of Brexit. Today I shall provide an economic picture emanating from Brexit with particular reference to Indo-UK economic relations. To get an immediate perspective, Figure 33.1 reveals how India has surpassed UK in share of world GDP in PPP terms over the last two decades post-liberalisation. In 1994, both languished between 3-4 per cent. While India doubled to about 7 per cent by 2014, UK's share declined to 2-3 per cent or by a percentage point. This points to the distance UK needs to travel to enhance its global economic participation.

It is interesting to make comparisons in other indicators of UK's economic relationship with India to track recent changes. Figure 33.2 shows that growth in FDI (foreign direct investment) flows from UK to India vacillated since 2001. Resultantly its growth rate has also flip-flopped during this period. On India's part, Indian mutual funds have increased their investment in UK, the share increasing from just over 1 per cent in 2009 to 7 per cent in 2014, remaining the same in 2015 (not shown). Clearly with a 15 per cent post-Brexit depreciation of the Pound versus the Indian Rupee, these trends are not only likely to continue but may be expected to pick up speed. In other words, UK should benefit from further investment from India but FDI into India would be costlier for UK.

If benchmarked, UK's trade relationship with India is not ranked terribly high. Table 33.1 shows, in terms of UK's exports and imports, India occupies only 13th and 12th position, respectively. On the flip side, Figure 33.3 shows India's total trade—exports plus imports—while growing significantly since late 1990s, has declined since 2014. This mainly reflects trade with UK and US as opposed to China. In fact, lamentably, Figure 33.4 shows that India's overall trade balance catapulted since 2007 overwhelmingly due to China with which India rapidly built up a negative balance. Interestingly, India has run a positive balance with both UK and US. This phenomenon is more starkly revealed by separately plotting Indian exports and imports to and from these countries (not shown).

Table 33.1

UK: Selected Trading Partners, 2014

	UK Exports			UK Imports		
Country	*Ranking*	*Value (£ billion)*	*% of Total*	*Ranking*	*Value (£ billion)*	*% of Total*
US	1	88.0	17.1%	2	51.6	9.4%
Germany	2	43.3	8.4%	1	70.6	12.8%
China	7	18.7	3.6%	3	38.3	7.0%
Japan	11	10.1	2.0%	13	9.9	1.8%
India	13	8.8	1.7%	12	10.3	1.9%

Source: Office for National Statistics (ONS), UK.

Figure 33.1

UK and India: Shares of World GDP (PPP), 1994 to 2014

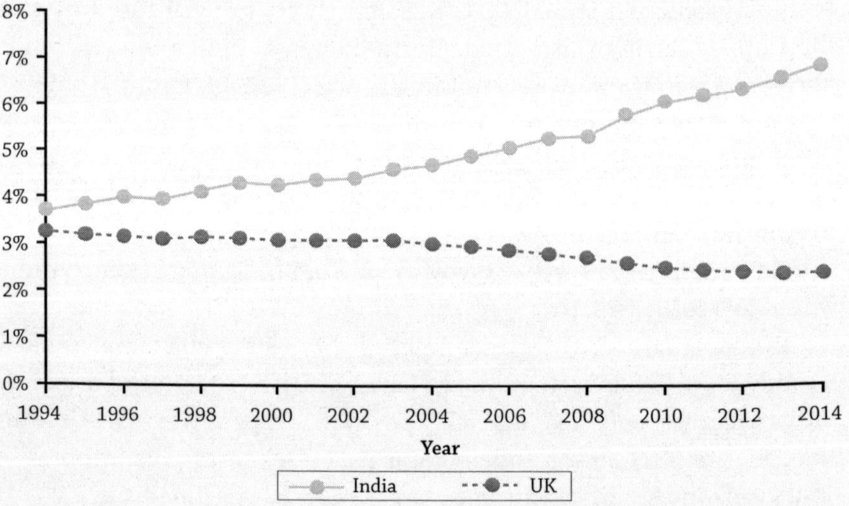

Source: IMF.

Figure 33.2

FDI Flows into India from UK

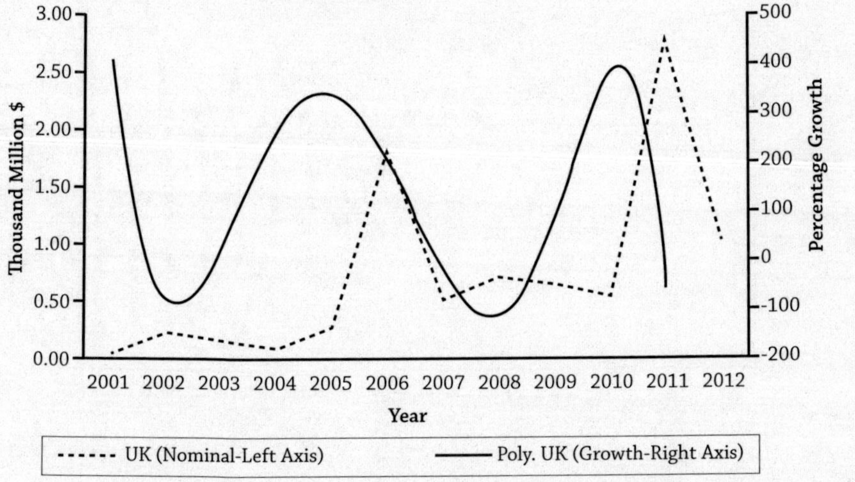

Source: UNCTAD Foreign Direct Investment/Transnational Corporations Database.

Figure 33.3

India—Total Trade ($)

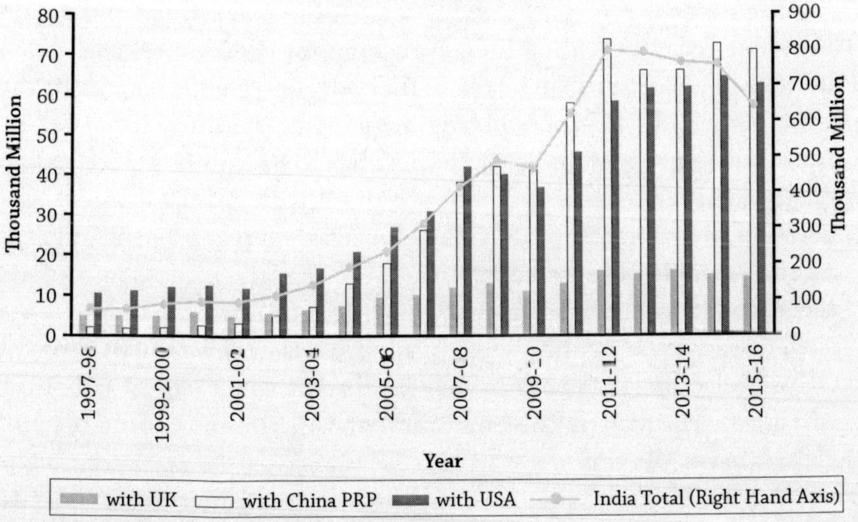

Source: Department of Commerce, Government of India.

Figure 33.4

India—Trade Balance ($)

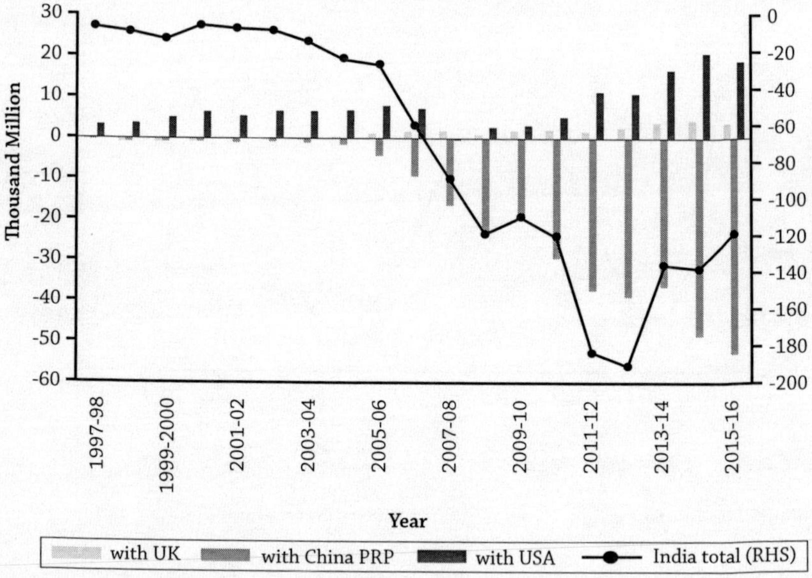

Source: Department of Commerce, Government of India.

The rupee depreciated steadily against the dollar, yuan and pound in recent years, providing India a cushion for exports (despite which it has had export problems). Now that advantage with respect to the UK is lost. Clearly, UK should have a greater opportunity to correct its trade imbalance with India while India has to be cautious since Indian goods and services will cost more to the British. In this context, the decision to stall or stop the sale of its UK steel plant by the Tata's is a good example of retained investment in the UK since its immediate recoupment would have fetched much less in any non-UK currency such as the dollar or the rupee. In addition, new investment into the UK will also be less costly to make; thus UK could expect enhanced foreign investment if the environment is accommodating, a point elaborated at the end.

On the UK side, one area in which it could increase export to India is advanced technology including defence. India, on its side, should use the opportunity to quicken its pace of technology and defence acquisition from UK. At this moment, it should be easier also to link imports with knowledge transfer and further cooperation in the wider defence field. Indeed technical assistance having become cheaper, India should identify areas where UK could provide technical assistance and advice. This could initiate a new era of cooperative development over and above the assistance that DFID, UK's foreign aid arm, or its Foreign Office that has a small technical assistance wing, currently provide. This would be a win-win situation for both parties.

Figure 33.5

Economy Ranking

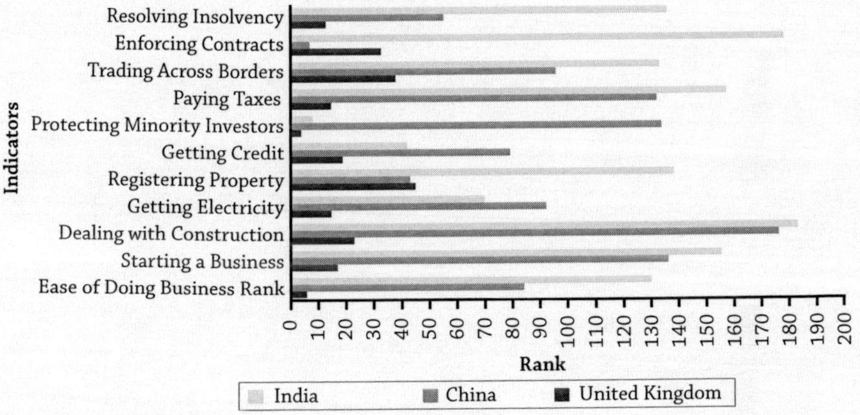

Source: *Doing Business*, June 2015 (World Bank Group).

Before concluding, in pointing to UK's possible advantages from Brexit, UK still is among the best places to conduct business. Figure 33.5 reveals that, in 2015, World Bank ranked India 130, China 84 and UK 6 in ease of doing business, in a sample of 189 countries. India was even worse than 130 in indices such as starting a business (155), dealing with construction permits (183), paying taxes (157), trading across borders (133), enforcing contracts (178) and resolving insolvency (136) when compared to China or UK that scored much better. UK is at an advantageous position of depreciated exchange rates to utilise its unique opportunity and surge ahead. However, as I have argued last month (chapter 54) and earlier, the resolve to tighten its belt and get to work is yet to be witnessed in an environment that punishes work effort. It is to be seen how UK tackles the vacuum in the labour market, having confidently created it.

Business Standard, 06 September 2016.

34

India's Strategy—Both Japan and China? The Answer is No!

Mr Modi recently visited Japan which was followed quickly by a visit to India by the Chinese President. Both promised India considerable FDI, China predictably more than Japan. Mr Modi's ease of manner with the Japanese Prime Minister gave Indians yet another proof of the former's ability to reach out. His confident manner with the Chinese President gave them reassurance in particular as he did not shy away from raising the border issue. Which of the two is a surer and safer option for India to partner with?

India's risk and uncertainty in engaging with China are obviously linked to the inevitability of China being a bad neighbour. Numerous and increasingly intensifying incursions are occurring across the Indian border, the most recent during the President's visit. The blatant objective, declared by their army, was to build strategic border roads. It was followed by the President's statement upon return exhorting the army to prepare for a regional war. It is unlikely that the reference was only to the South China Sea. It could comprise the Ides of March for India if it commits the folly of letting such mongering pass.

The risk is also associated with China's long-standing approach in sharing responsibility in global growth before the global economic crisis and, after, with its resistance to fair burden sharing. Table 34.1 reveals some stark contrasts that have emerged over three decades from the 1980s. Between 1981-2013, India's GDP increased from $19.7 thousand crore to $188 thousand crore, and China's from $19.4 thousand crore (lower than India's) to $924 thousand crore (about five times India's). Japan's GDP grew from $120 thousand crore (more than six times India or China) to $490 thousand crore (half of China and two and a half times India's).

Table 34.1

GDP Indicators (Current International $)

Year	China			India			Japan		
	GDP ('000 cr)	*GDP-PPP ('000 cr)*	*GDP Per Capita*	*GDP ('000 cr)*	*GDP-PPP ('000 cr)*	*GDP Per Capita*	*GDP ('000 cr)*	*GDP-PPP ('000 cr)*	*GDP Per Capita*
1981	19.4	-	195.0	19.7	-	275.0	120.1	-	10,212.0
2001	132.5	400.6	1,042.0	49.4	230.6	466.0	416.0	337.7	32,716.0
2009	499.0	1,083.3	3,745.5	136.5	491.4	1,147.2	503.5	408.1	39,473.4
2013	924.0	1,615.8	6,807.4	187.7	677.4	1,498.9	490.2	462.4	38,492.1

Source: World Bank.

China's phenomenal growth compared to Japan and even more so in relation to India is not strictly admirable in terms of human rights or international trade. The decades-long absence of labour rights is finally resulting in selective manifestation of labour unrest, albeit quickly crushed every time. The absence of political rights was recently manifest in emotional student protests in Hong Kong. And the global crisis finally impelled trading partners to protest China's international market manipulation through artificially low exchange rates with the objective of pushing exports significantly above expected growth in terms of quality or technology. Consequently, it initiated a currency appreciation, albeit reluctant and slow.

Japan has been demonstrably more cooperative in international relations. The secularly high trade surplus with the United States of the 1980s was broken by its acceptance of reducing the quantum of automobile exports, a quantitative policy *verboten* in the context of international trade. It protested mildly that the Japanese did not appear to prefer American cars when the United States further asked why the Japanese were not importing more of them. Throughout, Japan has revealed more willingness to go along with the international community in both trade and diplomacy. Indeed, Japan's prolonged economic recession, with periods of depression, is likely to have had its origin in that period of inarguable obeisance to the United States, robbing it of a way of life established from the mid 1800s by industrial houses such as Mitsui, Mitsubishi and Sumitomo in cooperation with Government. The squatters' park in front of the Tokyo Museum and the deserted department stores are presently its stark and constant reminders.

Figure 34.1

Exports and Imports

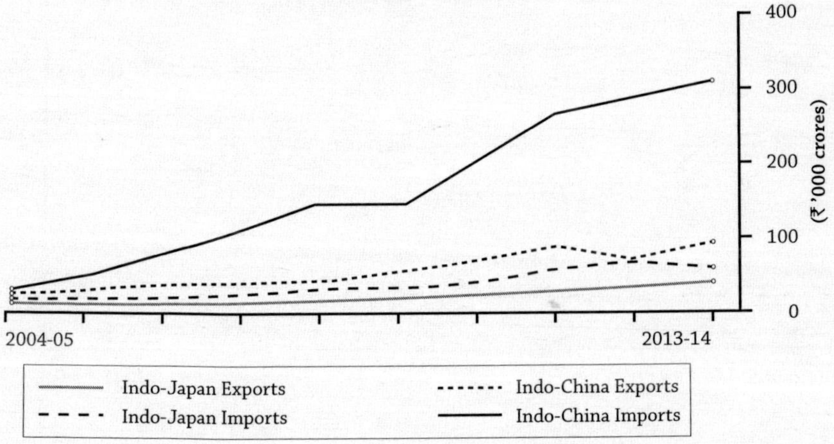

Source: Export Import Data Bank, Ministry of Commerce & Industry.

Post-War Japan's concept and practice of human rights are akin to those of India. It is pleasurable to see the variety of human behaviour in Tokyo's Shinjukuku where human hair assumes colours from the vibgyor and pedestrians are seen walking with their pictorial cellphones in front of their eyes. By contrast, seeing (twice) China's own citizens being handcuffed and ushered away from Tiananmen Square for lacking a "visa" to visit Beijing, their own national capital cannot be erased from memory. Is it even imaginable that an Indian could be excluded by decree from Delhi? Indeed, a Delhi NGO went to court and ensured that some 80 ragpicker families would not be removed from their shacks atop a hill despite the Vasant Kunj connector remaining a bottleneck at that point.

With luck, Indians should never suffer the Emergency ever again. Bedding with habituated human rights abusers is not, and should never be, Indian practice even for the direst economic reasons. Those countries that have fallen prey to this fallacy will only further enable China's inexorable economic and political rise since it will continue to obfuscate and apply its own rules while the rest of the world tries to abide by globally configured principles.

Figure 34.2

Share of Total Exports and Imports (%)

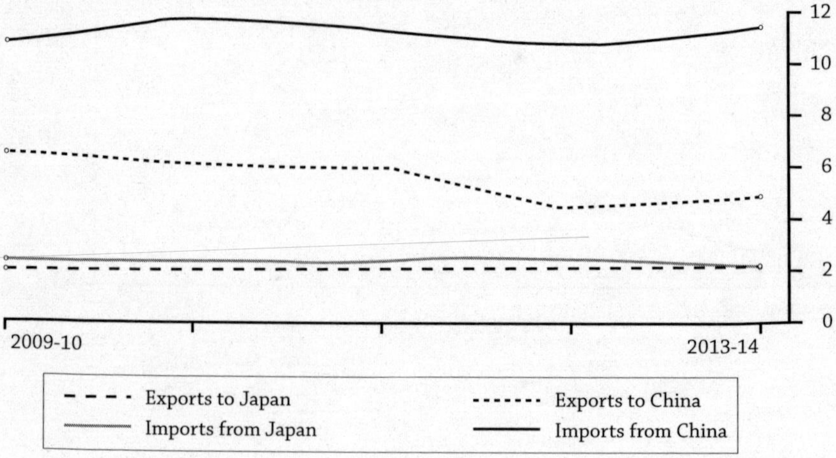

Source: Export Import Data Bank, Ministry of Commerce & Industry.

Indo-Japan and Indo-China trade patterns are pointers. Figure 34.1 shows that, though India exports to Japan a bit less than it imports from it, in the case of China, India's imports are three and a half times its exports. Figure 34.2 shows India's imports and exports from and to Japan have remained similar in the last five years at about 2 per cent of India's global imports and exports respectively. However, in the case of China, it represents 11 per cent of India's global imports but only 5 per cent of India's global exports. Does India wish to become even more dependent on, and acquire a higher deficit with China, a country that projects its naked power at every available opportunity? There is no need for India to be impolite but the clear policy should be an assiduous adherence to enhancing border security, strategic transport access through roads and airpower, and a continuing demonstration of fearlessness on the seas. And, paired with a clear turn exclusively towards Japan.

Unfortunately, India loses direly in its inability to control corruption including in defence if wide ranging reports are given credibility while China can take quick action, including using capital punishment, to contain it. India need not replicate medieval remedies but it must control corruption for, otherwise, all arguments made above would stand on quicksand. At the moment, hopes are high that Mr Modi will improve things, perhaps even radicalise the issue. If not, it is expectable that the disaffected majority would find solutions sharper than Naxalism.

Business Standard, 15 October 2014.

35

The India-Pakistan Phenomenon

Ready for Economic Deconstruction

One of the best recent novels is *The Reluctant Fundamentalist* by Mohsin Hamid, a non-resident Pakistani, an NRP so to speak, educated at Princeton and Harvard, employed at one point in New York and now living in London. Of several reviews, the most apt was New Statesman's "Admirably spare and amazingly exciting" reflecting the subtle tones that weave the transformation of an upper-class, soft-spoken Pakistani boy educated in America, a janissary for the West, to a bearded protagonist who returns to Pakistan.

But this is not a book review. The reason for its use lies in its final pages where the author emotes against India through the protagonist's voice, derailing his "spare" narrative, and essentially leading to its collapse. Post-9/11, "the threat of war with India reached its highest point ... the heat was too great for an Indian offensive in the desert, then because the monsoon's rains made driving treacherous for Indian tanks in the Punjab." There is no mention of Kargil. "America felt justified in bringing so many deaths in Afghanistan and Iraq, and ... in risking so many more deaths by tacitly using India to pressure Pakistan." Thus, the determining factors for India, the would be attacker, not to attack are attributed to weather, war strategy and confidence emanating from an Indian-American nexus.

The question is why otherwise enlightened Pakistanis would feel this way. On this side of the Line of Control, or the LoC, their Indian counterparts find it far-fetched that an American-Indian nexus exists, leave alone persists, in light of the extraordinary tensions between them that have historically existed, will continue to exist, and perhaps will intensify in light of recently emerging world economic and political events. The clearly unsuccessful 31 July day-long talks in New Delhi between the foreign ministers of both nations and their open admission to "a lot of homework" to do and "divergence" are its latest evidence. I recall a 2006 visit to a venerable educational institution in Karachi where the faculty and students and persons of eminence embraced my presence even while, in everyone's speech, India was referred as if not doing so publicly was socially indefensible. I remember wondering why we in India are not similarly afflicted despite nuclear capability on both sides.

Because India is, physically and normatively, more expansive; clearly, India has to play the larger role by persistently extending its hand in cooperation. Prime ministers Atal Bihari Vajpayee and Manmohan Singh tried albeit with very limited success. Despite the latest continual provocations, confidence-building measures have to be deepened by our new prime minister. Indo-Pak trade remains little compared to Indo-Bangla. Figure 35.1 reveals that while India's imports from Bangladesh and Pakistan have been comparable, the former has surpassed the latter. Further, India's exports have been far higher to Bangladesh than to Pakistan. India's integrated border posts at Attari with Pakistan and Petrapol with Bangladesh that oversee the procedures for trade and security reveal the difference in trade volumes handled despite the former's larger infrastructure to handle expansion. Pakistan's being a considerably smaller economy than India's, it seems natural that India should consider to unilaterally and comprehensively liberalise trade with Pakistan despite the latter's shorter positive list for which it allows trade with India. After all, as Figure 35.2 shows, India's share of trade with Pakistan to its total trade remains minuscule, at 0.7 per cent of its total exports and at 0.1 per cent of its total imports in 2013-14, lower figures than with Bangladesh. Opening up trade with Pakistan fully, to begin, India's exports would jump leading to both pecuniary and non-pecuniary gains. Pakistan's exports should also improve.

Figure 35.1

Exports and Imports

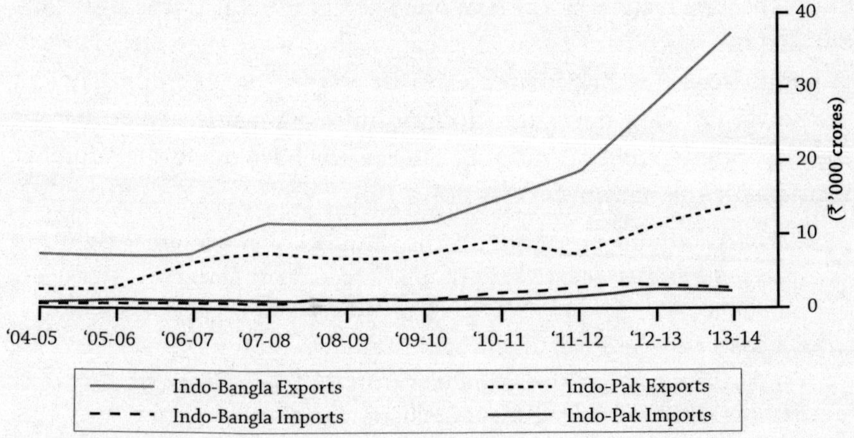

Source: Export Import Data Bank, Ministry of Commerce and Industry.

Figure 35.2

Percentage Share of Total Exports and Imports

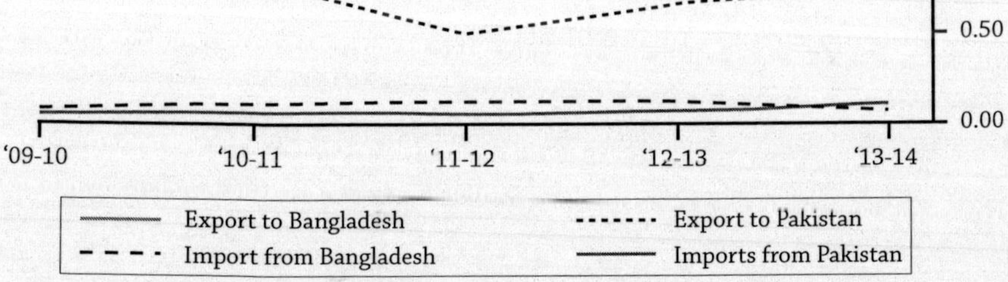

Source: Export Import Data Bank, Ministry of Commerce and Industry.

A visit to the Wagah border and witnessing the drill and mock show of force by our soldiers, both men and women, arouse feelings of patriotism. Yet, the subsequent two shakes of hand by bedecked jawans on both sides of their divisive gates raise the fraternity quotient. Resultant of the statecraft of foreigners and assimilation by our respective leaders of the day, one needs to squint the eyes to view our distancing cousins across the gates. They wave their flag. A wave of hands from this side invites a similar wave of hands from theirs.

Yet great wars have been fought among cousins. On return to the city, one learns that more of our jawans have made the supreme sacrifice for the nation, for our protection.

> Gathered round preceptor Drona, Pandavas in armour bright
> Like the five star constellation round the radiant Queen of Night,
> Gathered round the proud Duryodhan, dreaded for his exploits done,
> All his brave and warlike brothers and preceptor Drona's son.
> Wrathful sons of Dhritarashtra, born of Kuru's royal race!
> Righteous sons of noble Pandu, Godborn men of godlike grace![1]

The big placard just inside the Indian border proclaiming "Respect All, Suspect All!" that had earlier invited smiles from passersby suddenly appears relevant. No doubt our neighbour's ceaseless incursions set more goalposts for our leaders to cross. We could begin by dazzling our neighbour with free trade as a unilateral gesture and wait to see the response. Improbable as it may sound, fully free trade should improve its economic prospects, contain its burgeoning internal strife, hopefully abate its relentless compulsions for attack, and bring positive externalities to our own soil. But it won't be easy. It has to be achieved by leapfrogging hurdles that would rear their head from far corners of the bureaucracy.

---

1. *Mahabharata* (circa 1300-1400 BC) in English Verse, Romesh Dutt, CIE, J.M. Dent and Co. London. 1898.

Business Standard, 15 September 2014.

36

Developed and Developing Societies

A Behavioural Hypothesis

Historically, social scientists, in particular economists, have been deeply concerned with how to ascribe development. The long accepted common sense approach uses GDP (gross domestic product) and GDP per capita. A variation is to use PPP (purchasing power parity). The Leftist postulate has been exploiter versus exploited. A more recent boutique approach has been the Happiness Index that eschews cardinal measurement and selects an ordinal index that ranks how joyful a people are. Here, a distributary of traditional microeconomics, called behavioural economics, has made inroads by including social behaviour through new analytical techniques. I am sympathetic since it is leading to successful outcomes by moving away from traditional methods of investigation and instead using actual behaviour as observations. Through this process the scope and coverage of economics is imperceptibly expanding and growing. In sum, economists increasingly believe that many, if not all, aspects of human behaviour can be successfully explained through techniques that they have developed or will develop.

One observed behavioural difference between developed and developing countries is a family's grasp over its progeny. A societal value system that generally prevails in the former is to leave children be after a certain point in their nurturing and to let them choose their life path through their own trials and tribulations. In other words, let them experience life in its fullest and find their calling before settling down in the straitjacket of life. Many may fall by the wayside in this process while several others explore and experience, traversing distance and time to find their niche. Discoveries and inventions and resultant economic advancements of galactic proportions have occurred, continue to occur, and will occur in the process. The vast majority of those populations enjoy the fruits over time including the advantages of lowering prices for access to advanced technology in its myriad manifestations from electric knives and surround-sound TVs to mobile phones, laptops and notepads. Thus, some would become couch potatoes but society can, by and large, afford to mollycoddle them since, heuristically having accepted that everyone has risen to his or her level best in the encounter with life, broadly acceptable redistributional policies take care of those who may be otherwise left behind. The larger world also enjoys positive externalities from such technological progress.

I remember well being treated to a rock concert in 1991 by the secretary (minister) of finance of the state of Sao Paulo after a long day of meetings when, to my astonishment, he proudly declared that the rock star was his son. Neither can I forget a 1973 luncheon in a Miami Spanish-style hacienda with what seemed like a billionaire family. I was proved correct by the gait, poise and confidence of the hostess who floated in with that certain flair to welcome her guests. Soon thereafter, a gaunt woman in a yellow and orange uniform sauntered in and was introduced as her daughter. Quite unable to contain my curiosity over their apparent difference in appearance, I waited anxiously until, in the conversation, it emerged that the daughter was a crane driver at a construction site. Yet parents and daughter seemed in the best of terms and spirits and shared the same dining table for lunch with their foreign guests.

Such events remain etched in memory since they stand out from one's usual experience in India. To begin, children are driven to take up a field of specialisation of their elders' choice. Many children as a result can never dream of independently taking up a profession, becoming someone they want to be, since they know they will finally have to abide by the wishes of others in their selection of a lifetime occupation or lifestyle. There is another deleterious impact of this. The child may not develop responsibility to self, reflecting his knowledge and comfort that it is someone else who should answer for failure along, not only the course of education, but oftentimes through life. Thus, there is a further outcome. Parents feel obligated and remain perennially interested in pushing their children to find "stable" jobs, and are forever seeking jobs for them by pressing family, friends or strangers. I can safely surmise that, in my circle, I can think of only three friends or family who have steered clear of this erroneous policy on behalf of their children.

In such an environment I myself do not refrain from lending a helping hand when besieged, with the excuse that I should not be stone-hearted at an individual level until society changes itself, thus setting aside a basic principle of economics that macro-societal economy is a blowup of micro-individual economic agents and not vice versa. Interestingly, my generation, by and large, did not receive such beneficence. Nor do I encounter this behaviour pattern in the West even today with one mega caveat, though thankfully only occasional, in their highest rungs of society whereby mediocrity unabashedly get into the best universities on the back of huge donations. Alarmingly, such people have risen to their highest offices and, given their global reach, with unimaginable ramifications on populations far and beyond.

In India in the meanwhile, every aspect of life has descended to a family business, a phenomenon that did not reveal its fangs so clearly until the 1980s but then spread unabashedly. Efficient and productive politicians bring in their children, deemed children, and family, visibly irrespective of the latter's qualifications for the job. The productivity quotient for the unit crumbles compared to that of the single original if one uses a simple average as an index. The film world commits the same error, and even the music world with ghastly consequences on the audience, thankfully ephemeral. Second- or third-generation industrialists, more often than not, do not reflect their forefathers' brilliance. And, in society at large, overall productivity declines since few people appear to be in an occupation of first choice or ability where they could have excelled. This marks a developing country where family comes first at all costs and country remains in the background, on the back burner, so to speak. This behaviour difference between developing and developed societies and its impact on productivity and growth remains to be modelled as yet by behavioural economists.

Business Standard, 18 August 2014.

37

China Must Look Within

As China enters a new decade of changed leadership, it faces many international and domestic economic challenges. The 2008-09 global economic crisis and the 2011-12 euro-area sovereign debt crisis have raised the question whether current account surplus countries have appreciated their exchange rates to reflect market realities. It is increasingly recognised that China has appreciated the renminbi not insignificantly against the dollar, euro and pound sterling during 2007-2012, broadly from 20 to 35 per cent.

Recall that the REER (real effective exchange rate) is the NER (nominal exchange rate) multiplied by the ratio of foreign to domestic inflation (CPI). Using this formula, changes in the REER and NER of the renminbi against the dollar, pound and euro for 2007-2011 are plotted in Figure 37.1. Data on CPI (base 2005=100) are obtained from the IFS database of the International Monetary Fund (IMF), and the NER is from Data Stream.

Figure 37.1 shows that, between 2007 and 2011, the renminbi appreciated in real terms against the dollar, the euro and sterling by 20 per cent, 19 per cent and 33 per cent respectively. Similarly, movements in the NER suggest that the renminbi appreciated during the same period by 15 per cent, 13 per cent and 32 per cent respectively. The higher appreciation against sterling reflects a large depreciation of the pound during the first crisis of 2007-2009. And the renminbi has continued to appreciate steadily in 2011-12, with the general view taking hold that China is at present serious in its currency appreciation policy.

Figure 37.1

RER and NER of Chinese Renminbi against Major Currencies

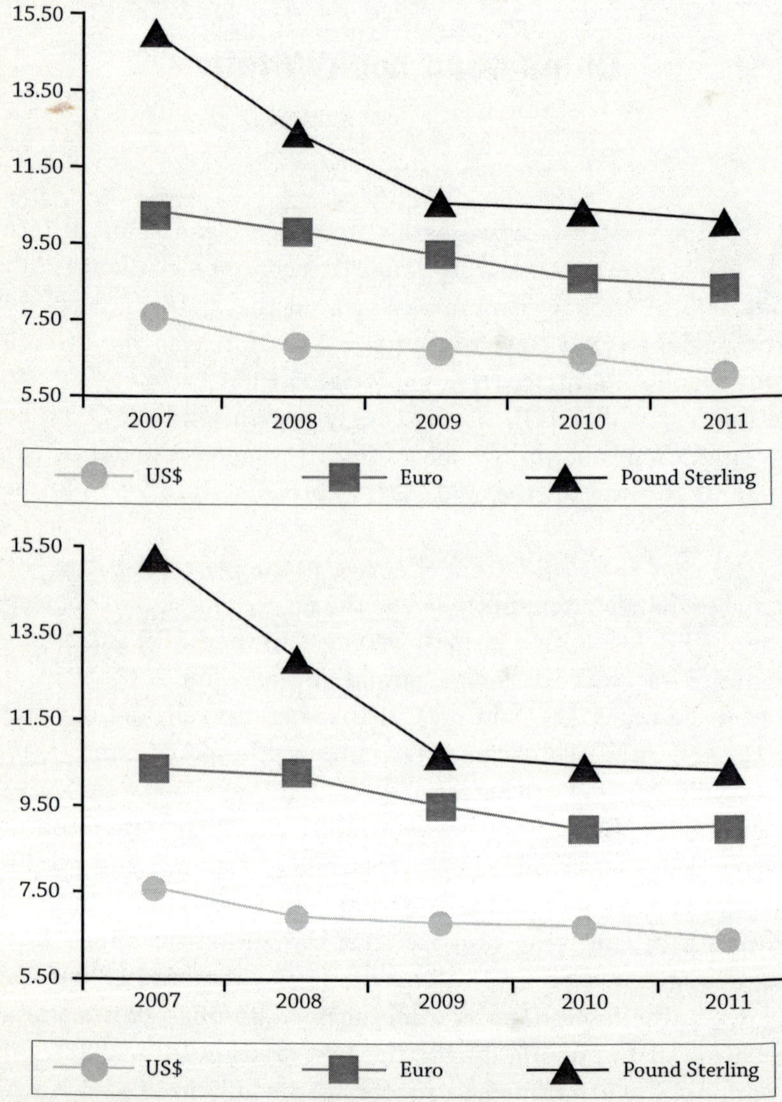

Source: Estimated.

It is also being recognised, however, that currency appreciation alone will not be sufficient for China to contribute successfully to global rebalancing. Further action would need to emanate from its domestic sector—for, after all, the imbalance of exports in excess of imports in the external sector translates exactly into the imbalance of excess of savings over investment in the domestic sector. Thus, what could such domestic actions comprise?

Typically, there are structural catalysts that underlie a macroeconomic disequilibrium. In China, demand for imports of commodities—that have comprised raw material for building economic infrastructure—is already high. In fact, as this author has pointed out earlier in this column, China has come under criticism, somewhat inconsistently, from the developed world for taking up too much of the global supply of commodities even while being asked to raise demand. Under the circumstances, one area where China could raise demand is to increase the government's inadequate levels of social expenditure. Public expenditure on social security, health, and education is likely to be negatively related with the current account imbalance. High public expenditure would indicate a lower need for personal savings to meet these demands, which would translate to a lower current account surplus.

Figure 37.2

Public Expenditure on Health and Education (Ratio of GDP)

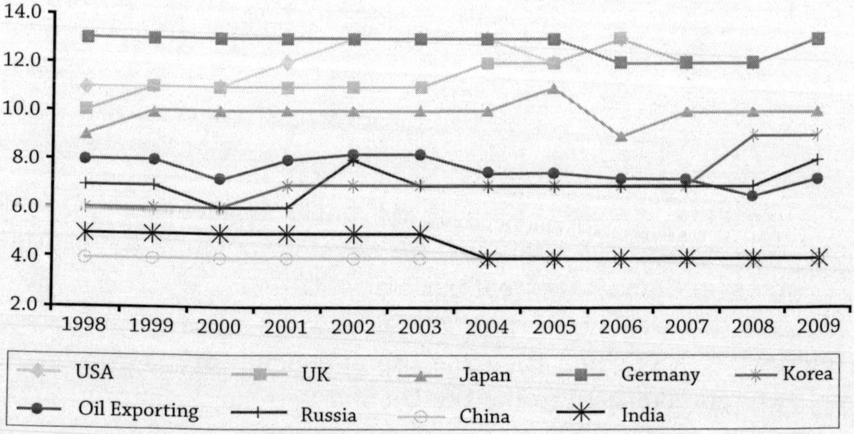

Source: *World Development Indicators*, World Bank, 2011.

Instead, the lack of well-developed social protection systems induces households to set aside a large portion of their disposable incomes to cover life-cycle risks related to health, accident, old age and unemployment. Social protection systems that help mitigate these risks can assist in bringing down such precautionary savings, and thus in rebalancing the current account. Recent international research suggests that an increase in government expenditure on social safety nets reduces private savings, and the impact is higher for developing compared to developed countries.

Figure 37.3

Per Capita Public Expenditure on Health and Education (in current US$)

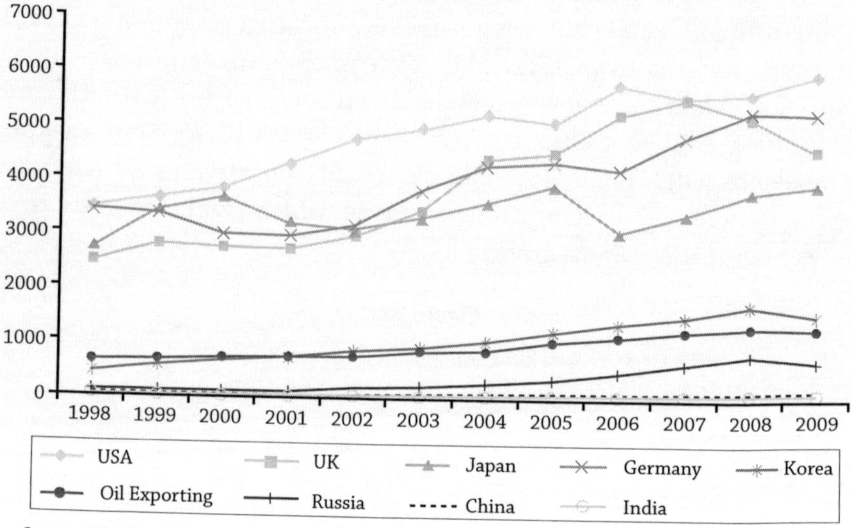

Source: *World Development Indicator*, World Bank, 2011.

This probably reflects the fact that public expenditure on health and education is relatively low for developing and oil-exporting countries. In China it was four per cent of GDP in 2009. It was seven per cent of GDP in oil-exporting countries, comparable to Russia (Figure 37.2). Further, their per capita expenditure is also low in dollar terms compared to the US, UK and Germany (Figure 37.3). In China this appears to be an important reason that contributes to high precautionary savings on the part of households. Recent research from the Organisation for Economic Cooperation and Development, or OECD, suggests that an increase in public health spending would reduce China's current account surplus by as much as 2.5 per cent of GDP out of a total surplus of 10 per cent of GDP.

Thus, higher public provision of social services and more extensive social safety nets would enhance consumer confidence and boost consumption, thereby reducing China's precautionary savings rate.

In conclusion, China's cautious policy has certainly paid off so far in advancing its global presence. It has secured a permanent seat in the United Nations Security Council. Over the years, it has increased and holds a good share of US public debt. It has obtained higher representation in multilateral institutions, etching out for itself the position of deputy managing director at the IMF. Over and beyond its overwhelming presence across Asia, its presence in Africa has steadily grown where its command over natural resources has been more than minimal. Its entrance to Latin America is also apparent and significant.

China should now be making changes in its economic stance from its commanding heights. The government has already made huge investments in economic infrastructure, thus pushing up demand. It has now got to raise social expenditure in health and education and thus buttress public sector demand further. A significant rise in such public expenditure will, first, raise the economy's overall consumption level and, second, reduce the need for huge precautionary savings of the household sector. This is clearly a win-win situation for China. Thus, while facilitating global rebalancing, it also offers China a great opportunity to use its surplus to catch up with developed economies in social expenditures (in proportion of GDP) and thus make another giant leap forward towards achieving fully developed status. Yet, China appears to continue to be cautious in redirecting its policy stance significantly. It is time for it to do so convincingly.

Business Standard, 19 November 2012.

38

Solving the Euro Zone's Problems

The euro zone's doldrums are never over. When a silver lining appears, dark clouds gather from another direction, obliterating small gains from fiscal tightening or commensurate monetary policy. One advantage of southern Europe from adopting the higher-valued euro was cheaper imports. After a period of excessive consumption, the balance of payments became unsustainable as exports got priced out. As they entered the EU, Europeans became used to early retirement and a consumption boom—but had to abandon them, even though after stubborn resistance.

At first glance, it therefore appears that, apart from fiscal correction and belt-tightening, the euro zone has to look elsewhere to bring itself back to normalcy. Europe has to work again. Work can be generated if they once again export competitively. Export enhancement will be feasible only with an appropriately depreciated euro. What is that level? One option is to link the euro to the dollar. Today the rate is euro 1 = $1.28 but it could be pegged at euro 1 = $1. The EU would immediately experience a 25 per cent advantage for exports. An even deeper link would be dollarisation of the euro, but that is not to be considered; why so, will become obvious below.

One problem is that the euro zone is a heterogeneous entity with surplus and deficit countries. One size does not fit all. Let us focus on the deficit ones to analyse the case for how to enhance exports of those deficit states. At first glance, looking at Figure 38.1, the dollar depreciated against the euro by 9.7 per cent over a year from September 2011 to August 2012. Thus, first, pegging to the dollar at 1:1 and, second, expecting the dollar to further depreciate against other hard currencies, could certainly promote the euro zone's exports.

However, history reveals that pegging to the dollar has led to woe in several instances. In the Bretton Woods system prevailing in the 1960s, the pound came under severe strain through persistent balance of payments pressures. The Bank of England attempted to defend the fixed exchange rate against speculative attacks by selling foreign currency, rapidly depleting its reserves. Finally, in 1967, it was forced to devalue the pound.[1]

In the more recent 1997-1998 East Asian crisis, pegging to the dollar also afflicted those economies.

> Many countries had effectively linked their currencies to the dollar at a time when the dollar appreciated relative to the Japanese yen and the Chinese renminbi. With the Thai baht, Indonesian rupiah, and other Asian currencies rising relative to the yen and the renminbi, the products of Thailand, Indonesia, and other Asian countries grew more expensive relative to those of Japan and China.[2]

What is instructive is that the UK and Asian economies had pegged their currencies to the dollar to protect themselves against too much depreciation, while the experiment that we have embarked on here is the opposite: whether the euro should peg against the dollar to reap gains in exports from effective depreciation. What we show below is that the advantage may turn out to be one-shot. If the dollar begins to appreciate, the end result will be similar to the UK and East Asian experiences, and the euro zone will lose international competitiveness.

While the pegging would give the euro significant initial advantage, and even though the dollar depreciated over the last year, what we observe is that, recently, the dollar has been steadily appreciating against the euro. Between July 17 and September 12, a two-month period, the appreciation has been about 5.8 per cent (Figure 38.1(B)), as if about to nullify the depreciation in the previous year. Thus, in the case of the euro as well, dollar appreciation against major currencies would effectively imply appreciation of the euro

---

1. Bordo, M.D., R. MacDonald and M.J. Oliver (n.d.). "Sterling in Crisis: 1964-1969". Available on *http://viessmanncentre.ca/wp-content/uploads/2011/06/Bordo_Mac_Oliver.pdf*
2. Glick, R. and M. Hutchinson (2011). "Currency Crises", *Federal Reserve Bank of San Francisco Working Paper Series*. September.

Figure 38.1

Euro Trail

(A) Euro over US Dollar

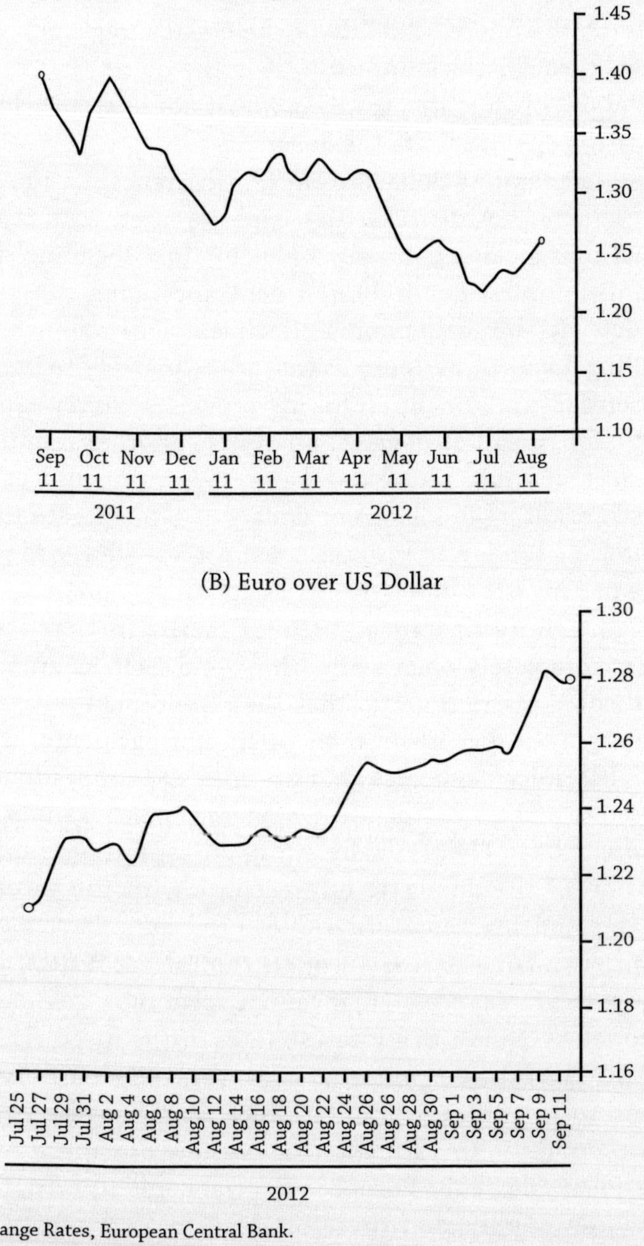

Source: Exchange Rates, European Central Bank.

against those currencies. Or, despite a fixed exchange rate, the EU would begin to lose competitiveness, worsening the trade balances of the eurozone members under consideration. The crux of the matter is, therefore, the unpredictability of the dollar's trajectory. Over the long haul, through thick and thin, it is the dollar that comes out strong and on top, and this is why it would not be to the euro zone's advantage to peg the euro to the dollar.

Worse is complete dollarisation of a currency. Latin American countries such as Argentina that experimented with it suffered disastrous consequences, initially indulging in a spending spree and accumulating dollar-denominated debt and, later, plunging into foreign debt default, abandoning effective dollarisation, suffering a freely falling domestic currency as well as the inability to import even basic essentials and, finally, suffering previously never experienced intensity and spread of poverty. Of course another ramification is the haircut that lenders have to take on the sovereign debt of those economies, resulting in billions of dollars of actual losses to those—such as mutual funds and insurance companies—that had presumed that they had invested in relatively risk-free sovereign debt.

The euro zone has an additional factor in that its capital account is completely open while China and East Asian economies have had some restrictions so that they could manipulate the end result—surplus or deficit—in their balance of payments. The phrase "impossible trinity" indicates that an open capital account, a fixed exchange rate and an independent monetary policy cannot function at the same time. Theoretically, an open capital account implies equalisation of the domestic interest rate with the international interest rate and any departure will lead to capital movement. Thus, when the euro zone—with an open capital account and a fixed exchange rate—faces recession, it cannot solve the recession problem using monetary policy. Say interest rates are reduced. This pushes up domestic investment initially. However, reduced interest rates would lead to an outflow of capital which would negate any positive impact on domestic investment. The outflow of capital would also trigger a dollar sale by the European Central Bank. In turn, this would reduce money supply, and therefore lead to an interest rate rise, thus obviating the initial reduction in interest rates and, ultimately, having little success in alleviating the recession.

Thus pegging to the dollar may be an immediate panacea but, in the medium term, it is unlikely to lead to a current account benefit. Instead, the euro should be steadily depreciated; indeed it is likely that it will eventually need to decline well below the dollar. Let Europe not be Wednesday's child. Its final solution is in domestic belt-tightening after all, in the form of fiscal rectitude, reduction in public debt, longer hours of work, postponement of the retirement age to way beyond thus far contemplated, and acceptance of a permanent downward shift in its warranted rate of growth until fulfillment of such economic measures is able to pull it up once again.

Business Standard, 17 September 2012.

39

The Just-Emerging Asian Economy

Myanmar is poised to enter the global economy with its mineral resources, fertile soil and potential for attracting foreign investment. It is perhaps also the last inhabited exotic destination boasting hotel lobbies with on the counter displays of rubies, sapphires, emeralds and other precious stones, reminiscent of one of this subcontinent's tales from a bygone era—of Indians exiting Burma without any saving other than sachets of precious stones. In the recent past, with maintenance of cordial relations, Myanmar supplied India with the variety of lentils that only they grow other than Indians, thereby keeping lentil prices below the stars.

Myanmar's decades old autarky protected and preserved a quiet religiosity. The pagoda I visited, climbing a flight of wide indoor stairs that seemed to rise five or six storeys, ended in a terrace under an open sky with intricate canopies under which sat scores of larger-than-life jade and marble Buddhas. Many of them were washed in gold that was visible everywhere including, of course, the steeples. The temple is said to possess 56 tonnes of gold, amply displayed on its deities and other adornments. Scores of Myanmarese meandered about, lighting incense and small lamps, the flickering glow imparting a sense of ShangriLa. The only other places so surreal that compare are possibly the uninhabited Okabango River Delta—with lotuses and flying white-plumed birds, and its contiguous Moremi National Forest with packs of animal species flocking around—or Tula, the long abandoned flat pyramid with whistling winds flowing through a maze of tall, stone-faced pillars as if beckoning extraterrestrials and, most recently, perhaps the glistening neon colony in *Avatar*, Hollywood's path-breaking 3-D creation.

Interestingly, the direct India-Yangon flight was from Kolkata, hidden as Myanmar remained all these years. I understand that Calcutta was the second busiest international airport in the 1950s; certainly it was Art Deco with style, impatiently as we now await its new international airport to become functional. The fact that some Indians did remain in Myanmar was revealed in co-passengers who seemed to emerge straight out of the rural Tamil Nadu of the 1960s, adorned in Kanjivaram saris and cubes and globes of gold hanging from heavily weighed-down earlobes. Others wore opaque glasses, as if modern eye surgery was yet to reach its shores. They were obvious local residents. But there were new explorers too. A friendly young man from Burra-bazar declared that he was visiting Myanmar for the first time because he had heard that there were spices to be bought and traded.

I arrived in this milieu being fortunate in leading the first international mission on taxation to Myanmar.[1] There was nitty-gritty analysis to be done. We got about our business by first proceeding to Naypyidaw, the new capital in the interior, five hours from Yangon on a four-lane highway with one service area halfway through. Entering the capital, we passed through a broad boulevard with countless five-star hotels. Soon we passed a sprawling building with pointed towers exquisitely painted in varying colours. Its scale was large enough to give it the appearance of a collection of buildings. We learnt it was the new parliament. Each ministry, newly painted and polished, was housed in a hollow between adjoining hills, with officers riding scooters from one hill to another, to reach meetings on time. As we were ushered into our hotel rooms atop another hill, I felt it was a dream as each room, a bungalow in itself, looked out exclusively over a sloped valley, green with teakwood trees and covered in nestling clouds. I knew the objective of my trip was to impart TA (technical assistance) in taxation but felt that it should have been R&R.

Myanmar's tax-to-GDP ratio is around 3 per cent. I recalled Guyana from years back, which had a number over 30 per cent,

1. Organised by the International Tax and Investment Centre (ITIC), Washington, DC.

revealing the problem with the measurement of GDP in nascent economies. Even if Myanmar's number were to double, it would still be low in a cross-country comparison. There is indeed non-tax revenue from state-owned enterprises but much is also expended on them, so that their net outcome remains unclear. The government's challenge, therefore, is to secure tax revenue. It has a schedular income tax system that charges different rates for different sources of income; hence it is possible to move towards an amalgamated broad-based structure that would be revenue-productive and impart progressivity into the structure at the same time. Myanmar also operates a large taxpayer unit, apparently somewhat better than India has been able to perform on this front.

Myanmar's domestic indirect tax system resembles India's early excise structure—indeed, by and large, the tax laws derive from the same pre-independence Codes—with limited ITC (input tax credit). And exports are not effectively given ITC, rendering them not so internationally competitive. And there are expectedly other anomalies that will be improved and corrected for sure. In the absence of a GST (goods and services tax), India's ITC mechanism also suffers from limited scope. As a result, its Centre-state indirect tax structure cascades at several points. The embedded taxes in the production-distribution chain result in a high indirect tax burden on manufacturing, posing serious challenges to the international competitiveness of Indian manufacturing. Myanmar also needs to reform its indirect tax structure in a likewise manner. Interestingly, Myanmar's customs administration and structure are also reminiscent of India's some years back.

Against the challenge of revenue productivity, the Myanmar authorities need investment, in particular, foreign investment. And they are drafting a new SEZ (Special Economic Zone) law, reflecting China and India's more recent tax incentives policies for buttressing economic growth. Of course caution is called for in arriving at an optimal balance between the competing goals of revenue and investment. And the known pitfalls in administering a successful SEZ policy should be avoided. If SEZs are designed primarily to attract foreign investment, a concomitant challenge would be to provide a level playing field for domestic entrepreneurs. Members of the primary chamber of commerce and industry expressed strongly why differential treatment should be minimised as Myanmar moves from protection to an open economy.

The authorities are ready for change and eager to learn from the rest of the world, including India. India is conveniently poised to provide TA in the economics field, be it trade policy formulation or the public finances. There is another area, that of ICT (information and communication technology), in which India has a particular comparative advantage. It may not be well known that the Indian government provided TA in ICT imperceptibly to post-crisis Vietnam at little cost. Today Vietnam has not only entered the field internationally but is competing with India. One matter that was clearly observable in Myanmar was the dearth of ICT accessibility in any form. India could fill the vacuum by providing TA to Myanmar. And, reflecting its eagerness, Myanmar could soon become India's second competitor in its own image.

Business Standard, 20 August 2012.

40

Has the Euro Matter now been Solved?

The euro zone should consider allowing countries to leave and rejoin.

For the first time, it appears that the European Union (EU) has taken an appropriate structural measure in their recent meeting in Brussels that could allay market fears for a time. They have decided to create, with haste, a Euro 500-billion European Stability Mechanism as early as July 2012. It will be permanent, and perhaps would be able to borrow directly, as needed, from the European Central Bank (ECB). In a complementary, confidence-seeking short-term gesture, they also agreed to ask their respective central banks to give the International Monetary Fund (IMF) Euro 200-billion to buttress the Euro 440-billion European Financial Stability Facility. These do represent moves in the right direction, and should enable these institutions to quickly come to the rescue of their ailing members.

What self-imposed belt tightening would the 17-member EU undertake? They have agreed to more centralised oversight and control of the fiscal budgets of individual countries, and possible sanctions for countries that break public debt understandings. Figure 40.1 reveals the continuation of higher than trend fiscal deficits in selected EU economies, and the need for correction. However, only time will tell if they would, or could, adhere to agreements this time. Recall that, after all, the Big Two broke the Maastricht Treaty guideline of a three per cent fiscal deficit with respect to GDP. Regarding a public debt ceiling, Figure 40.2 indicates the scale of the problem in 2011 compared to 2007, and the need for rules.

But these rules cannot be designed with a cookie-cutter. A lacuna for imposing a single fiscal rule for all of the EU is that, in practice, economists know well that the same fiscal deficit-to-GDP ratio leads to different multiplier effects in different economies—depending on their particular characteristics, such as trade openness, exchange rate regime, stage of development and others. Despite empirical evidence to the contrary, if the EU decides to redeploy the generic flawed criterion/indicator that they have already broken in the past, and then expect that Moody's or other rating agencies would suddenly retreat from downgrading some of their economies, it would be fallacy. Instead, the rules would have to be designed for each country through IMF-type programmes. The Fund should revert to traditional financial programming and apply a modified and improved version across the board, rather than being perceived as selective. Clearer signals are needed that the EU too is willing to consider the acceptance of such individually-guided, corrective programmes for its member countries.

Figure 40.1

General Governments Defict/Surplus

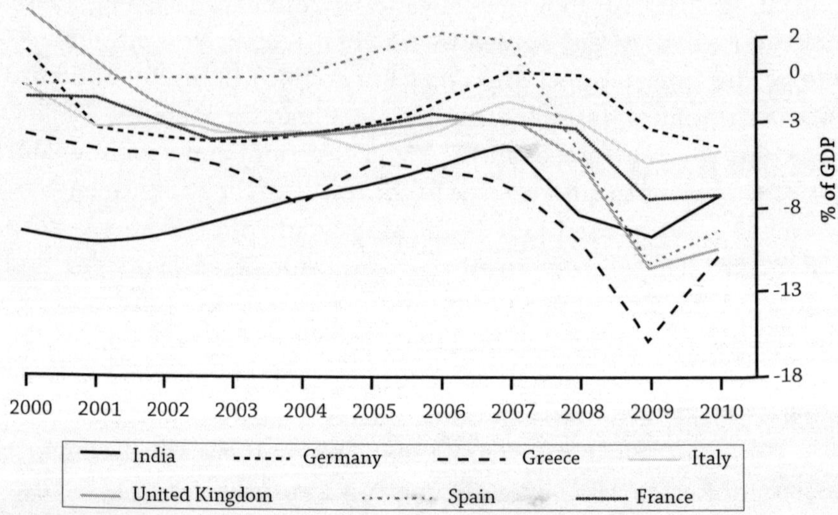

Source: Eurostat and RBI, India.

The consideration should, therefore, remain on the table that euro zone members that have no realistic long-run alternative but to severely curtail domestic consumption and lurch into an export-driven recovery might move off the euro and devalue—in the process countering somewhat the undervaluation of selected Eastern currencies. In effect they would be like the UK, being a part of the EU but not of the euro zone. Figure 40.3 illustrates selected figures for crosscountry balance of payments; it should make obvious where the

Figure 40.2

Public Debt

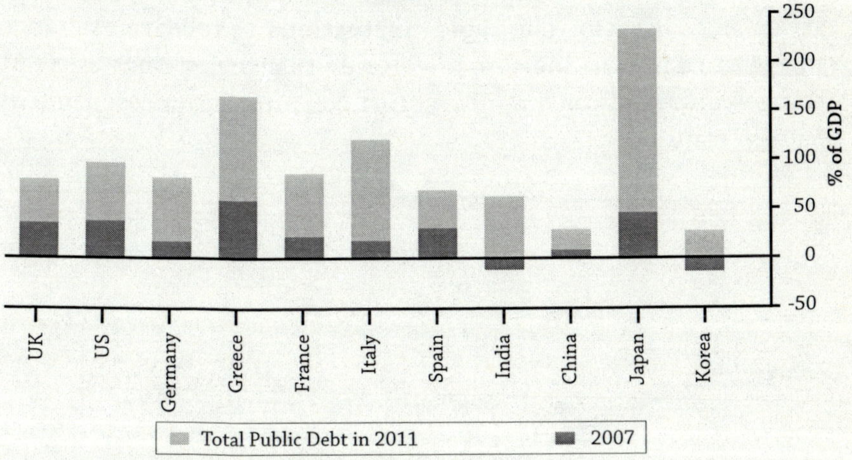

Source: *World Economic Outlook*, IMF.

Figure 40.3

Balance of Payments Current Account

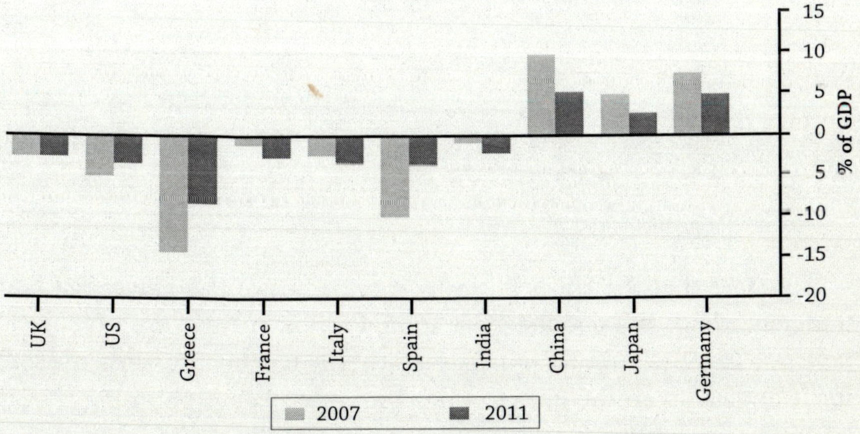

Source: *World Economic Outlook*, IMF.

need for continuing correction lies, even though between 2007 and 2011, adjustments among surplus and deficit countries have indeed occurred.

Once solidly on the path to recovery, the exited EU members should be able to rejoin the currency union equally smoothly. Arguments that such a course—comprising altering membership of the euro zone, and presumably more fluctuations in the currency itself—might cause disruptions in the global trade and payments system is post facto. The rapid fluctuations in relative exchange rates with respect to the euro are already challenging lines of credit arrangements and causing discomfort for future, trade-dependent business plans.

Figure 40.4

GDP Growth

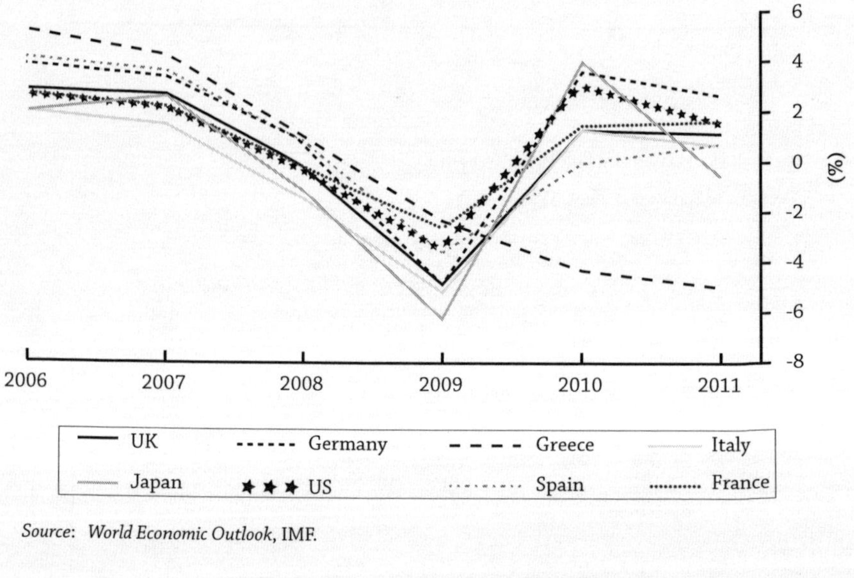

Source: World Economic Outlook, IMF.

The fact that the UK is basically staying out of the newly-reached understandings is a good sign. It should follow its conservative fiscal policies. There should be no surprise that it has been a slow process for it to pick up on the growth rate. The severe belt-tightening that it has opted for is akin to that of Korea, which voluntarily did the same after the 1997-98 East Asia crisis. It served Korea well. If the UK clings to its current fiscal path, it will emerge stronger in the longer term, and with less of a burden on posterity.

In the same vein, any speculative debate over how to resurrect GDP growth quickly is not based on realism since this is not an achievable short-term scenario. Figure 40.4 shows recent GDP trends. These economies should be guided to accept that not only has there been a dive in their GDPs, but the future trend GDP growth rates will be lower than past trends for some time to come. How long it will take to get back on the pre-2007 rate path will depend on how much they are willing to tighten their belts and leave more of their product for export. They can achieve this at realistic exchange rates, rather than be seen as continuing to need bailouts. Markets have perceived the shortsightedness of continuing with the previous century's East-West divide in economic ratings, with lopsided prescriptions for correction primarily on one side. Commensurately, rating agencies have become less and less oblivious and forgiving.

A final word. There remains little option for the EU but to infuse confidence among its counterparts in the G20. Their mettle will be proved with the strength of correction that they actually undertake, rather than with their mere agreement to take action. The world can wait until the summer of 2012—but not too much longer.

Business Standard, 19 December 2011.

41

Countdown to Cannes

As the G20 leaders' summit of November 3-4 approaches, different streams of thought have taken hold. First, there is a divergence over the utility of the process that has turned out to be relatively slow in achieving consensus on mutual assessments among countries. Second, there is continuing disagreement over the relative importance of artificial exchange rates, loose fiscal stance, and reluctance to provide support in, broadly speaking, Asia, America and Europe. Be that as it may, G20 is still the vehicle that a group of economically diverse, advanced, large and emerging nations have put together which, at present, is the only vehicle that offers the potential of leading the way out of a deep and continuing global economic and reemerging financial crisis. And, within G20, BRICS–Brazil, Russia, India, China, South Africa—have appeared as a formidable bloc from which greater contribution is anticipated.

The G20 Mutual Assessment Process (MAP) is designed as a reasonable, multilateral process to develop a set of indicators for noting internal and external imbalances and indicative guidelines for assessing those imbalances. Will an Action Plan be adopted at the Cannes summit that would draw up triggers for corrective action? A September 22 communique of finance ministers and central bank governors released at the G20 meeting in Washington promised to

> Commit to take all necessary actions to preserve the stability of banking systems and financial markets as required. We will ensure that banks are adequately capitalised and have sufficient access to funding to deal with current risks and that they fully implement Basel III along the agreed timelines. Central banks will continue to stand ready to provide liquidity to banks as required. Monetary policies will maintain price stability and continue to support economic recovery.

Interestingly, the emphasis is on domestic policy rather than on international agreed triggers that would compel domestic policy. Thus, whether there is scope for sharp changes in policy direction is to be awaited at Cannes but opinions are stacked in favour of slow progress. Even if it is "slow but steady", advanced economies would be charting the right course and emerging economies would be delighted.

A second feature at Cannes should be the role and prevalent use of capital controls. Some countries have been, and some are contemplating, imposing them to contain surges in capital inflows caused by untamed quantitative easing elsewhere. However, such controls should only be a measure of last resort rather than a substitute for sound macroeconomic policy. Cannes should take a position on this. After all, there is broad agreement in research findings that capital controls cannot compensate for fundamental macroeconomic imbalances. Governments, however, could temporarily improve the quality of capital flows by curbing shorter-term, and encouraging longer, maturity flows. There is also built-in futility in using capital controls, for, unless quantitative easing or loose fiscal policy in advanced economies is directly addressed, capital is bound to flow, find locales offshore, and suffer increased volatility. Only progressive international cooperation in monetary affairs through MAP can counter this, not unilateral imposition of capital controls.

A third feature at Cannes has to be G20's long-term agenda based on the Seoul summit's Development Consensus for Shared Growth and the recent Washington communique of the G20 Ministerial Meeting on Development. In policy circles, however, there is the expressed preoccupation that G20 has overreached itself in defining nine pillars of development that will be addressed: infrastructure; human resource development; international trade; private investment and job creation; food security; growth with resilience; financial inclusion; domestic resource mobilisation; and knowledge sharing. These appear to challenge the singular focus that is needed to address the most crucial systemic fault-lines that should be closed for restoring stability in financial flows. The broadening of objectives assuages the developing countries that claim recognition of their long-term structural concerns as a group. However, it carries the danger, and perhaps the reality, of diluting the immediacy of instituting strong and meaningful global indicators that should quickly enable automatic triggers for tightening, or loosening, macroeconomic—financial and fiscal—policies that most advanced economies should be implementing now or in future. Perhaps the development agenda is a way for the G20 to maintain its relevance beyond the present global crisis and to reach out to countries beyond its own membership. In turn, the question that arises is, how should G20 relate to G24, of which India has just taken over the chairmanship for a year?

Finally to BRICS. Advanced economies are interested in what they can do pro-actively as a group. Some within the group are keen to make a contribution in terms of financial resources. Thinking out of the box, however, would it not be more helpful if BRICS took a combined position in advancing their agendas over remaining aspects of liberalisation of their economies, an issue that advanced economies harp on during ordinary circumstances? In the case of India in particular, financial sector liberalisation including banking and insurance would help buttress supply opportunities for mature economies, improve the allocative efficiency of investment, and reduce expenditure in mature economies through a scaling back of global demand for their government securities.

Liberalising the retail sector would help advanced country firms find a new source of unmet demand and improve their global supply chain. This would, in turn, rationalise the cost of production and enhance net exports of these economies. That would act as a catalyst in reviving global demand. In the process, BRICS, and India in particular, would reap the benefit of organised retailing, investment in local supply-chain management and storage capacity, areas in which improvement is required immediately. An efficient service sector would make a better enabling environment for more foreign investment, thus engendering a second round of correction in global imbalances. Making a contribution towards redressing global imbalances through domestic policy reform by BRICS, rather than through making a token contribution of financial resources that can at best represent a drop in the bucket, would be a more proactive, albeit deeper and more challenging, route for them to adopt. Let us await Cannes.

Business Standard, 08 October 2011.

42

Hola! Yo Soy America Latina

Hello? And I am India! Language is a terrible barrier but the walls are coming down. Latin Americans speak Portuguese in Brazil and Spanish elsewhere, reflecting the division of commercial interests in the continent centuries ago. But they are learning English, though Indians are reluctant to learn their languages, still preferring, curiously, to learn French or German. That should change rapidly as trade and cultural links spread and firm up. Fifteen years ago when I spoke of the ABC economies (Argentina, Brazil and Chile) at a seminar in Delhi, an unimpressed researcher lamented that he was tired of examples from banana republics. Recently, a scholar from Jawaharlal Nehru University visited São Paulo and exclaimed, "São Paulo is New York! How can we compare Brazil and India?" Clearly, times have changed.

For cross-country comparisons from India's viewpoint, it is best to think of Latin America in groups: (1) Brazil since it is part of BRICS (Brazil, Russia, India, China and South Africa); (2) Argentina, Colombia and Chile (ACC), noting that our exports to Colombia are greater than to Argentina; (3) Mexico and Venezuela (MV), because they are oil producers; (4) Bolivia, Ecuador and Peru (BEP), since they are heavily indigenous and India could establish synergies with them; and (5) Uruguay, Paraguay, Cuba, Nicaragua and Guyana (UPCNG) comprising small yet varying interests. To put per capita incomes into perspective, Figure 42.1 demonstrates how small India's per capita GDP (gross domestic product) is relative to Latin America's. It also reveals that Brazil's per capita GDP is not the highest in Latin America; it is in the middle. One could allude to India's population challenge. At 1.2 billion, India is double that of Latin America in terms of population. Brazil is 200 million, Mexico 100, Colombia 50, and Argentina 40.

Figure 42.1

GDP Per Capita (Constant US$)

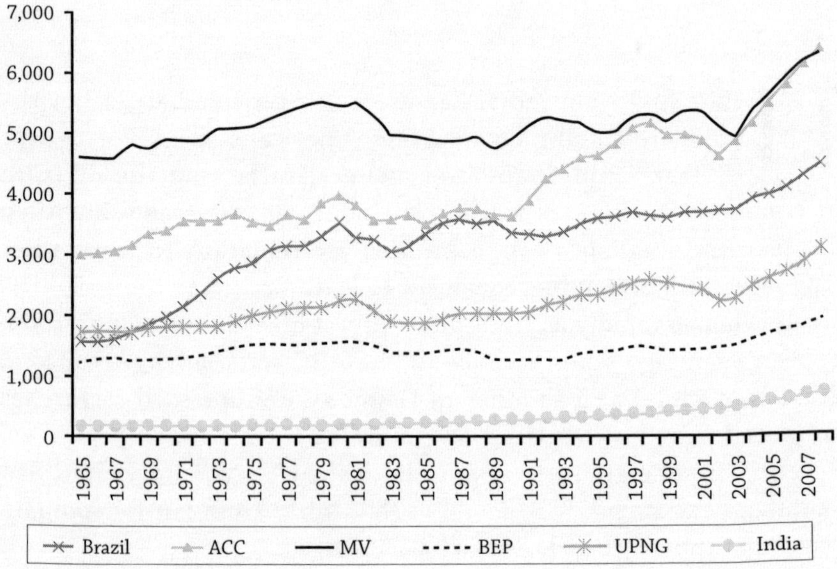

Source: *World Development Indicators*, 2010.

In the February edition of *Diplomatist*, R. Viswanathan, India's ambassador to Argentina, provided trends and potential in trade and investment in traditional manufacturing and services, agribusiness and farmland, and culture and entertainment. In 2009-10, Indian exports to Latin America increased by 20 per cent, reaching \$9 billion but India's imports were \$14 billion, implying a considerable trade deficit for India and, therefore, potential for export. India's export and import trends are shown in Figure 42.2 and Figure 42.3. They demonstrate how India's overall trade relationship with Latin America has expanded. But considering that the region imported \$700 billion in 2010, India's share is minuscule. Clearly, the potential is huge.

Figure 42.2

India's Exports to LAC

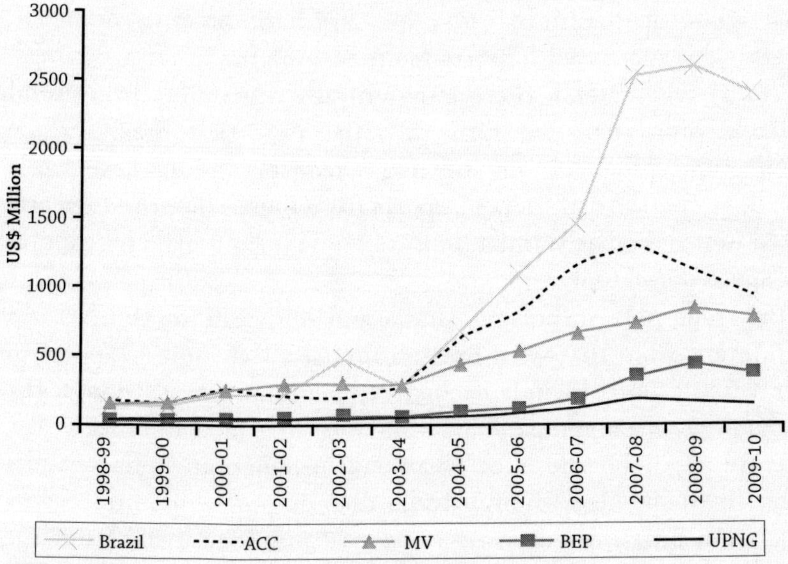

Source: Export Import Data Bank, Ministry of Commerce & Industry.

Figure 42.3

India's Imports from LAC

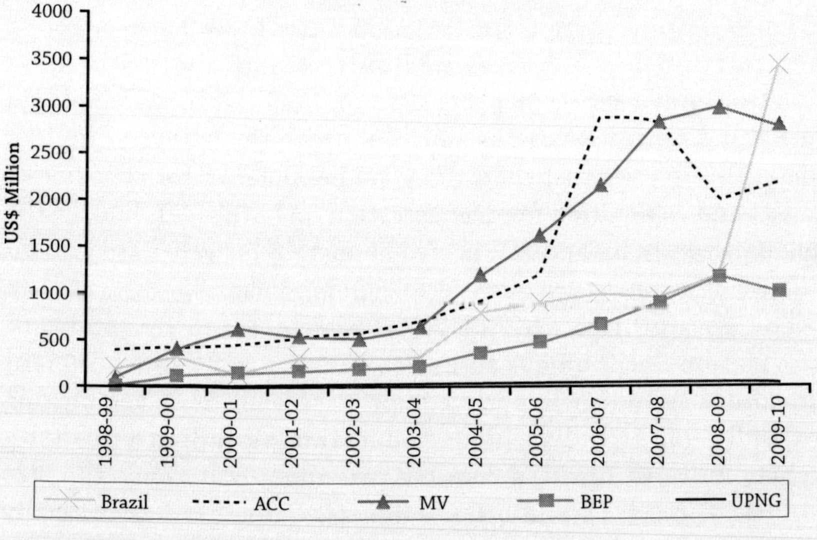

Source: Export Import Data Bank, Ministry of Commerce & Industry.

Figure 42.2 reveals India's exports to Brazil and to the rest of Latin America were almost equal. Figure 42.3 shows India's imports from Brazil did not match those from the rest of Latin America combined, though they surpassed imports from each of the other groupings. Beginning with Brazil, there is essentially a manufacturing-food exchange. More than two-thirds of Indian exports to Brazil include manufactured products—engineering, chemicals and textiles—while more than one-third of India's imports from Brazil comprise food and related items. Similarly, India imports crude from Brazil and exports high-speed diesel to it.

The trade pattern between India and ACC, BEP or UPCNG is a bit different from that with Brazil—almost all of India's exports to these three groups include exclusively manufacturing, though the commodity range is comparable to Brazil's. But, unlike in Brazil's case, there are negligible diesel or petroleum products in India's export basket to them. Also, though India does import a manufacturing range from Brazil, there is no import of manufacturing from the others to India except a very small amount of chemicals and textiles. Instead, from those three groupings, India mainly imports metal ores and scrap, a lot of food and wood products, some wool, and a bit of crude (see Table 42.1).

Thus, despite some intra-variations, the India-Latin America trade relationship has remained quite traditional with India exporting much more of processed or manufactured products and Latin America exporting much more of the primary product variety. This implies that there are good possibilities for cooperative strategy and exploration for diversification on both sides. Finally, the trade between India and MV is also almost exclusively based on an exchange of manufacturing for petroleum products.

The possibilities are not restricted to trade in goods. IT (Information Technology) as Indian exports and entertainment and culture as Indian imports comprise services that are picking up rapidly—so is Indian higher education as Indian university teachers move to Brazil, a country two-and-a-half times the size of India, to teach IT and other subjects. Colombia has officially recognised Ayurveda as a medical system and Ayurvedists are regular peripatetic visitors there. Embracing their culture and language, and participating in their reform process, I realised that Indian traditions of hospitality, healthcare systems such as Ayurveda, Yoga, Unani, and classical dance and musical traditions are vehicles waiting to be snapped up by the eager and trusting Latins.

Table 42.1

India's Trade with Latin America

	Exports from India (100 %)	*Imports to India (100 %)*
Brazil	High speed diesel (37)	Petroleum crude (31)
	Chemicals & related products (19)	Food & related items (35)
	Engineering goods (19)	Chemicals and related products (7)
	Textiles (19)	Capital goods (6)
ACC	Chemicals & related products (33)	Metaliferrous ores & metal scrap (44)
	Engineering goods (37)	Food & related items (27)
	Textiles (14)	Petroleum crude (16)
	Petroleum products: Waxes, Motor Spirit (1)	
BEP	Engineering goods (44)	Metaliferrous ores & metal scrap (57)
	Textiles (27)	Petroleum crude (20)
	Chemicals & related products (16)	Wood & wood products (9)
	Petroleum products : Lubricating oil (0.4)	
UPCNG	Chemicals & related products (39)	Food & related items (16)
	Engineering goods (28)	Textiles & readymade garments (9)
	Textiles (4)	Chemicals and related products (5)
	Petroleum products: Lubricating oil (0.4)	Wood & wood products (30)
		Wool raw (16)
MV	Chemicals & related products (32)	Petroleum crude (91)
	Engineering goods (34)	
	Readymade garments (9)	
	Textiles (9)	
	Petroleum products: Motor Spirit (5)	

Source: CMIE

Business Standard, 13 August 2011.

43

Volatile Times

Regulators and experts recently met in Brussels to analyse market volatility in food and agricultural commodities, fossil fuels and energy, and industrial raw materials, and to debate what regulators can and should do, and how multilateral institutions might respond coherently.

French President Nicolas Sarkozy delivered an impassioned speech on why markets should be regulated. A handful of players are controlling large chunks of most markets, driving and determining prices. Further, huge gains are being made from orchestrated price movements rather than availability based on production and weather conditions, or changes in demand for products owing to economic growth or natural disasters. He implied that an intolerable situation was developing and that regulation had become imperative. He indicated that he was giving the speech in anticipation of the following week's Paris meeting.

That G20 agriculture ministers' meeting took place in Paris to discuss measures against volatility in global agricultural markets. The members could not conclude concretely. They, however, agreed to collect comparable information with the Food and Agriculture Organisation's involvement, committing to an Agricultural Market Information System. It is an onerous task since the US, which is the only member that publishes reliable data, remains unwilling to regulate the markets effectively. But data are not enough. It is important to ask how the data would be used for indicators, and if the indicators are meaningful.

Only after the first stage is completed could agreements be meaningfully drawn up on regulation to contain prices and volatility. But volatility is not the only concern. The world is also worried about extreme price rises and, based on evidence, the increased volatility as prices rise. Two explanations follow. First, the rapid change in the nature of market operations, with price determination in commodity markets moving closely with financial markets. And second, the real demand-supply gap in global markets.

On the first, price rise and volatility have been closely linked to the increasing financialisation of commodity markets that Mr Sarkozy denounced, unless regulated. Commodities have become an asset class. They now comprise investor havens for hedging against higher-risk sources, low interest rates and a depreciating dollar. Hedgers take speculative positions on commodities, and exploit arbitrage opportunities in markets through index funds, pension funds, mutual funds and the like. These activities would not have been questioned but for the emergence of instruments that do not necessarily reflect market fundamentals such as hedge funds, swap deals, exchange-traded funds and exchange-traded notes, where passive traders track commodity values and act on them. Thus, commodity index futures are operating much like financial market indexes, creating bubbles intermittently. Their regulation must, therefore, be along the same lines.

The regulatory indicators should, therefore, target such trend spotters who have little or no intent of taking futures to delivery. They ride the wave, accelerating and enlarging both price upswings and downswings. Speculative position limits have to be stipulated to prevent excessive speculation and assist in monitoring potential violations in the market. It can be implemented through surveillance of individual and institutional traders' activities to contain, if not obviate, an oligopoly in market power.

In the absence of full agreement on the course of action, monitoring based on traditional macroeconomic indicators remains in vogue. It cannot be sufficient since links between an economy's macro performance and financial/commodity market-driven global doldrums are tenuous. Unfortunately, there is a stubborn continuation in, and overemphasis on, using macroeconomic indicators such as savings rate, fiscal deficit/GDP, or current account balance as indicators linked to all ills. But fiscal deficits have different impacts—multipliers—reflecting country characteristics. Similarly, the current account indicates net financial flows, while we need gross flows from trade in goods and services to obtain trade in financial assets that comprise the bulk of cross-border financial activity. In fact, gross financial flows make current account positions look small. Claudio Borio of BIS, Piti Disyatat of the Bank of Thailand, this author and others are pointing to the need for indicators that are more directly linked to global market movements.

The problem is that many of them are financial indicators that the US seems reluctant to touch despite the experience of the 2008-2009 financial crisis and its continuing fallout. Fortunately, the large trader reporting system has been endorsed by the Dodd-Frank Act, which has accepted the importance of collecting data to implement aggregate position limits for certain physical commodity derivatives. The G20 process must push forward on this issue. While the French chairmanship appears to be a silver lining, the outcome of the Paris meeting is not sufficiently reassuring.

What are the better indicators? These have to be found from observed associations between volume and value in the lineup of global commodity markets measured by indices such as S&P GSCI Commodity Spot, CRB Spot Index Fats & Oils, and others that can be related to prices of corn, wheat, crude and minerals on the one hand, and movements in major asset classes such as the Dow Jones Industrial Share Price Index and FTSE Global Bond Index, and global liquidity such as global money stock (M1) as a percentage of real GDP, on the other. Further, the correlation between the financial asset classes and off-index commodities (commodities not included in commodity indices) will shed more light on the impact of portfolio rebalancing on indexed commodities.

Price stability can be achieved by putting together a framework of triggers based on observed strong associations. Otherwise we are heading for another vortex of price escalation and volatility that would fuel the next global recession. Further, there is a continuing lack of resolve to tighten belts or control runaway financial innovation.

Now to the demand-supply gap—the second explanation on global price movements. Take China. At an overarching level, China is criticised for excessive savings and current account surplus. Yet at the Brussels conference, China was singled out for overconsumption of global resources. China consumes over 50 per cent of the global supply of cement and iron ore, and just under 50 per cent of steel, copper, nickel and zinc. Its per capita consumption of these metals is higher than developed countries'. Hence China is over-consuming. Finally, this author found himself in the awkward position of having to speak on the argument's internal inconsistency. At the macro level, China has too much current account surplus and excessive savings; at the micro commodity market level, it is over-consuming. So, should China stop producing and only import finished products when global demand reflects otherwise? Additionally, that China consumes only 10 per cent of global oil supply was ignored until pointed out. And since oil prices and their volatility are central to the prevailing inflation, price volatility and potential resurgence of global recession, should the solution not lie in rapid fiscal and monetary tightening elsewhere?

I felt a strong desire to escape from the real world and found refuge in Brussel's museums showcasing Bruegel's unreal miniatures and Magritte's surreal vision of the world.

Business Standard, 9 July 2011.

44

Venice to Verona via Vittorio Veneto

Venice is invariably on Indian tourists' travel route. They ride excessively priced gondolas through its canals, gazing at dilapidated, photogenic homes with sculpted exterior mouldings, hanging clothes and blooming flowers. Stopping to pick up exquisitely crafted Murano glass or Cameo pendants for loved ones and gorging on seafood and wine are other musts. The more adventurous tourists criss-cross the waterways in crowded Vaporettos or navigate narrow lanes in sneakers, doing the rounds of the Bridge of Sighs or the hidden treasures of San Rocco, where frescoes by Tintoretto led it to be termed the Sistine Chapel of Venice. The Moor sounding the gong of the clock at St Mark's Square reveals the millennia-old dependence on Africa for physical tasks. Yet, such were the rigours of the Venetian Republic that once the Doge, its administrator, was elected and entered his palace, he never emerged from it again, like the living child goddess of Kathmandu. Of course, the Doge's decisions were final.

A well-heeled tourist looks for more and ventures out of Venice. One cannot but notice striking similarities in the political economy of India and Italy. In the post-Roman period, Italy had been fragmented into city states and kingdoms until, after an extended tumultuous period, it was unified in the 1860s. Reflecting the different economic stages of the regions—the poor south including Sardinia and the rich north including Venice to Verona—a complex system of fiscal federalism emerged. Even today, tempers tend to run high among Italian regions on the matter of interregional transfers.

Moving east to west, Vittorio Veneto is located between Venice and Verona. Its calendar-perfect historical neighbourhood is from when it was in the Venetian Republic until annexed to the Kingdom of Italy in 1866. Not only did it produce a pope, but the final battles of World War I were also fought here. Its gracious environs produce Amarone, the best Italian wine. There to celebrate a friend's hallmark birthday, I found myself among friends from Colombia, Venezuela, Canada, the UK, and other Italians, a veritable mix. At dinner, I realised that Italians could be louder than Indians over meaningless banter, in a relaxed ambience of perfect camaraderie. Their menu could be more extensive than ours with antipasto, cheeses, pasta, fish and meat dishes, and various desserts, comprising a cuisine finessed over millennia from the epicurean Romans. No wonder then that the modern Italian feels comfortable in an Indian milieu with our chaotic debates over delectable food.

The highway to Verona revealed a super-developed region of manufacturing units. It led me to think of Indo-Italian trade. How we are, or might be, linked, I thought. Reaching Verona, though I failed to find the Two Gentlemen of Verona, I did make it to Juliet's little balcony and the small courtyard from where Romeo would have climbed up to her. Moving on, an unforgettable asparagus risotto topped with Amarone at Botega del Vino, a timeless boutique restaurant, completed the visit.

Coming back to my query, over the last decade, India's exports to Italy as a share of exports to the European Union (EU) fell from over 12 per cent to 10 per cent (see Figure 44.1). The share of imports rose from 6 per cent to 10 per cent. Further, Indo-Italian bilateral trade suffered in particular in the 2008-09 global economic recession. A negative growth rate of over 10 per cent was registered in 2009. However, since the recession, it grew 22 per cent in 2010-11 albeit from the shrunk 2009-10 base, reaching $8.85 billion. The number of traded commodities also expanded. An Italian diplomat recently expressed optimism that Indo-Italian trade would reach $17.5 billion by 2014. After all, since Italy is not the largest trading partner of India among EU countries, possibilities are not saturated.

Figure 44.1

India's Trade with Italy

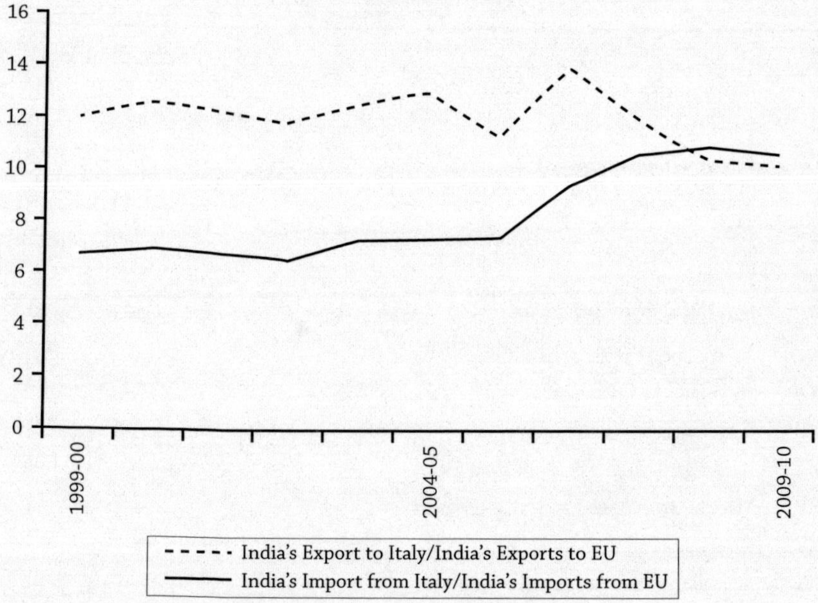

Source: Export Import Data Bank, Ministry of Commerce & Industry.

Selected important items in Indo-Italian trade are shown in Tables 44.1 and 44.2. India exports textiles, vehicles and transport equipment, base metals, chemicals, machinery, leather goods, gems and jewellery, engineering goods, iron and steel products, automobiles and auto parts (Table 44.1). It imports machinery and mechanical appliances such as precision tools, articles of base metal, chemicals, vehicles and aircraft, plastics and rubber, and optical instruments (Table 44.2).

But has Indo-Italian trade neared its potential? Economists measure bilateral export potential by using the RCA (revealed comparative advantage) index and then combining it with some assumptions. RCA is defined as a ratio of two shares. The numerator is the share of India's exports of a commodity in its total exports. The denominator is the share of world exports of the same commodity in total world exports. An RCA value higher than one for the commodity indicates India has a comparative advantage in exporting it to the world.

Table 44.1

India: Main Exports to Italy 2009 (US $ Million)

	HS Classification	*Actual*	*Potential*
I	Live animals	53	485
II	Vegetable products	131	492
IV	Prepared foodstuffs	27	760
V	Mineral products	34	6289
VI	Products of the chemical or allied industries	350	1488
VII	Plastics and Rubber	99	1353
VIII	Raw hides and skins, leather, furskins and articles	187	518
XI	Textiles and textile articles	750	3169
XII	Footwear, headgear, etc.	222	403
XIV	Pearls, precious or semi-precious stones, precious metals, etc.	128	1438
XV	Base metals and articles of base metal	399	3842
XVI	Machinery and mechanical appliances	299	662
XVII	Vehicles, aircraft, vessels and associated transport equipment	483	1751
XX	Miscellaneous manufactured articles	26	277
	Others	95	
	Total	3283	22927

Source: Export Import Data Bank, Ministry of Commerce & Industry.

Table 44.2

Italy: Main Exports to India 2009 (US $ Million)

	HS Classification	*Actual*	*Potential*
VI	Products of the chemical or allied industries	337	920
VII	Plastics and Rubber	133	309
XIV	Pearls, precious or semi-precious stones, precious metals, etc.	33	435
XV	Base metals and articles of base metal	537	1302
XVI	Machinery and mechanical appliances	1727	7803
XVII	Vehicles, aircraft, vessels and associated transport equipment	185	783
XVIII	Optical, etc. Instruments and Apparatus	92	439
	Others	400	
	Total	3444	11991

Source: Export Import Data Bank, Ministry of Commerce & Industry.

But is there potential for India to export it to Italy? For this, we select India's RCA commodities in Italy's import basket that have a share of at least 0.5 per cent in Italy's total imports. And we use two criteria. One, India could export all exports of a particular commodity to the world (that Italy imports from India) to Italy alone. And two, Italy would shift all its global imports of a particular commodity to India alone. The lesser of the two is selected and is used to indicate India's export potential of the commodity to Italy (Table 44.1). It is an upper bound of India's export potential to Italy. It reveals that India's potential exports to Italy are $23 billion. Similarly, Table 44.2 shows Italy's potential exports to India are $12 billion.

Comparing the actuals with potential in Tables 44.1 and 44.2 reveals that in both cases exports could increase significantly. But the difference between actual and potential exports from India to Italy is much higher than that from Italy to India. There is optimism in the air but India needs to seek Italian markets more aggressively.

Business Standard, 8 June 2011.

45

Globalisation and G20

In the context of G20, let us scrutinise selected aspects at its epicentre, revealed by changing international trade patterns. First, using merchandise exports statistics, we define globalisation and its evolution and course. Second, we note a striking change in the composition and direction of trade among selected countries. Third, we point to a commensurate shift in regional trade balances. Accordingly, fourth, we can assess the role of G20 despite dampened expectations.

Figure 45.1

Worldwide Merchandise Exports

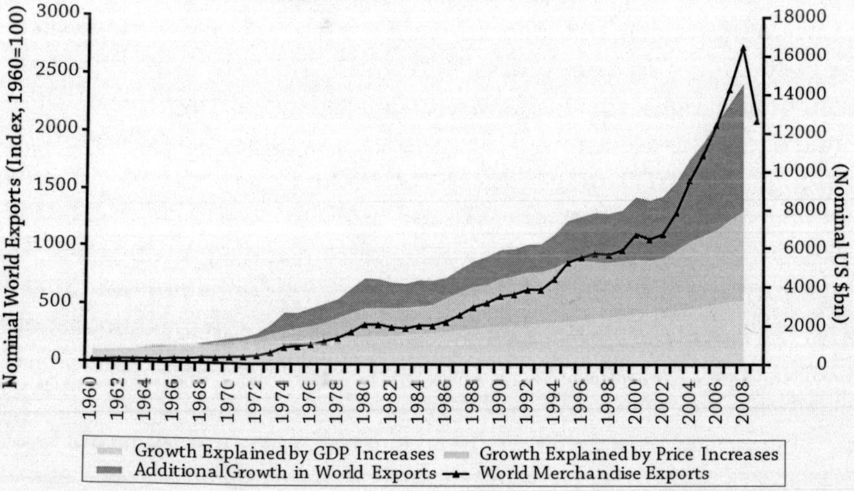

Source: World Trade Organisation (WTO).

Over 50 years, we witnessed an exponential rise in merchandise exports (Figure 45.1, right axis). Yet, the global crisis resulted in a

20-25 per cent fall in world exports in 2008-09 alone, a manifestation of a finally unsustainable heterodox consumption-driven economic stance in many advanced economies, reflected in stubbornly negative household savings.

Looking to the antecedents of the crisis, Figure 45.1 (left axis) breaks down growth in the global trade index. The bottom portion shows how much trade would have grown with GDP at constant prices or, if fixed at the 1960 share of GDP. The middle portion adds in the effect of prices. The top portion then shows the additional growth in trade over this period, reflecting trade's increasing share in world GDP. Without this, trade would have been 45 per cent lower than that actually experienced in 2008. It is this portion that reflects globalisation. Many have blamed it not only for its inability to control depletion of global non-renewable resources but also for failing to provide appropriate signals for the self-regulation of the international marketplace.

So, how did trade grow over real economic growth and inflation? First is an economic rationale—cost advantages of large-scale specialisation in particular countries resulting in greater supply than domestic demand. Second were complementary technological improvements in communication and transport (air shipment, containerisation), increasing use of billing and tracing through the Internet, to name a few. Third were reductions in trade barriers through the WTO that reduced tariffs and quotas, and customs unions such as ASEAN, the EU and NAFTA. Fourth, globalisation accelerated with escalating consumer demand and a growing taste for high turnover and product differentiation. This consumption-linked aspect became simply unsustainable. Just as an individual household cannot dissave in the long run, so must economies at the macro level eventually be constrained by dissaving.

Figure 45.2 breaks down net trade (exports minus imports as a percentage of total trade) for selected countries. The space above zero shows net export sectors, while below zero are net import sectors. Indicators for 1980 reveal China and India exporting low value-added raw materials and agriculture, with the UK and the US having the advantage in services and manufacturing. The change in comparative advantage by 2008 is equally clear: China developed a strong advantage in manufacturing and is now a net importer of raw materials, while India gained advantage in commercial services. Indeed, between goods and services, services grew steadily in relative terms, from 15 per cent to 21 per cent between 1980 and 2009. Though still small in global share, India nevertheless contributed to this changing pattern, with IT (information technology) comprising a major component.

Figure 45.2

Trade by Commodity Type

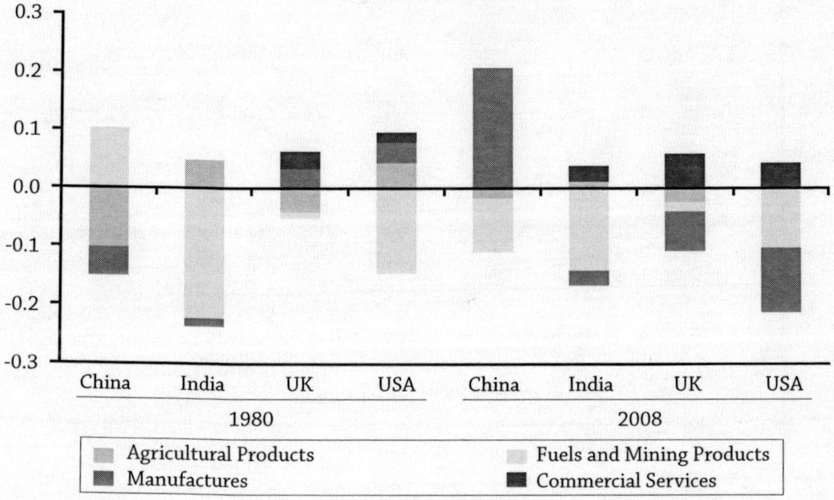

Source: WTO.

Changes in regional trade balances in Figure 45.3 reveal how North America—primarily the US—moved into deficit over recent decades, while Asia moved towards trade surpluses. The changed trade balances are symptomatic of the much-maligned "global imbalances", cited as one of the key indicators of the need for global economic rebalancing.

The IMF has historically argued against overconsumption. In the early annals of the IMF, its executive board did not desist from reining in post-War Europe from excessive consumption. In the 1970-1980s, Latin American countries faced opprobrium that, in the 1990s, East

Asian economies did not escape either. In the 2000s, the US and Europe, the historical rule-setters, themselves fell into unsustainable consumption, suffering its deleterious impact on economic growth. Reflecting the changed world economic order, G8 expanded into G20 for future global economic and financial dialogue, and revisions of IMF quotas could not be stalled any longer.

Figure 45.3

Regional Trade Balances: Net Trade as a % of Total Trade

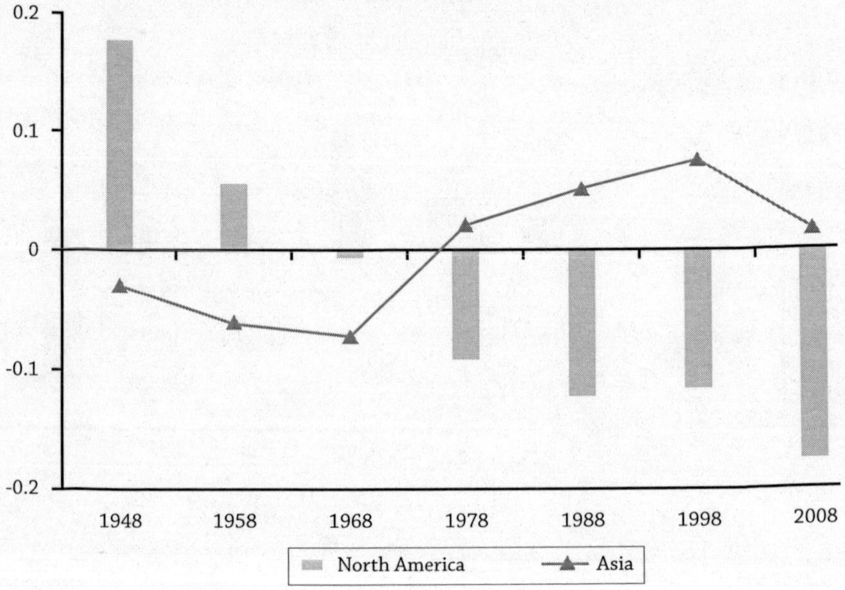

Source: WTO.

A huge socio-economic change is needed to get back to the basic habit of household savings in advanced economies where untargeted subsidies in various sectors and in multiple forms have curbed incentives to work or save, and have resulted in heavy expenditure burdens on government. This is where the need for rebalancing is most apt. Households, government and private businesses comprise an economy. They cannot all be in deficit, filling it perennially from abroad. That is unsustainable in the long run. It also leaves an unjust debt burden on posterity. Recognising this, more advanced countries are of late embracing tough, unpopular belt-tightening measures.

Thus, it is pertinent to ask what G20 can achieve to usher in less, yet better, global consumption that could form the anchor for a new exports road map from developing countries, rather than exclusively emphasising relative exchange rates or pushing artificial trade barriers. Perspicacity and reform in demand from advanced economies would naturally result in a realistic exports trajectory from developing nations, that could: (i) slow the rush; (ii) allow space for more intelligent use of depletable resources; (iii) minimise environmental degradation; (iv) enhance internationally comparable labour standards; and (v) minimise the use of child or indentured labour. G20 has included development issues in its Seoul Summit. To end on a cautionary note, it is necessary on the part of the Sherpas to ensure that crucial objectives are not lost in a creeping incrementalism of agenda items, as was evidenced in revisions in the IMF's agenda after earlier global crises.

Business Standard, 13 November 2010.

VII

Socio-economic Policy

46

Compassionate and Palliative Care

Compassionate and palliative care relate to the quality of the process of dying. After suffering their absence during and after a deeply grievous demise, I belatedly explored the literature on India by both international and Indian researchers, after my broaching the subject produced disinterest and disdain from the doctors who I spoke to. No wonder; little has been achieved in practice due to lack of Budget allocation despite the recognition and subsequent introduction of selective public policy. In a 2015 Economist Intelligence Unit (EIU) study of end of life care (EOLC) services comparing 30 advanced and 10 developing countries, India was ranked 40th in the quality of death.

Various authors coincide in defining compassionate care as the provision of medical, health and social care services with compassion, derived from the roots *passio* (suffering) and *com* (with)—or, to suffer with another. Studies reveal that compassion could be taught and has advanced significantly as an area of interest in the UK. It recognises a set of values: care, compassion, competence, communication, courage, commitment—and actions: leadership, positive approach and appropriate skills for working with people, and providing high quality care, all of this while ensuring the independence of service users, or patients. It encompasses locations comprehensively: communities, people's homes, doctors' offices, hospitals, hospices —and roles: nurses, midwifes, doctors, physiotherapists, health assistants, administrators, managers—and outcomes: health and wellbeing of all population segments, particularly the elderly. The result of research, policy relevant discussion, policy formulation and meticulous application is that in 2010, the EIU ranked the UK first in a quality of death index.

There is little discussion, leave alone policy, in India on compassionate care. A fledgling attempt was made by Delhi's Medical Humanities Group of University College of Medical Sciences (UCMS) which organised a workshop on compassionate care in May 2015 with a lecture from Greenwich University, UK. The aim was to encourage compassion and its practical application in healthcare; but its recognition or inclusion has not moved forward reflecting internet information.

Palliative care, discussed by Dr Carlos J. Moreno-Leguizamon and others is a subset of compassionate care, comprising end of life palliation in particular for terminal illnesses. India lags behind even in this though there is academic discussion by Dr Stanley C. Macaden, Dr M.R. Rajagopal and others, and government committees; hence there is some helpful policy. A National Programme for Palliative Care (NPPC) was enacted in 2012 and the Narcotic Drugs and Psychotropic Substance Act was amended in 2014, making morphine available to end of life patients. Thus, the discussion of palliative care in India appears to be centred on the non-availability of narcotics though globally its ambit is much wider. However, the binding constraint for palliative care remains the virtual absence of budgetary provision despite continual, though slow, recognition of its need; the NPPC received two per cent of its original Budget proposal with a handful of states benefitting from it.

Policy recommendations have invariably included the need for training and education of professionals, for example by Dr Macaden et al. There have been several proposals for undergraduate courses as well as in medicine and nursing. Nevertheless, none has been approved by the Medical or Nursing Council of India, revealing where India's medical profession stands on palliative care, leave alone compassionate care. However, Kerala stands apart. More palliative care centres operate in Kerala than in the rest of India put together. As early as 2008, palliative care policy was integrated into healthcare and implemented through institution building with WHO collaboration in research and training.

As in the UK, the Indian experience is a tale of tenacity of enthusiasts, Indian and foreign, in taking forward the thinking, policy making, and application of palliative care. Yet it is astonishing how little the willingness of the Indian medical profession is in incorporating it in medical practice, leave alone allocating financial or human resources for it. The outcome is chaos at end of life moments reflecting an ingrained unwillingness and, thus, stark inability of the medical profession to impart compassion or palliation due to a gaping lack in training.

In 2014, Dr Macaden et al. made strong recommendations for EOLC in India. First, there is no legal framework or policy guiding clinicians on dignified death which should include deliberated consensus decisions with a humane touch. Second, EOLC should recognise patient choices as a human right and as the cornerstone. Third, instituting or escalating aggressive medical intervention comprises malfeasance and amounts to harm and assault. Fourth, all medication should maximise comfort. Sedatives should be titrated and used minimally. Regarding government policy, first, the Government of India should enhance and speed up legislation. Second, EOLC should be included in all hospital care and healthcare delivery. Third, doctors, nurses and allied health streams should undergo mandatory EOLC training.

Those practices militated against my experience. I could give no choice to the patient who pleaded to be taken home such was the pressure I felt from the specialists in the ICU to apply the last available biomedical techniques despite the emaciated body in extreme pain. Even on the day of passing, a specialist recommended a liver function procedure. When asked if it would end the coma, the answer was in the negative. I further asked why such horrendous measures even at the final stage of life and was informed it was their responsibility to make available all procedures until the very end irrespective of other practices elsewhere. Female and male nurses hurried about pushing and shoving the inert body, robbing any peace, contemplation or prayer. Where was palliative care? When she did leave, not a single doctor or nurse came by; only a new one appeared to issue the death certificate. Where was compassionate care? Later, a doctor, proud owner of several hospitals, explained to me that doctors hide due to the wrath of relatives. I wish I had educated myself earlier with Dr Macaden, Dr Moreno-Leguizamon, Dr Rajagopal and others so that I could have been more assertive and my mother, as she had pleaded, could have died at home.

Business Standard, 17 May 2016.

47

Supply Constraints for Private Sector Healthcare

Supply of healthcare in India is among the lowest in the world on a per capita basis. This is especially so as we go down the income scale, at the bottom of which there is little availability of hospitals or even health centres, doctors, nurses, or surgical and laboratory equipment. For example, World Health Organization (WHO) guidelines recommend 3.5 hospital beds per 1,000 population. While the global average is 2.3 beds per 1,000 population, India is at 0.7 beds per 1,000 population.

Successive governments have introduced measures that they supposedly believed would raise supply of healthcare and accessibility for the poor, the fondest demarcated by the number of hospital beds or distance of location from urban centres. Such incentives have not worked because they do not reflect market or field realities. The incentive criteria keep changing through various Budgets as if such changes are backed by survey-based micro-information, which does not exist in actuality. And there is little practice of meaningful impact assessment of changing government expenditure policies in order to redirect policies towards a more rational path. India, thus, remains backward among fellow nations in terms of design, application, regulation and assessment of government policy, including healthcare.

The bottom line is that it is lamentable how little the government has been able to empower the daily wager in terms of nutrition, healthcare or marketable education. I mean not the poor by using official indices, but the daily wager for whom it is a miracle that he, and increasingly she, makes do at the end of the day and for whom there is a trite regional idiom, "*din ani, din khai*". I would say they comprise two-thirds of our population or 800 million.

Under the circumstances, the least the government can do is to get out of the way of the private sector, where it is experimenting with innovative frameworks to provide socioeconomic welfare. Focusing on healthcare, I recently read about a solution-oriented model being followed by a private Indian group where patients are charged reflecting their ability-to-pay. This has enabled a three-tier charging system giving access to the poor of the same quality healthcare as the richer households. Another model comprises a small investment by an organisation combined with a somewhat larger government contribution, while the primary reliance is on private donations. This model has enabled almost half a million prosthetic limbs to be fitted across the globe by a single Indian organisation. These are good examples of existence and survival sometimes with, but mainly despite, government. The government should increasingly enable more of such worthy private sector models by cutting out bureaucratic hurdles that have tended to thwart widespread progress.

For that to happen, the government should recognise the special features that characterise the healthcare industry. It typically has high setup costs, followed by high operational costs, reflecting the need for high-skilled manpower, expensive equipment often embedding imported medical technology that usually has around seven-year investment cycles, medicines and consumables. Such characteristics, in turn, render it prohibitive for most Indians to avail high-quality healthcare.

A gap in domestic manufacturing obliges hospitals to import major medical equipment, such as MRI, CT scan, linear accelerators and others. Hospitals pay a CD (countervailing duty) of 12 per cent on imports that is equivalent to the central government's domestic excise. Similarly, a SAD (special additional duty) of 4 per cent is imposed to achieve comparability with the state-level VAT (value-added tax). Thus, it is understandable that these two taxes have to be paid. However, customs duty on imported equipment is additionally imposed at 7.5 per cent to 10 per cent. This is typically couched in the old argument of protecting "infant" industry, though, in reality, it is an easy means of collecting revenue, a practice increasingly rare in emerging economies.

In addition, recalling continuing exchange rate depreciation of the rupee, the cost of imported equipment has escalated. And note that, with exchange rate depreciation, all three above-mentioned duties also rise in terms of the rupee, posing additional net cost to the healthcare sector as long as they cannot pass on the full burden to patients. By contrast, equipment required for hydro projects, equipment for setting up planetariums, solar energy equipment and research equipment are exempt from customs duty.

Again, the Reserve Bank of India (RBI) encourages banks to extend long-term loans to the infrastructure sector with flexible structuring to absorb potential contingencies. Public infrastructure projects can raise loans at lower interest rates (150-200 basis points) than that of commercial projects and have repayment periods of 10-25 years as against 5-7 years for commercial projects. The government has not yet accorded infrastructure status to hospitals. On the whole, therefore, healthcare cannot be said to be a preferred sector.

A recent decision of mine to move to Bengaluru reflects its attractiveness of year-long pleasant weather that I experienced during countless visits I made during my membership in the Karnataka Tax Reforms Commission 15 years back. But it also reflects the availability of an excellent healthcare network offered by various private sector groups, whose existence I became familiar with while crisscrossing the state at that time. Hence, I possess a natural interest in the conditions under which this sector is functioning here.

In Karnataka, electricity rates for hospitals are slightly higher than for heavy industries. Hospitals are charged ₹6.4 to ₹6.9 a unit, whereas it is ₹5.75 to ₹6.15 a unit for industries, workshops and R&D (research and development) centres. There are variations across states. For example, in Rajasthan and Gujarat, all commercial consumers are charged based on connected load. Hospitals, due to the high-end equipment installed, invariably fall in the highest bracket and tend to pay high tariffs.

Yet hospitals are prescribed to provide treatment under the Employee State Insurance (ESI) and central and various state government health insurance schemes at regulated rates prescribed by the central and the state governments. The rationale for those rates remains to be explained; hence, they appear to be anomalous and inconsistent. They are revised at infrequent and unpredictable intervals without justification through appropriate analysis. An example for pricing anomaly is the Central Government Health Scheme (CGHS) prices for single-valve and double-valve replacement. CGHS Bangalore recommends ₹1,19,157 for a single-valve replacement and ₹60,950 for double-valve replacement.

Karnataka recently launched a health insurance scheme for APL (above-poverty-line) households. The scheme, known as Rajiv Arogyabhagya (RAB), covers 449 medical procedures at the same base package rates as that of the BPL (below-poverty-line) insurance scheme, Vajpayee Arogyashree (VAS). With little effective cost sharing for reducing input costs while creating a price cap by stipulating provision of health insurance to APL households at BPL rates, a financial burden is being created for hospitals and their operations. In addition, irregular and delayed payments by government are straining their cash flow. In the Bengaluru region, CGHS has pending payments above 30 days of close to ₹0.7 crore and, in the Kolkata region, it has pending payables of close to ₹1 crore.

To conclude, without meaningful collaboration from government, catching up with WHO guidelines is unlikely to occur in India's healthcare. But the paradox is that the first step is for government at every level to effectively eradicate bottlenecks and constraints placed along the way of growth of the private healthcare sector.

Business Standard, 16 June 2015.

48

Anatomy of Aswachh Bharat and Alchemy to Swachh

Nirmal remained unattained. Now we want to graduate to *swachh*, also a laudable objective if its broad contours are to be imagined. To begin let me ask rather obviously, was there any centrally sponsored *nirmal* scheme that went to local as opposed to state-governments for which central ministries were responsible? Has there been any impact assessment of programmes undertaken under *nirmal*, and have states been pursued regarding their promise to set up state finance commissions to ensure constitutionally guaranteed financing of municipal and *panchayat* programmes? Or is *swachh* to turn out to be another unfulfilled wish?

It is one thing to expect the middle class not to litter Indian streets. But the depth of the problem lies elsewhere. Unless all Indians are assured a basic right in relieving themselves decently and in privacy, that is, have access to at least septic tank or slab/open pit, leave alone modern latrines, how could they be expected to throw their garbage in bins, presuming, of course, that adequate number of bins are provided?

Coming to brass tacks, let us examine relevant figures. Based on Census 2011, Table 48.1 reveals that about one-fifth of urban and more than two-thirds of rural households do not have inhouse facilities; most of them use open fields. Table 48.2 lists the top 10 states' shares of night soil removal by humans, one of the most degrading human occupations. Unsurprisingly, by far the highest occurrence is in Uttar Pradesh, though surprisingly dismal performance persist also in rural West Bengal and urban Tamil Nadu. Rural conditions of Jammu and Kashmir are also poor, noteworthy in light of pre-election promises being made to Kashmiris on development.

Table 48.1

India: Sanitation Use

	Urban	*Rural*	*Total*
Number of Households (mn)	79	168	247
Within-House Latrine (%)	81	31	47
Piped Sewer System	33	2	12
Septic Tank	38	15	22
Slab/Ventilated Improved/Open Pit	8	13	12
Night Soil Disposal/Open Drain/Human/Animal	2	1	1
Without In-House Latrine (%)	19	69	53
Public Latrine	6	2	3
Open	13	67	50

Source: Census 2011.

Table 48.2

*India: Top 10 States' Night Soil Removal by Humans (%)**

States	*Urban*	*Rural*	*Total*
Andhra Pradesh	3.41	0.55	1.30
Assam	2.97	2.72	2.79
Bihar	1.83	1.67	1.17
Jammu & Kashmir	8.48	27.43	22.46
Maharashtra	2.56	0.73	1.21
Manipur	1.90	1.04	1.27
Odisha	3.62	3.23	3.34
Tamil Nadu	8.36	1.75	3.48
Utar Pradesh	51.21	37.44	41.05
West Bangal	6.91	19.78	16.41
Total	91.25	96.34	95.02

Note: * India = 100%.

Source: Census 2011.

Table 48.3

Cross-Country: Open Defecation (% of Population)

Country	*1990*	*2012*	*1990-2012 Reduction*
Ethiopia	92	37	55
Nepal	86	40	46
Vietnam	39	2	37
Cambodia	88	54	34
Angola	57	24	33
Bangladesh	34	3	31
Pakistan	52	23	29
Peru	33	6	27
Haiti	48	21	27
Benin	80	54	26

Source: WHO and UNICEF, 2014.

Using Census 2011 should not be terribly erroneous in light of little improvement over time. A 2014 World Health Organization UNICEF cross-country comparison in Table 48.3 lists the top 10 countries that have achieved the highest reduction in open defecation since 1990 as a percentage of population. In the subcontinent, it shows a rapid decline in open defecation in Bangladesh, Pakistan and Nepal. Reflecting the numbers on the use of open fields in Table 48.1, it is not surprising that India does not feature in Table 48.3 at all, while Sri Lanka does not feature for the opposite reason that there is likely to be little open defecation there. Also to be observed are that Ethiopia's reduction is most striking, while Bangladesh, Peru and Vietnam have rapidly reduced their incidence to single digits.

In Table 48.4, the same source reveals that India's inclusion significantly worsens southern Asia's performance between 1990-2012 or 2000-2012. Clearly, India has been, and continues to be, an outlier by far. As one indicator, 12 per cent of rural plus urban southern Asia other than India uses open defecation. But since in India it is 48 per cent, southern Asia's number jumps to 38 per cent once India is included in it! Indeed, globally, India represents almost 60 per cent of open defecation.

Table 48.4

Southern Asia: Latrines (% of Population)

Region	Year	Urban				Rural				Total			
			Unimproved				Unimproved				Unimproved		
		Improved	*Shared*	*Other Unimproved*	*Other Defecation*	*Improved*	*Shared*	*Other Unimproved*	*Other Defecation*	*Improved*	*Shared*	*Other Unimproved*	*Other Defecation*
Southern Asia	1990	55	15	8	22	12	3	5	80	23	6	6	65
	2000	59	16	9	16	20	5	7	68	31	8	8	53
	2012	64	18	9	9	31	7	9	53	42	11	9	38
Southern Asia without India	1990	68	11	15	6	25	8	17	50	38	9	15	38
	2000	69	12	15	4	36	11	18	35	47	12	16	25
	2012	73	14	11	2	49	15	17	19	57	15	16	12

Source: WHO and UNICEF, 2014.

Thus, the statistics for India on sanitation, in the above discussion on latrines in particular, are no less than shocking. Should any policymaker expect *swachh* Bharat from those who suffer such ignominy through life? The answer is decidedly in the negative, and even less so from those who hand carry excreta through urban and village streets, not unusually the subject of mockery for being of a low caste. These very fundamental challenges have to be addressed through rational allocation of financial resources to the appropriate level of government, ex ante and ex post IA (impact assessment) and tight M&E (monitoring and evaluation) of an intelligently designed Swachh Bharat programme.

Implementation of the programme has to be followed by wide induction in awareness of the dignity of labour and social equity more broadly. When Mohandas Karamchand Gandhi iterated, "Karo pahale, kaho pichhe", he actually cleaned out night soil of the Bihar Harijan, or so my generation was taught in junior school. In that light, by the time the joy of middle to high school came to be experienced, tasks following Gandhi's example were meted out to us to be applied in urban slums. Rhetorically, how many children are going through a culture of this kind of activity today?

In sum, Swachh Bharat is a correct policy revival but will fail unless buttressed by a robust, palpable implementation structure. The prime minister has to show his mettle by revealing his plan to make India clean and smart. Luckily, there exists a handful of municipalities from where one could derive inspiration. One such is the 2013-14 Budget of Berhampur Municipal Corporation in Ganjam district of Odisha that details its Budget allocation in garbage collection, solid waste management, drainage, public toilet, water supply, housing, roads and bridges, street lighting, parks, livelihood, infrastructure and project assistance. It elaborates that it wants mandatory public disclosure of documents and allocation, to ensure citizen participation—common in developed societies—increase allocation for the urban poor, and for basic services including water, garbage, drainage and public toilets, and implement a development outcome budget to ensure effective government management and accountability. It is rejuvenating for it sets an example for other local governments to follow. Central government bureaucrats should pick up such examples consistently and give concrete shape to the prime minister's vision though the leadership in this endeavour has to continue to be his.

Business Standard, 16 December 2014.

49

Indian Railways: Nostalgia and Reality

India's new government presented a fresh Railway budget on July 8. Its thrust comprised (1) an upward revision of ticket prices using a cost-plus approach reflecting international fuel prices; and (2) the introduction of a PPP approach due to the government's lack of resources to fund investment. Both measures reflect essential corrections for past policy errors and corruption. Undoubtedly it will hurt passengers' pockets unused to transparent or direct inflation corrections for holy cows such as rail tickets, petrol, or fertilisers. They pay indirectly through a steady deterioration of product quality such as in railway services and infrastructure, road conditions, or soil quality and livelihood.

I recall railway journeys in the 1960s when Madras-Calcutta took 2½ days, Calcutta-Bombay 2, and Calcutta-Delhi 1½. When my father was on official family leave, we travelled in large first class compartments impeccably cleaned at stations at father's will, where liveried bearers served food of your choice, continental or Indian. I still remember the aroma of chicken soup served in a white flattish platter. Nevertheless, I preferred my grandmother's dry delicacies: fish fry, mutton chops, prawn cutlets, parwal dorma, trifle and, of course, luchi and aloo dum despite father ceaselessly reassuring us railway food was safe because it was "antiseptic". My siblings got down with him at every extensive stop, traversing the length of the platforms, Kharagpur and Gorakhpur being the longest, though quizzes of this type invariably felled our knowledge to his devouring hot samosas, kachouris and tea while I stayed put on the top berth with a novel under my mother's protection. Water came from the station's potable water tap and was quickly stored in a terracotta *kalas* to keep it cool. When he was not on such leave, father would take us all over India, "practical" education being the objective, on corridor trains, equally clean if not that spacious but with the promise of making ever new friends. There was a jolly mood through and through, once leading to the Mohan Bagan soccer team travelling with us and then landing at our Madras doorstep on the pretext of desiring ethnic food. That, in turn, led to the inevitability of my being shunted out of my own room to the living room during their stay. I thought I must mention it in this world soccer season!

Those journeys were dreamlike. In search of a bygone era, and to satiate my wanderlust, I continue to take occasional train journeys, though it may seem like an oddity. Recently I took round trips from Delhi to Gorakhpur and Dehradun, the objective being to visit remote villages in their hinterland to spend time there. In eastern UP, I encountered abject poverty, describable only in the grossest terms. I distributed blankets and lunch boxes. Those who received blankets seemed younger than me but had laboured so hard that they were too arthritic to raise their arms high enough to receive the simple gift. All those who received lunch boxes had knotted hair, ragged frocks or shirts, and dusty faces in a land with water bodies all around. The recent report on poverty criteria that modified the numbers from a recent past seemed irrelevant, if not amusing, faced with actual rural poverty.

My hospitable hosts took me to many a temple whose deities I recognised except for one. She was Samay Devi. I was impressed but obviously not surprised to have encountered yet another Indian omniscient; how appropriate I told myself, for one cannot capture or reverse time through known Physics or Complexity, and wondered how much time India had left to correct herself. The other village further from Kemti Falls near Mussourie seemed better. First, local Block elections were on with 220 voters who were all being given invitee status, safe from the morbidity of local elections in "advanced" states. The ground was heaped with fruit, though abandoned due to lack of transport. The villagers looked healthy though the conditions of ancillaries such as teeth were abominable and the texture of their pinkish skin revealed a life of toil under a mountain sun. The homes had beds, sofas, TV and, most agreeably, overlooked beautiful ravines or valleys. I didn't want to return.

Also because I did not look forward to the return journey by train which has become an increasing, almost forbidding, challenge. On both journeys, the forward journey was several hours late without a single explanatory announcement. The latrines were unusable except through self-hypnosis. The food was murky. The compartment was filthy. Yet the families remained optimistic. The children played in the aisles without complaint, happy just to create a ruckus. The adults reassured one another that the train "will make up time". Referring the matter to Samay Devi, I continued to write a pending report.

A short super-fast rail link between Mumbai and Ahmedabad could perhaps be digested as an accommodation to a new regime since it also appears to be focussing on O&M and infrastructure improvements. The public will accept the government's price increases since they perceive it by and large as correct. But it will not wait too long for things to transform. To recall, the total route length of India's railway network is 65,000 km, with *dailymail.co.uk* reporting that India already possessed 53,000 km shortly after independence. The additional kms in almost 65 years is hardly impressive. The results of the new policy would have to fructify rapidly. ₹55,000 crores of project allocation were reported by the media to have yielded a one per cent project completion by the exited government. Rhetorically, one could perhaps ask, why blame the Railways alone when irrigation or public services such as health and education may have even out-competed the notoriety?

Screaming matches sponsored by the visual media seem to suffice aspirations for reform. On the Railway Budget evening, one anchor assembled five critics and apologists to discuss the Budget. Amidst the cacophony, I wondered how many of them had taken a train ride in India during the last Plan period or two. Had they actually experienced the deterioration or were they merely occupying pigeonholes in a singsong of vacuous chatter. I recommend that debaters have some field experience in any matter that they deem themselves competent to debate.

Business Standard, 23 July 2014.

50

A Sense of Independence

Children are taught by their parents in their early years. Thus my mother taught her children a song by poet Dwijendra Lal Ray:

Dhan Dhanya Pushp Bhara Hamara Yah Vasundhara—
Our earth, with its abundance of crops and the richness of flowers
Holds within its midst a land that is the most beautiful of all lands
This land is built of dreams and bound by memories
This, the land of my birth, the queen of all lands, is ne'er to be found anywhere else
...I pray that I breathe my last in this land where I was born.

That memory of the overflowing sound of her pedal organ as a cacophony of kids chimed in the words and the competing intoxicating aroma of the surrounding flora has lasted intact.

It is August 15. I ready myself for a morning constitutional. Underneath, I feel upset. Independence from what? From abject hunger? Farmers commit suicide on their parched, unirrigated lands under debt burdens that break their soul. Cowed down, few question. Yet guaranteed dig-and-fill employment ensures unresponsive labour supply at harvest time. A quarter of Indian babies are wasted and half suffer from malnutrition or stuntedness. Save the Children claims India is worse than Bangladesh. The vast majority of them leave high school to have to feed themselves. The basis on which the term "demographic dividend" is used is mysterious.

Squalor surrounds urban and rural environments. It beats countries in Latin America, Asia or Africa. The Metro to Delhi's airport is suspended reportedly due to cracks in its holding pillars; there is no shared information on who is responsible. After every shower, roads reduce to dirt patches. Ostriches. Nero.

Inflation (except most recently) has remained abnormally high. There is no dearth of lower numbers floating out of crystal balls. Crops rot or are meals for mice. GDP growth has crashed. Given our labour supply, a growth rate of 5-6 per cent should be considered natural in economic parlance. Any genuine effort should achieve higher growth. Manufacturing is weighed down by excessive, distorted and inequitable taxation. Its indirect tax burden, when considered in light of embedded, and cascading, taxation is among the highest in the world. Yet we have not enacted a GST (goods and services tax). Indeed, the proposed GST structure is at such odds with the world that it may be better to return to the drawing board. Ditto for the direct taxes code, where simplicity, clarity and certainty should be reinstated by revisiting the earlier versions and recognising that the world of taxation has moved on.

International rankings of the cost of doing business and corruption reveal how challenging it is for economic activity to take place in India. Productive activity is confronted by bureaucracy that, by global standards, enjoys greater freedom from accountability and little need for specialisation. In the productive sector, what is crucial is to deepen competition. Why the reluctance to open up to international competition in the services sector? Can't we observe how difficult it is to receive insurance benefits, especially by the lower deciles when they make legitimate insurance claims? Have we not experienced better banking with more foreign bank branches becoming available? Has opening up single brand retail in clothes or shoes obliterated domestic sectors? Would not the supply chain benefit, and farmers be better off than having to suffer crops being abandoned for lack of transport or people to move them?

The prime minister said last Thursday: "The mindless atmosphere of negativity and pessimism that is sought to be created over ... corruption can do us no good." Also, "Experience has shown that bigticket corruption is mostly related to operations by commercial entities. It is, therefore, also proposed to include corporate failure to prevent bribery as a new offence on the supply side." The chaotic yet crowdpulling expressions against corruption that are gathering storm all around us point towards the need to not ignore the demand side either. The daily life of civil society has become near impossible. The lack of water and electricity even in upper class neighbourhoods recently brought out their denizens hurling stones and bricks. With the rains, dengue has made its inevitable return, nesting in stagnant water that isn't cleared despite being budgeted for. Urban slum dwellers pass 10 or more hours daily without electricity, and often receive just an hour of water. Let us not even ponder rural civic amenities.

I enter my neighbourhood. I see the bust of Netaji and the tricolour unfurling. I enter Rabindra Sarobar. I see youth in imaginative uniforms in a drill under a commanding officer of sorts. I move under a canopy of neem and gulmohar trees along the meandering Lakes to my right. Loudspeakers blare patriotic songs from across the Lakes. I see Scout troops standing at attention at a distance, and guests across the water at the Rowing Club gathered for the flagraising function.

I walk on. The sounds mellow. I find myself at a blue pandal set against an ample banyan tree and glistening waters. An orchestra is seated. It comprises six violins and a violin master, a cello, a viola, a percussionist, a synthesiser, and a guitar. Sanjib Mondal and his men, linked to the Calcutta School of Music Chamber Orchestra, and Youth Orchestra, are playing Scottish-Irish ballads familiar in Tagore operas. I sit down carefully amidst the attentive audience. There is chamber music; I recognise Mozart's Symphony #40 in G Minor reminiscent of *Itna na Mujhse Tu Pyar Badha*, sundry western pop of yesteryears, alternating with Tagore's marching songs as well as *Saare Jahan se Achha*. The programme ends with *Jana Gana Mana* to gentle applause.

I rise chastened with a sense of independence. People are celebrating by being out in droves. They have made the effort to organise enjoyable yet meaningful events. They seem to believe in India. Where else could you hear such a potpourri of world music? India is inclusive despite hiccups and heartburn. In spite of adversity, the poor do not loot. The startling mandated upward movements in the political and the commensurate social and educational status of the backward classes are unique to India. It gives Indians hope. Indians are an active people. Economic activity reigns over slothfulness. As I end my walk, I know why I keep returning to India and why nowhere else compares. It is the Indian peoples.

I have a pen pal whom I have never met. He reads what I write. As I lamented the lack of a next topic to write on, he emailed back, "It would be great if you can write on development that has taken place in India in the last decade. Our cities have become like global cities, infrastructure, including rural infrastructure, has improved much, public transport has seen a sea change, and our economy is still one of the fastest growing in the world. India is blessed. Can any country take care of a 120 crore population ... only India can do this with pride. I firmly believe that India should always think positive, act positive, as it can be the biggest economy in the next 30-40 years."

Business Standard, 15 October 2012.

51

A Walk from Kolkata to London?

The chief minister of West Bengal has proclaimed that she will convert Kolkata to London. The idea did not raise much interest or hope, but deserves consideration. To begin, she has had Kolkata's public spots, walls, park grilles, and road dividers painted in white and shocking blue—reminiscent of Mother Teresa—though, the other evening on television, Mamata explained that the blue was for the open sky, an acceptable enough explanation. There are also new streetlights and pavement tiles, though neither reveals the robustness that was the hallmark of older versions. Clearly, however, attempts are on at a certain level, of initiating and implementing decorative change.

Morning constitutionals in Kolkata, for example around Park Circus Maidan, or along stretches in the Ballygunge Lakes between Menoka Cinema and Anderson Club, give a glimpse of the challenges she faces. Night-time strolls along Southern Avenue and, after crossing the Tollygunge connector, to and beyond Kalighat, or onto Bhawanipur Road past the Greek Orthodox church, are no better. Alternative walking routes from Gariahat Junction to Park Circus to Park Street Extension, Mullick Bazaar, Linton Street, and into Dr Sundari Mohan Avenue (CIT Road) enhance the scale of complexity. Such extensive forays, despite demanding the use of all one's reflexes to avoid physical clashes with other pedestrians or animals or being run over by every manner of vehicle, raise the alertness level, enable engagement with one's immediate surroundings that car rides can never make possible, and facilitate contemplation that a drawing-room dialogue in Delhi would never encourage.

A walk around Park Circus Maidan reveals the segments of society that Kolkata embraces—from the corpulent upper class, of whom there are a handful, to the very bottom of the ladder, destitutes, bathed in dust, who cannot even sit upright from a perennial stupor. In between are layers of economic and social groups—energetic young joggers in cheap keds; couples who walk briskly or slowly; gossipers who sit and chat and possibly report taking long walks when back home; a myriad of boys who play cricket and occasionally football, march and drill in uniforms that need ironing, or cluster with their respective girlfriends; and elderly or amputated beggars who have the energy to beg, their money collected intermittently and openly by touts. A walk into the Maidan in the evening brings to view once again the young population thronging around tree trunks and floating in and out of religious festivities or country fairs.

A morning walk in the Lakes is quite different. The strollers are mainly upper- or upper-middle class, keeping pace in their Nike or Bata jogging shoes. The walking path along the long stretch of water is canopied by resplendent Gulmohar and other trees. The only bother is the possibility of bird droppings—for that could be the only reason why so many men and women wear caps as they walk in the shade. The bulging young population is not to be observed here. Just outside of this path, both inside and outside the Lakes, rubbish heaps pile up, and animal and human excreta have to be avoided.

A night walk from Southern Avenue through Kalighat and Bhowanipore begins to reveal the work to be done. Even Southern Avenue, boastfully declared to be the only remaining boulevard—garden-like greenery and flower beds in the narrow middle of a wide road—in Kolkata, has been abused. Some past local politician is said to be responsible for a grotesque construction in one such middle block that passes as a women's swimming pool, the exterior wall of which serves as a men's room; one block has been converted into a garbage sorter, for which the garbage is first collected there; another block has been partly taken over and built upon by the Kolkata corporation itself, and so on. Some time ago, a group of enthusiastic school children selected one block to clean up its garbage, and enthusiasts brought sandwiches and cold drinks for them. The project seems to have trailed off now.

As one approaches Kalighat, sights of the most abject poverty appear, defying description and making one wonder what happens to these families during April nor'westers, now in full sway. Behind one such family, one climbs a few steps to go into a boutique selling exquisite pieces of art and sculpture from Southeast Asia. They are a beauty to behold. It is easy to conclude that, for these poorest of the poor, it hardly matters if they are in the bottom 35, 30, or 25 per cent. The fact that a 62-year old society is willing to live with such abominable differences in living conditions without being able to pull itself up with its bootstraps, when matched with the perennial excuse that India has democracy, brings forth a measure of disbelief.

Getting on to a tramcar on Gariahat Road, skirting Park Circus into Park Street Extension and getting off at the crossing of Acharya Jagdish Chandra Bose Road and Linton Street exposes the victory of concrete over grass—for the lawns over which tramcars had plied have been paved over, facilitating the million footfalls and tyres that have to be accommodated along those familiar routes. Entering Linton Street, which forms a meandering H belt connecting A.J.C. Bose Road and CIT Road, is another eye-opener, with its mounds of garbage spilling over into its distributaries. The nausea that ensues is hard to control except for the prayer that it must dissipate soon.

A top Delhi technocrat once commented that there must be a PDS (public distribution system) ration shop every 50 yards in Kolkata. It remains as a metaphor for the distance between policymakers and the representative Indian. The shopping centres coming up—though their existence is not being questioned here—are for a negligible few. The vast majority of Calcuttans live a different life. The communists just had their congress in Kozhikode. Their statements remained tactical, shying away from matters that might be expected to be central to their concerns. West Bengal's communists came out as ineffectually as they had in preceding crucial episodes, such as the popular possibility of prime ministership of Jyoti Basu, or the continuance as Lok Sabha speaker of Somnath Chatterjee, succumbing to their Delhi bosses. Little can be expected from them.

Paradoxically, Mamata Banerjee's stridency in refusing to increase any burden on those with lower ability to pay is beginning to make sense. The solution is not to increase taxes, or indulge in more wasteful expenditure by expanding the budgets of pompous bureaucrats. The country should begin to challenge budget incrementalism and to demand more out of less. Efficiency has to be increased through monitoring and evaluation. There should be a budget freeze and squeeze across ministries. The international media—*Financial Times* and *The Economist* from the UK and *International Herald Tribune* (The New York Times) from the US to name some—have reached the point of ridicule when reporting on India, due to its corruption and lack of leadership and management. Drastic change is needed and can come only from within.

Ms Banerjee's dream can come true, but not through traditional means. She has to use imagination to achieve her goal. She has to reinvent the use of the latent workforce that is in view everywhere in Kolkata—armies of young people waiting to be called upon with a promise of recognition and involvement. Social, rather than merely political, engagement can be used as a contemporary tool in schools and colleges without exception or excuse for children of politicians or the rich. Appropriately-guided social projects should be included in the marking system.

Vitalising our youth is not merely a contemporary idea, however. Earlier generations, through socially motivated school and college programmes, were infused with a fervour that no amount of traditional accomplishments could diminish. Tasks included a variety of endeavours—taking care of the terminally ill in slums and government hospitals; helping people who met with accidents after passing a First Aid course; erecting tents for people in emergencies; learning Hindi through the Hindi Prachar Sabha in non-Hindi speaking regions; as well as hiking long distances, learning the constellations in the night sky to find one's way if lost, the Morse Code, swimming, cooking one's own meal, to name a few.

Ms Banerjee should show concrete steps towards re-engagement with societal development. She should continually express and maintain her interest in cleaning up Kolkata, without allocating excessive additional financial resources. She should benchmark her outcomes with successes in Bhopal, Chennai, Hyderabad and other Indian cities. Only after that can she realistically think of London. Second, she could clean up government hospitals from their prevailing diabolical state. Third, she should focus on the condition of school buildings and infrastructure. Fourth, she should encourage the painting of the facades of homes in designated areas under specific colour guidelines, as is done in Paris or La Boca in Buenos Aires in Argentina, or Santa Marta in Rio de Janeiro in Brazil or other global cities (why focus only on London?).[1] For this last task, she should empower and demand Kolkata's high society—whom she seems to be accessing in her other efforts—to take the lead, rather than directing only its Gulliveresque bureaucracy. Arousing the spirit of Ram Mohan, Anthony Kabiyal, Michael Madhusudan, Vivekananda, Vidyasagar, Netaji, Rani Rashmoni, Rabindranath, Nivedita, and other forbears from the mothballs in which they have been put to slumber over four decades, she must involve Kolkata's youth with specific tasks and witness how they perform.

Mamata should not stop imagining. But she must be specific and clear in defining programmes and methods, get society's involvement, and show positive outcomes. Otherwise she will not succeed. She is being closely watched, no longer for her spritely ways, but whether they can bring results.

1. See Kimmelman, Michael (2011). "Rescuing the Poor by Design", *The New York Times*, in *www.chinadaily.com*, 30 October, for more such urban projects across the world.

Business Standard, 16 April 2012.

52

Children's Condition: Wither Demographic Dividend?

India and the international community have been talking about the demographic dividend that India should reap until mid-century. United Nations Population Division data indeed reveal that the share of the working age group of 15-64 years in total population will grow in South Asia until 2040, in some until 2045, and in Afghanistan until 2075. The challenge is to convert this population into productive citizens through nutrition and education. It is just like the challenge of converting savings into productive investment rather than into non-performing assets as has emerged increasingly in Indian banking experience. Also, the rural-to-urban migration will be steep in all of South Asia, with urban India reaching 50 per cent of population by 2050, adding a further onerous dimension of absorptive capacity and implied social infrastructure—health and education—needs into this witch's brew.

Who will finance this need in India? In 2010, those with a daily expenditure of $10 to $100 a day comprised less than 5 per cent of India's population in contrast to 20 per cent for Sri Lanka.[1] This marginal economic class should find financing social infrastructure—nutrition and health—an uphill task unless every paisa is well spent in this endeavour. On top, the state of child nutrition and health is shocking. In 2005-06, 45 per cent of rural babies under three years were stunted, more than 40 per cent underweight, and more than 20 per cent wasted.[2] For urban babies the numbers were 10 to 20 per cent less bad. Mother's education had a strikingly salient

1. Ghani, Ejaz (2011). *Reshaping Tomorrow: Is South Asia Ready for the Big Leap.* World Bank. Washington DC: OUP. p.7.

2. *National Family Health Survey, 2005-06.*

effect on outcomes. Almost 55 per cent of babies of mothers who had not completed 10 years of education were stunted, 50 per cent underweight, and 25 per cent wasted. For mothers with that education, these numbers were 30 to 60 per cent less bad, quite a remarkable difference.

Education numbers appear less alarming. There is 100 per cent rural and urban primary (I-V) school enrolment for 6 to 10-year-olds. For secondary (VI-VIII) level, it is 80 per cent for rural and 90 per cent for urban; for IX-X, 60+ per cent for rural and 80+ per cent for urban and; for XI-XII, 40 per cent for rural and 60 per cent for urban.[3] Female attendance ratios decrease with levels of education, are 5 to 15 per cent less than those for male, but nevertheless are not as bad as one might expect.

Figure 52.1

Share of Age-Group 15-64 in Total Population

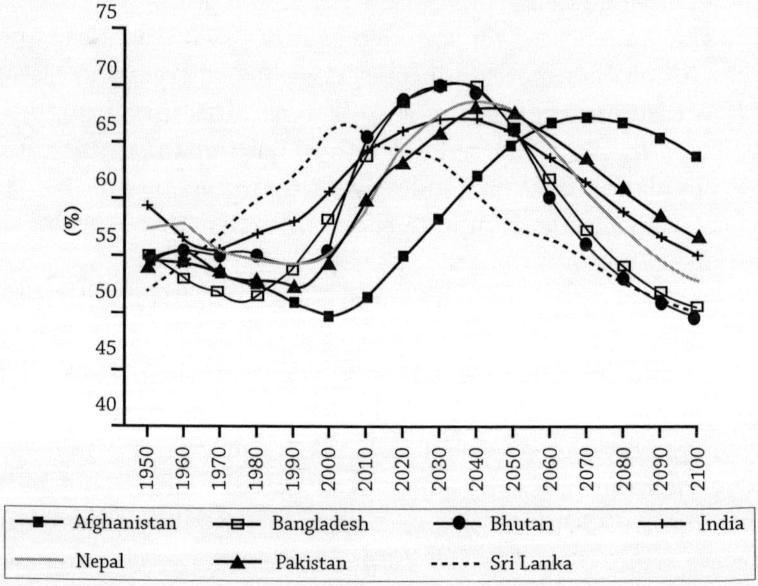

Source: United Nations Population Division data.

3. National Sample Survey, 2007-08, Education.

Discontinuation of education vitiates the enrolment figures. It increases with age, from negligible under 5 years of age, and 2½ per cent between 6 and 10 years, to 40 per cent among the 16-17 in rural, and 30 per cent in urban cohorts. The reasons for discontinuation are wrenching. Top reasons are financial constraints and disinterest. Strong corresponding reasons include the need to join the labour force and completion of desired education level. Discontinuation reveals a male-female divide on two grounds—marriage, and parents not interested in further studies of females. Thus, while Indian children are enrolling, many of them leave before completion reflecting the need to work primarily for males, or because females are packed off to marry; and the vicious cycle of underage, undernourished mothers bearing undernourished babies keeps repeating. Some government programmes such as midday meals have helped retain children in school despite their many challenges and shortcomings, but the quality that makes education interesting is also a major factor in discontinuation. More revealing information can be gleaned from the surveys cited. From statistics alone it is clear that a demographic dividend cannot be realised at the current rates of nutrition and education.

Moving from the quantity of education, its quality is particularly suspect by Western standards for the majority of even privileged children. There is little standardisation in curricula, lesson plans or requirements, and testing varies widely. Even within a state, the method varies in different schools. One pervading expectation is that students should be able to memorise rather than be allowed to think freely or innovate.

The questions to ask here are: are we successfully changing systemic rote learning so that students are able to think independently? Can they appreciate a painting or have time to read a book and judge its merit by the time they are out of school? Are they allowed to express themselves, even if chaotically, if they wish to without being reprimanded? Can they critique the teaching of their teachers in class?

An incongruity appears to be the emphatic commendation of high achievers and a focus on the poorly faring—paradoxically, lucky—

students whose performance needs to be improved in the interest of the school's reputation. The middling majority is, more often than not, left to fend for itself, as it neither brings any glory nor poses any serious threat of disrepute. What lessons exist from other countries?

Figure 52.2

The Reasons for Discontinuing Education (2007-08)

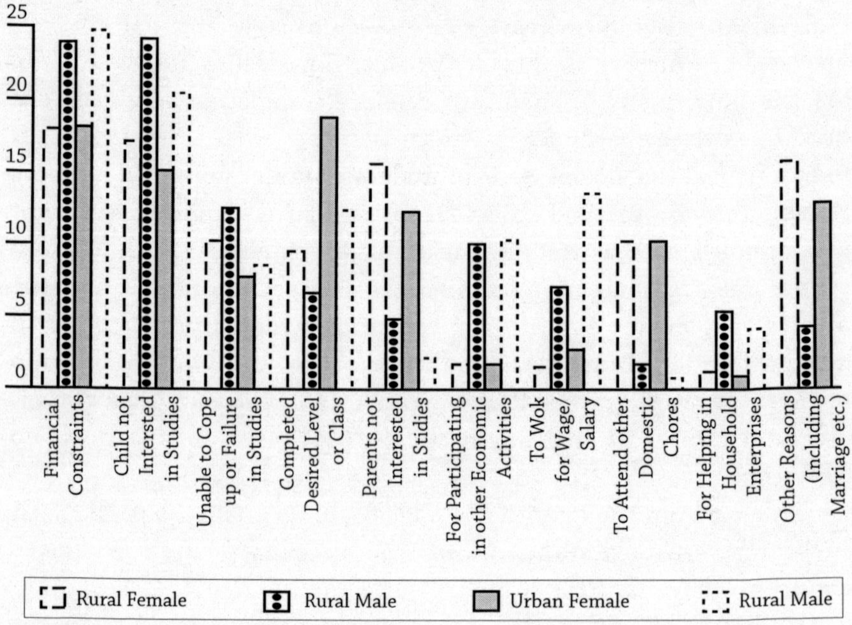

Source: National Sample Survey, 2007-08, Education.

Let us remind ourselves that we celebrated Education Day this month. To take up the challenge of turning a probable demographic nightmare into a dividend, we have to be on a war footing. That could occur only with strong control and rapid dissipation of moral hazard, leakage, graft and corruption. That should, in turn, improve public expenditure productivity and outcomes by monitoring if school funds are being siphoned off or a child is being robbed of the right to a school meal. There is little time to lose or to get to work.

Business Standard, 21 November 2011.

53

West Bengal vs Tamil Nadu

Chennai and Kolkata, where I equally divided my school days, are two of my favourite places. I like to recall them as Madras and Calcutta, with their unique cultures, habits, beliefs and practices. Calcutta's Park Street lined up Peking, Waldorf, Skyroom, Flurys, Kwality and others where we would be hauled once a month; the adults also had the option of Mocambo and Trincas, made famous by novelist Sarat Chandra Chatterjee's *Parineeta*. Hollywood, (Calcutta's) Tollywood and Bollywood films were aplenty, shown in numerous cinema halls at 3, 6 and 9 pm with 10 am Western movies on Sundays. There were many pujas and gala weddings that extended through the evening, sometimes into the wee hours of the morning. Cousins and friends would regularly visit from elsewhere for education or medical purposes. At Hindi High School, we sang Saraswati Vandana every morning. The intricacies of yoga, arts and crafts, music and dance—and not just traditional mathematics, history or erudite English—were taught by famous personalities of the teaching profession.

Arriving in Madras in 1960, Kwality was the only restaurant. Pal and Savera came years later, where I discovered Usha Iyer, who later became famous as Usha Uthup. Weddings took place in the morning, putting my mother in a quandary over how much to dress my sisters and herself. Accompanying evening receptions tended to serve Coca Cola, betel nut, *beerha*, *kumkumam*, *chandanam*, *vibhuti* and jasmine. My father explained that the best meal was breakfast and that dinner should be light. Gestures were new: a rapid fist movement as a generic inquiry from domestic help would have my mother reeling. Slowly, she learnt some Tamil words, though she was eventually sent a domestic aid from Calcutta after word about a crisis travelled back.

I joined Don Bosco school. I recited *Our father who art in heaven* every morning as did every Tamil-Brahmin or Dalit classmate. We were taught by Czech, Indian, Irish and Italian priests. They also taught us to cycle, play tennis and table tennis, and swim—sometimes in their cassocks—at scout camps. Though I could sense my nationalist father's unease about his children going to missionary schools, my mother's responsibility to her children easily allowed her to put us in "English medium" schools given my father's transferable service.

My reading and music interests broadened to include Jules Verne, the Beatles and Beethoven. Films were few and far between. There were *Beau Geste* and *Seven Days in May*, but I went with classmates to watch *Parthal Pasithirum*, *Nenjil Oar Alayam* or *Kadalikkai Nerum Illai*. My parents were perplexed, though my father was distinctly happy at my "national integration". Much to the chagrin of my mother, who had to help me make up for lost lessons, my father would take us out of school willy-nilly when he went on a trip to the interiors in an air-conditioned bus or train for his work. He believed that it would give us superior education. He could not have done better in exposing us to temple sculptures and ablutions, taut ethnic food, dresses (*veshti* for me and *pawarai* for my sisters), bharatanatyam arangetrams, music, kachheri season and temple festivals, when a platform boat would float round the temple tank with Carnatic vocalists and instrumentalists.

My attachment to both places continues intact. Over the last two decades, however, the impression is that there has been a decline of West Bengal and a rise of Tamil Nadu. I would want them to be on a par, partial as I am to both. Tables 53.1, 53.2 and 53.3 (from the Reserve Bank of India, Central Statistical Organisation, Planning Commission and *Economic Survey*) compare the two states.

Table 53.1

Selected Indicators

	1981-90	*1991-00*	*2001-09*
Growth in NSDP (%) #			
Tamil Nadu	3.7	6.3	6.2
West Bengal	4.8	6.7	6.3
All States	5.6	5.6	7.0
Per Capita NSDP Growth (%)			
Tamil Nadu	3.9	5.2	5.3
West Bengal	2.7	4.8	5.1
All States	3.2	3.5	5.4
Revenue Expenditure as Percentage to GSDP			
Tamil Nadu	14.3	15.8	14.9
West Bengal	11.2	12.6	14.0
All States	11.4	12.6	12.9
Capital Outlay as Percentage to GSDP			
Tamil Nadu	1.0	0.9	1.9
West Bengal	0.9	1.0	0.8
All States	1.9	1.5	2.1
Development Expenditure as Percentage to GSDP			
Tamil Nadu	14.0	12.5	10.5
West Bengal	9.6	9.5	8.5
All States	11.2	10.1	9.6
Social Sector Expenditure as Percentage to GSDP			
Tamil Nadu	7.1	7.3	6.6
West Bengal	6.0	6.2	5.6
All States	5.5	5.7	5.7
Per Capita Development Expenditure (Rupees)			
Tamil Nadu	459	1524	3677
West Bengal	319	942	2273
All States	417	1227	3152

Note: # These growth rates for 1971-1980 are 3.8, 2.1 and 2.7.

Table 53.2

Deficit and Debt

	1999-2002	*2003-2006*	*2007-2009*
Deficit/GSDP			
Tamil Nadu	-3.7	-2.1	-2.3
West Bengal	-7.5	-5.0	-4.5
All States	-5.2	-3.7	-3.0
Public Debt/GSDP			
Tamil Nadu	25	27	25
West Bengal	40	48	43
All States	36	40	33

Table 53.3

Social Indicators

	1961	*1991*	*2001*	*2008*
Infant Mortality Rate (per 1000 live birth)				
Tamil Nadu	86	57	49	31
West Bengal	95	71	51	35
All States	115	80	66	53
Literacy Rates				
Tamil Nadu	36	63	73	
West Bengal	34	58	69	
All States	28	52	65	
Gross Enrolment Ratio (Classes I-VIII)				
Tamil Nadu	-	-	95	115
West Bengal	-	-	86	97
All States	-	-	82	100
	1973-78	*1983-88*	*1993-00*	*2004-05*
Percentage of Population Below Poverty Line				
Tamil Nadu	55	48	28	18
West Bengal	62	50	31	21
All States	53	42	31	22

In the 1990s, economic growth of Tamil Nadu and West Bengal was higher than all the other states but fell below them in the 2000s. It's heartening that per capita growth in West Bengal has almost caught up with Tamil Nadu, but the issues remain. West Bengal's revenue expenditure as a percentage of GSDP (gross state domestic product) increased more rapidly and its capital outlay as a percentage of GSDP declined, while the latter for Tamil Nadu increased significantly. West Bengal's development expenditure as a percentage of GSDP and social-sector expenditure as a percentage of GSDP are quite below all states while those of Tamil Nadu are far above. West Bengal's per capita development expenditure has improved but is far below that of Tamil Nadu.

West Bengal's fiscal situation is worse. Deficit as a percentage of GSDP has improved but remains double that of Tamil Nadu. Also, the public debt is nearly double. On both indices, West Bengal is far worse than the national average while Tamil Nadu is far superior. It is safe to conclude that West Bengal's growth and per capita growth have been more on the back of posterity than Tamil Nadu's.

Also, a comparison of social indicators reveals certain facts. In both states, infant mortality and literacy rates have remained better than the rest, though West Bengal has lagged behind Tamil Nadu. But it's inexplicable how between 2001 and 2008 West Bengal's school enrolment ratio fell below all states. Finally, the percentage of population below poverty line improved in both states. Both states were ahead of the rest up to the 1980s. But Tamil Nadu improved above all states in the next two decades, while West Bengal just managed to reach that level. The next government will have a harder time in West Bengal than in Tamil Nadu. It should increase school enrolment and, more widely, reduce the inter-generational burden.

Business Standard, 09 April 2011.

54

Water Wars: Yesterday, Today and Tomorrow

Thirst for water has expressed itself among competing societies for millennia. In India it has emerged in grotesque terms in the last two decades. It has not mattered much to an inured Indian society when poor farmers commit suicide by the hundreds in Vidarbha or elsewhere. Not that long back, the state government's interest in an enquiry to trace the use of thousands of crores of rupees spent to achieve one per cent of budgeted irrigation objectives appeared to be quashed by the same political party at the Centre possibly reflecting that the coffers had been managed by an allied party in the central coalition.

Water pollution has affected parts of India in a particularly harmful manner. The granary bowl of India, Punjab, once the pride of the country and the home of the Green Revolution, today stands vitiated by chemicals in its soil, its farmers impoverished and, from all accounts, being obliged to seek sustenance from the worst imaginable sources of income including the transportation—and lamentably even the consumption—of drugs from across the border. A state that was also the pride of India for its jawans, now amazes with its youth easily lamenting the long wait for immigration visas to Canada, New Zealand, the UK or the US.

Another emerging phenomenon is water wars. West Bengal's unwillingness to share water with culturally comparable Bangladesh, her neighbour across the Ganges/Padma, even while the Centre has been willing to share, reflects the emotions that fear of water scarcity can stir locally even if far flung Delhi can appear charitable. After all Delhi is not affected materially by magnanimous gestures.

The latest eruption in Karnataka is somewhat different in that farmers (though not those from Gulbarga) of the state are better off than those in Vidarbha. Kannadiga farmers would not have revolted unless they seriously feared bankruptcy if they shared water with Tamil Nadu. Thus the genesis was more economic than ethnic in particular reflecting that Kannada-, Malayalam-, Tamil- and Telugu-speaking peoples have lived by and large harmoniously in the vast lands of Karnataka for centuries.

But it would be myopic to ignore the intensifying local perception that ongoing influx into Karnataka is the outcome of poor management of floods and drought in other states. Bengaluru—and other towns—have become a catchment for employment not just for IT (Information Technology) or other white-collar professions, but for barbers, carpenters, cooks, movers, security staff and other blue-collar professions from Bihar, Jharkhand, Odisha, Rajasthan, West Bengal and elsewhere. The collapse of public service delivery of reasonable roads or collection of garbage that plagues Bengaluru is regularly attributed to immigrant influx than to corruption.

These erroneous beliefs and convictions comprise the ingredients of turning an economic into an ethnic conflict. Characteristically, there is little anticipation, so unprepared has India been in the analysis or preparedness for emergencies of this type. To recall, India suffered the worst violent episode in human history during Partition. Though that reflected religious differences, religion does not have to be the only separator. It is not as though ethnic incidents are not already occurring in Bengaluru against Keralites in particular. At the moment, it does not have official sanction of course.

That instantaneous conversion from economic to ethnic was starkly witnessed in Yugoslavia not that long ago. Admittedly Yugoslavia had been pieced together by the Allied Powers—Soviet Union, the UK, the US—at the end of the Second World War, bringing together Serbs, Germans, Croats, Slavs, Romans, Greeks, from the Eastern Orthodox Church, Catholics, Muslims and so on. Marshal Josip Tito (recall the founders of the Non-Alignment Movement—Gamal Nasser, Jawaharlal Nehru, Suharto, Tito—now just about defunct) subsequently built a modern economy with robust economic growth and social integration with cross-ethnic marriages a common phenomenon.

Economic dissension began with the mainly germanic Slovenians complaining of having to subsidise the rest of Yugoslavia. It became a war of economic resources. The economy began sliding with hyper-inflation around the corner. Slovenia, the western-most province contiguous to Austria, declared independence. In its worst revelation of its own ethnic preferences (until then hidden since its diabolical expressions during the Second World War), Germany immediately recognised Slovenia and brought it into the European Union in blatant contradiction of its much expressed pan-European vision. Croatia, the next contiguous western province, followed suit and its nationhood was also recognised. (Recall their fascist governments during the Third Reich)

Yugoslavia crumbled. Serbs who had been the dominant race viewed this as an affront. The next provinces to declare independence were dealt with harshly. Bosnia-Herzegovina—including its capital Sarajevo, an idyllic hideaway for a bygone Winter Olympics—was reduced to rubble. Cross-ethnic marriages, even existing ones, were terminated. Worse, concentration camps were built to starve and shoot men and boys to eradicate Islam or any ethic variegation. The province did get independence eventually. Other areas—little portions Kosovo, Macedonia, Montenegro—became rump states, while a few Serbs were taken to the International Court of Justice to be tried for genocide. But the original concept of Yugoslavia had died a horrible death. By contrast, the former Soviet Union did better in the process of its break-up though that equilibrium was not maintained reflecting continuing conflicting interests and covert and overt interference from the not-so-bygone First and Second Worlds.

Thus history has demonstrated time and again that economic—resource—wars, if not reasonably, rationally and quickly contained, result in ethnic wars with disastrous outcomes. The Indian water wars need examination in that light since buried in them are unanticipated, indeed unimaginable, outcomes for the Indian nation. Those who oppose economic progress have to reconsider their position. The Narmada Dam and other dams must be built in a country such as India. The solution is not to stop construction but to ensure environmentally friendly and technically robust construction and completion of rehabilitation—and that these are not thwarted by corruption. Admittedly, international indices put India's corruption at such high levels that it would be foolhardy to convey that it will be an easy task.

Business Standard, 11 October 2016.

VIII

Political Economy

55

A Socio-historical Perspective of Brexit

Brexit may have shocked but it should not have surprised. The phenomenon cannot be understood without a socio-historical context. Hence the focus here while, in a second article, Indo-UK economic ramifications will be provided.

If Delhi instructed how Bengalis should prepare the head of rohu for auspicious occasions or Tamilians were told off on their tayeersadam, it would be tantamount to what Brussels has been doing to the British, in particular, and to the Europeans, in general, over decades. A Cypriot closed down his hill-top family restaurant that fed multitudes of tourists and locals since he could not comply with the diktats of eurocrats with little knowledge of local modes, yet comfortable in designing and implementing guidelines across Europe. Even the Romans knew better than to consolidate social habits across their empire; they lived in their own style while allowing denizens to live the way they wished, however gross they might have appeared to the Romans. Indeed, English colonials went a step further and practised separation.

There is no doubt that the English have felt left out of decision-making in Brussels. Having ruled the world until not so long ago, the strain of occupying third place after Germany and France in almost all matters and decisions was apparent. Deepak Lal's emotion-filled article in *Business Standard* dated 27 June 2016, provided grist to this argument. Indeed, the lack of fairness descends even to ordinary life, for example, in the unfair ordering earned by Britain in the annual euro song contest in which Britain routinely ends up last or second last. Such low positioning seems unfair, having watched it for decades whenever chancing upon it, albeit more for its innovative stage sets and attire than for its musicality.

Intra-UK, it was not surprising that Scotland voted to stay in the EU—the opposite of England. England and Scotland merged only three centuries back (1707), before which there was constant war mainly reflecting differences between Catholicism and the newly established Church of England, epitomised by the 16th century hanging of Mary Queen of Scots by her cousin Elizabeth I, Queen of England, in 1587. One could arguably attribute the deep differences to Hadrian, the warrior-philosopher Roman emperor who, almost two millennia earlier, circa 122 AD, constructed Hadrian's Wall across the narrowest stretch of Britain, thereby successfully keeping the barbarians—apologetically the Scots—out to jostle in the cold North. The English soon were happy enough to don togas and take in the salts in the natural baths of Bath and other habitats in this farthest western Roman colony.[1]

Almost the majority of Scots—perhaps not the majority—see themselves as Scottish first. And, by their Brexit vote, they revealed that they view themselves as Europeans second and, as British in isolation, third. This contrasts with the urbane Londoner where Scots are part and parcel of Canary Wharf, the financial district what with, even historically, it was the Scots—since their merger with the English—who led with financial sector innovation, growth and reform. Tellingly perhaps, the Large Business Service office for the banking sector of Her Majesty's Revenue and Customs (HMRC) is located in Edinburgh. That is only one area in which the Scots have led or contributed, others being science and technology, horticulture and pisciculture from Aberdeen and Dundee towards the south, leave alone the more recent contribution of the North Atlantic oil industry based entirely off the coast of Scotland, or their prominent appearance in top politics, the most recent examples being Gordon Brown and Alistair Darling, prime minister and chancellor (finance minister), respectively, of the last Labour government. Thus, in Glasgow and Edinburgh, the thinking was different from London

1. Danziger, D. and N. Purcell (2006). *Hadrian's Empire*. London: Hodder.

and led by confidence. Indeed, Scottish cities went along with their agrarian relatives in the Scottish plains, where barley for their famed whiskey abounds, while voting in English hills and dales contrasted starkly with English large cities.

Yet, given that the outcome of the Brexit referendum is bound to have implications, its process begs commentary. There is no point in blaming the departed prime minister; indeed he deserves accolades for exiting with head held high though he could be perceived as responsible for calling the bluff on Brexit and being landed with a bitter pill to swallow. More inexplicable is that such a decision was based on a simple majority among only those who voted—70 per cent—so that actually less than 37 per cent of the entire population voted demonstrably in favour of Brexit and yet the UK has to leave Europe.

Further incomprehensible is that such an irreversible step occurred with Parliament playing no tatonnement role. It was just one-shot voting by the populace reminiscent of democracy in ancient Greece though, even there, voting rights were truncated through criteria. It thus remains incredulous to outsiders how Great Britain could have committed such a blunder. Could it have been the relative youth of the outgoing dispensation, pointing unmistakably to the value of experience, though this is not to say that leaders should only go out horizontally as occurs routinely in, let us say, the eastern democracies?

Finally, one should provide reason as to why Brexit could be a blunder for, after all, a 15 per cent currency depreciation should provide Britain space to catch up on exports, thereby raising GDP and correcting its trade imbalance with many economies including India. I shall provide economic reasons why Britain is theoretically in an ideal position to make up for lost time and catch up with emerging economies. However, having banished European workers from its shores and deflecting Asian professionals from joining the work force after receiving British degrees, the question to ask is if they themselves are now ready to get up, tighten their belts, and go to work. As I argued in *Business Standard* dated 17 May 2016, under the prevailing system of subsidies that protect unwilling and non-workers, Brexit is likely to remain at best a Pyrrhic victory.

Business Standard, 23 August 2016.

56

Vicissitudes of Modern Democracies

In March I was in London for a biannual talk at the Attlee room of the House of Lords to which tax heads of multinational companies and some lords and diplomats show up to listen and discuss the state of the world. Polite and seemingly enthusiastic as they always seem, this time I perceived a certain belligerence in their midst. Over the week, I perceived a similar discomfort among the British public and, placing them in the overall European context, Europe also seemed to be boiling over. What is happening there?

At the moment, the crucial matter in UK politics is Brexit or the referendum within the next couple of months that will decide whether Britain will be inside or outside Europe. Currently it is attracting opposite views. David Cameron, Prime Minister, comes on TV frequently to caution compatriots of the folly of leaving the European Union (EU). In turn, he was cautioned by François Hollande, French President, that, were Britain to jump ship, France may, in effect, throw open its Calais refugee camp that incarcerates would be African and West Asian immigrants to the UK thus enabling them to swim across the English Channel to find jobs.

Boris Johnson, Mayor of London and prime ministerial hopeful, is vocal about favouring Brexit though he should well know that few Britons want the jobs that East Europeans take up in the UK. But Mr Johnson's strategy has brought him up in the queue to succeed Mr Cameron. He knows that Britons do not like to be directed from Brussels by eurocrats. After all, "Rule Britannia rule the waves; Britons never shall be slaves." (A tabloid slipped out a titbit, true or not, that Her Highness is in favour of Brexit). Those in favour seem at peace ignoring the benefits of being in the EU—guaranteed exports of British products and continuous import of cheap farm and other labour from Eastern Europe that keep the wheel of British productivity going as service sector and farm employers insist. British youth by and large consider such jobs to be menial. They seem willing to remain jobless what with mindless state subsidies. When visiting the UK, a good anthropology pill is to watch any episode of the Jeremy Kyle Show—morning, afternoon or evening, so popular is this show presenting family encounters that test the DNA of absconding young jobless fathers.

The second source of discomfort in London was the anticipation that George Osborne, UK Chancellor (finance minister), would present a terrible Budget to Parliament on March 16. They had reason for fear. Earlier, he had attempted to cut back pensions when retirees cut him down. Sad that no Indian economist or bureaucrat seemed to have informed Finance Minister Arun Jaitley of the English calamity on pension reform. If the FM had been informed, he could have avoided the introduction of, and quick retreat from, his own pension reform in its presented form. That is why it is important to reconsider the Direct Tax Code in full once again, rather than dismissing it. But that is a separate story. FM has also adhered to his fiscal deficit number as has the Chancellor arduously, a fiscal option I myself had earlier praised on paper. But a point fiscal deficit cannot be a magic bullet reflecting the receding British economic climate or the deplorable state of Indian farmers. Economic conditions have changed. Whether virtue has become obstinacy becomes a legitimate question.

But there were also good lessons from the Chancellor's March 16 Budget. London barely took notice of the announcement to reduce the headline corporate tax rate from the prevailing 20 per cent (recently reduced from 28) to, hold your breath, 17 per cent in 2020. The boredom probably reflects pre-Budget stakeholder discussions of intended policy changes revealing the maturity of all parties affected by tax. Also uncelebrated were announced road maps to reduce standard deductions of income tax through 2017 or lower tax on small businesses from 2017. The Budget contained many more early announcements for India to glare at.

It is not possible to close a discussion on Europe without lamenting the tragedy of Shakespearean proportions that Angela Merkel, German Chancellor (head of government), is facing. Caught unawares by the intensity of voter derision in Germany's March regional elections, her party lost considerable ground while she remained unmoved from keeping German borders open for refugees even as her competitors promised to build virtual walls. Promising easier EU accession to a conservative regime such as Recep Erdogan's if he stopped the flow of refugees from Turkey also seemed ill-conceived. It is improbable that her European colleagues will support her when they have consistently revealed their bias against Turkey's accession even with earlier pro-Western Turkish regimes. Ms Merkel had demonstrated a rare combination of being likeable and being able to yield results. It is sad to see her in dire straits now.

Finally, a third source of English discomfiture was the question, would a Presidential system be better (I supposed such as in the Unites States). I raised the proverbial alarm expected from a foreigner, what would happen to the constitutional monarchy? It was politely set aside. Hence the US developments call attention. Shocked are speaking Americans of the ongoing Presidential campaign as to who among Republicans is so disgruntled as to produce a surging majority for Donald Trump. Is it too surprising though when Americans voted in George W. Bush for a second term and, for that matter, even Barack Obama could win a second term. That Mr Obama ascended immediately after Mr Bush could be perceived as anti-incumbency. But as argued, Americans often vote in second term Presidents and may even vote for third terms (Franklin Roosevelt) if that were still allowed. And the current or past Congress, the legislative branch of the US government, has refused to work with Mr Obama. This again provides good reason for India not to blindly praise Presidential systems for it would be a road merely from one logjam to another.

Business Standard, 10 April 2016.

57

Indo-UK Economic History in Space Age

Controversies in Indo-British economic history appear occasionally, swinging like a pendulum. Recently, reparations to compensate for colonial actions were demanded in an Oxbridge accent while, not that long back, admiration for the same was articulated in an unmistakable home grown lilt, both at Oxford University, it is likely, to the amusement of the grand masters of irony. British swings are equally striking. There is a statue on Trafalgar Square, indisputable heart of London, next to Nelson's Column, their most revered war hero, of H. Havelock K.C.B. condoling him "And his brave companions in arms during the campaign in India 1857" thus, "Soldiers, Your labours, Your privations, Your sufferings and Your values will not be forgotten by a grateful country". The same people have just usurped an icon and installed a statue of Mohandas Karamchand Gandhi aside their Parliament not farther than a kilometre from the first, enabled by the endeavours of an English Lord of Indian origin. Gandhi is the same person whose staying alive had been openly lamented by an irritable Winston Churchill, their much venerated warlike, Wartime Prime Minister.

The objective today is to address the issue of reparations. Admittedly one reason for its impossibility is the enormity of the scale of economic exploitation. Historical works such as Madhusree Mukherjee's *Churchill's Secret War* (2010, Tranquebar Press) and Partha Chatterjee's *National Thought and the Colonial World* (1999, Oxford University Press) are but a couple of instances that leave an indelible mark regarding its mind boggling dimensions. Earlier economic historians such as Nabendu Sen and Tapan Roy Chaudhury authored cryptic works demonstrating the nature of constrictive trade and other economic relationships that had prevailed. Thus, while ceding land to the British well beyond reasonable reparations in financial terms for the wars they waged was commonplace, its "compensating variation", an economist's concept to measure equal satisfaction, is surely not achievable in present times.

A deconstruction is nevertheless warranted, to reveal what may lie in the proverbial darkness under the lamp. The flip side of reparations generally left unconsidered should not be ignored. Take Victoria Memorial, that marble edifice in Calcutta commemorating the reign of the empress. It was constructed by Curzon, dissector of Bengal, with a preponderance of funds from willing (and, let us hope, some not-so-willing) Indian zamindars. In financial terms, what would be the "net" reparation for, certainly Indian acquiescence if not abetment in perpetration should be brought into the equation? Could it be denied that economic exploitation was successful substantially or partially due to Indian attitudes towards, and actions against, fellow Indians? If so, should the remaining properties of such Indian ex royals be expropriated today? Since few today would accede to that possibility even as a principle, the argument favouring reparations from Britain recedes pari passu.

Economic exploitation has many facets, consideration of which brings to light further challenges to resolution. It may be conceptually difficult to understand, leave alone convey, but egregious exploitation is often perpetrated by government itself through its misdirected tax-subsidy policies. They in effect expropriate resources away from the poor, sometimes the abjectly poor, for providing subsidies to industry that overwhelmingly benefit the middle and upper classes in the organised sector. To ensure that the social marginal productivity of such government action exceed the loss suffered by losers (at even the very last margin) is a mammoth task. Negative outcomes may be unintended or inadvertent but they do occur, mainly through a lack or failure to analyse, measure or track the ramifications of government policies on the poor. Anyway, the rich and powerful have infinitely more capacity to press government policy and action in their favour. And, indeed, the two elements become more conjoint every day.

Indeed exploitation of yet another dimension existed in our midst millennia prior to the arrival of any colonist. This is exploitation through exclusion that ensures economic benefits to excluders. Britannia cannot be exclusively crowned for racism. As early as in the *Mahabharata*, Draupadi refused to let Karna participate in her *swayambara* reflecting the uncertainty of his caste, a social and economic limitation that Karna could never surmount even from his birth mother. Catapulting to just two centuries back when, in an act of exclusion with utmost finality, the top caste burnt pubescent widows alive at the funeral pyre even as their own octogenarians married them and then died natural deaths. If modern India were to recognise the role of Bentinck and others in monetary terms who took risks to eradicate such barbarisms aplenty, what counter reparation value would that recognition represent in today's measurement scale?

Jumping to today, untouchables still are restricted from walking in front of, leave alone entering, certain temples. At the other end, shiploads of casteless Indians have been free to settle in the ex-colonist's shores and to never look back. That densely populated country has not closed its doors to space-age Indian youth from IIMs, IITs and NLUs who are found without fail in London pubs come close-of-business Friday. Wonder what causes, and continues to cause, that relentless westward march by the progeny of Midnight's Children who certainly don't seem deterred by the absence of reparations.

For argument's sake, even if reparations were agreed to as a principle, who would negotiate and how would the amounts be determined? Based on experience, India's incapacity to transparently negotiate requires no underlining even without mentioning the continuing immeasurable suffering of the victims of botched negotiations. Contrast this to the United States' recently demonstrated ability in the case of British Petroleum which will be obliged to adequately compensate for environmental and other costs of its disastrous oil spill.

Thus, reparations cannot be unidirectional. They are not practically feasible, financially calculable, negotiable, or efficiently and equitably managed. Suffice it to say that, on this soil, let in-depth analysis of Indo-British history continue while admitting that much of the data for such analysis reflects meticulous pre-independence data collection and maintenance. Keeping the issue alive and never to let it die is apt punishment, not reparations which would imply absolution. And woe to a mere statement of regret or apology which would comprise the easiest way out. But yes, if the Indian High Commissioner in London is tasked to negotiate the removal of that statue from Trafalgar Square, and he is successful, that would be acceptable expression of penance for their colonial history. Let it be known that Havelock's removal had been discussed by a London mayor who said that he did not even know who this man had been but the matter stalled due to local controversy. Since on these shores it is known who he was, it is felt that he may be removed.

History need not be expunged; neither should it be rehashed for good reason. Americans had their Boston Tea Party but did not insist later on compensation to counter "taxation without representation". Rather, they soon included their ex-colonial masters in their own global aspirations and strategies, reflecting the inexorable post-independence rise in their own economic and political fortunes. History can be squeezed only to a very limited extent. The clever would use it to their advantage in charting a future course and creating new history.

Business Standard, 18 August 2015.

58

Thoughts as Ideas

If one is called a thought leader, should one take it as a compliment even while fancying oneself as a nitty-gritty technocrat? That description is intriguing and worth exploring. In the minimum, there are two aspects to thought leadership: (1) generating ideas that change the way others behave or view a situation; and (2) communicating these ideas successfully.

On thought or idea creation, F. Czerniawska has observed in 2007 that a conducive environment for idea creation is essentially about a culture that allows as many individuals as possible to innovate. Thus, Google offices are laid out with laid-back furniture, delectable food and indoor games and magazines that make a "creative culture" and encourage brainstorming and innovation, with propitious outcomes. However, such a culture change cannot be a realistic, short-term or passive goal in established bureaucracies, though the "open office" concept is now becoming prevalent. An active strategy is called for to create a culture which encourages the generation of ideas.

Addressing thought leadership, R. Ryde in 2007 put forward the concept of "thinking channels". Humans use few ways to view and analyse a problem, automatically restricting the ideas created. Take deficit thinking. It is perhaps the most common and hard to break: finding faults and weaknesses is often associated with intelligence or rigour. So, colleagues immediately see problems with an idea. This prevents ideas being suggested. Second is common sense thinking: solutions use general or inexpert knowledge, particularly prevalent in areas that have few specialists in their field or high turnover of staff. Third is equity thinking: using consistency between groups as an overriding principle. This reduces ideas to the lowest common denominator. And fourth is binary thinking: presenting decisions as a choice between two extremes, using it as a strategic tool to force an agreement, ignoring alternatives that could realise the benefits from other options.

Considering alternative approaches is essential to creating innovative ideas. First is strength-based thinking: what is working well? Where has progress been made? Second is insight thinking: it relies on the insights of informed and experienced practitioners which may not generate brand new solutions but, rather, proven solutions from past experience. Third is 360-degree thinking: it views problems from different angles rather than focusing on the views of one particular group. Fourth is reintegrated thinking: it asks how we can integrate the benefits of different options.

Ryde concludes the obvious: the best way to influence the culture of an organisation is through senior managers leading by example. Infosys is an obvious example. "The long shadow of leadership" should supplement traditional thought channels with more creative ones. Then the organisation will follow, thus moving forward the overall idea generation culture. Czerniawska highlights that the road map to follow should be based on internal knowledge management processes. Thus the experiences across a large organisation would be aggregated to identify problems that persistently need solving, data to be analysed and solutions that could be generalised.

A growing demand for a strong evidence base would follow, with more emphasis on robust quantitative analysis rather than mere viewpoints and case studies. To enable this requires time and resources. In turn, it is important that leaders demonstrate a commitment to idea creation—giving staff the time required to generate the products and recognising those achievements. A primitive bureaucracy, on the other hand, avoids the recognition or use of analysis and allocates little resources to it. This is a poor choice for a bureaucracy to make.

How should such obstacles be avoided? At the outset, I highlighted effective communication. In a bureaucracy, those with the most influence are both short on time and bombarded with information. So, how could ideas from below get heard? Czerniawska suggests some ways. First is timing and salience: an idea must offer an actionable solution to a problem that is currently on a senior manager's or policymaker's agenda. Second is that it must be a new idea: repackaging old ones will not suffice. Third, an idea must be supported by evidence: while case studies help, mature ideas need significant analysis and evidence. Fourth is regular face-to-face discussion: it enables thought leaders to identify what senior leaders' major problems and priorities are, and to follow it up with new ideas as alternative solutions.

What are the pitfalls to be avoided? In 2009, J. Owen pointed to some of them. The first pitfall is providing "problem-free solutions": the use of latest fashionable ideas without addressing the concern or solving the problem. Second is providing "problem-free analysis": presenting technical analysis without considering which parts contribute to the solution. Third is confusing symptoms with the problem itself: solutions should be targeted at underlying problems rather than the symptoms.

Thus, I understand that the inexact science of thought leadership boils down to these essential aspects: first, creating ideas and successfully communicating them to others. A culture conducive to idea creation can be stimulated through leaders adopting new approaches to solving problems supplemented by structured knowledge management processes. Second, the key to successfully reaching ideas to influential senior leaders is to understand their priorities and then convey new ideas to them. For this, alternative channels need to be forged to reach senior leaders. Third, thought leadership involves taking some risk, moving away from a risk-averse bureaucratic stance. In 2008, M. Goldsmith and M. McLeod pointed out that it takes repeated exposure, apart from time and effort, to get recognition as a thought leader. I agree with them.

References

Czerniawska, Fiona (2007). "Ensuring Sustainable Value from Consultants", *http://dx.doi.org/10.4468/2007.1.05czerniawska*

Goldsmith, M. and M. McLeod (2008). "Thought Leadership", *Leadership Excellence* 25(2): 2-13.

Owen, J. (2009). *How to Lead: What You Actually Need to Do to Manage Lead and Succeed* (2nd Edition). Pearson Prentice Hall.

Ryde, R. (2007). *Thought Leadership: Moving Hearts and Minds.* Palgrave Macmillan.

Business Standard, 11 December 2010.

IX

Newest Concerns

59

Demonetisation

An (un) Necessary Evil?

Fears of a GDP (gross domestic product) setback from the government's demonetisation action are unfounded. At the macroeconomic level, whatever is the amount of black money coming into banks by December 31 and into the Reserve Bank of India (RBI) by March 31, would be estimated by RBI on March 31—what has come in and what has not—in comparison with the cash earlier issued by it. RBI will thus arrive at a calculation of change in its liabilities, and quantify mismatched assets and liabilities in its balance sheet. It will then return some government bonds it holds thus enabling government to increase spending and, in turn, restoring GDP to normal. Also, the view that black money holders will find refuge in gold is based on merchants assuming tax evaders' risk by accepting old ₹500 and ₹1,000 notes since, until December 31, that is legal. Unlikely again, since currently risk aversion is pervasive.

The problems lie elsewhere. First, consider why demonetisation was rendered essential. The lacklustre success of the income tax department (ITD) during previous and current governments to contain black money is one explanation. A white paper on black money listed measures they had taken to curb it. It was unconvincing since black money persisted despite those measures. Admittedly, Budget allocation to ITD's investigation function is too small compared to needs, in contrast to the Budget for fruitless routine assessment of all taxpayers, an uncorrected imbalance even after the Tax Administration Reform Commission (TARC) made its recommendations. If the recommended reallocation of staff resources were undertaken, black money could have been unearthed in a more unobtrusive, imperceptible and consistent manner.

Second, the government's Income Declaration Scheme (IDS) initially reported a base of ₹5,000 crore from undisclosed foreign accounts, followed by ₹65,250 crore of undeclared income in cash and other assets in India that was "likely to be further revised upwards". While the ₹5,000 crore base was believable, the ₹65,250 crore number requires deconstruction. It is likely to reflect to no small extent the expected outcomes of already ongoing actions of the tax or intelligence departments. After all, income tax officers are regularly carrying out investigation and search and seizure so that they continually gather information and possess expected collection estimates from such activities. Only if and when the government releases a breakup of the sources of the ₹65,250 crore could one assess the nature and reality behind it. Also, how much tax can be procedurally recovered from this tax base remains unclear.

It would be superfluous to repeat the inequity that emanates between good and bad taxpayers from repetitive tax amnesties irrespective of the government, a habitual quick fix of Indian policymakers that could only have exacerbated tax evasion behaviour over decades as is well known from international experience.

Lamentably, India continues to eschew benchmarking itself with other tax administrations or prevalent good practice elsewhere.

Third, tax avoidance—and evasion—occurs even in the organised sector through tax base depletion reflecting misapplication, misuse or illegal use of incentives and deductions, thus adding to the tax gap. The government's annual revenue loss calculation presented to Parliament in every Union Budget—we introduced this international practice in 2006—is testimony to tax base depletion. Yet this government too has done little to cut back incentives and has indeed given more of them for ever new so called leading sectors, benefitting primarily the already rich and wealthy. The Union finance minister's promise to bring down headline corporate tax rate to 25 per cent remains unfulfilled though he mentions its need occasionally.

Fourth is impact on the poor. To hear leaders opine that farmers can also put their money into banks is reminiscent of a policymaker of the previous government asserting to me that there must be a ration shop every 50 yards. The current authorities may take a few trips to India's deep interiors to view if all farmers do, or can, access banks and how far is their nearest bank; a mere statistic regarding new bank accounts is insufficient. Policymakers would realise that not just tax evaders, smugglers or terrorists use cash, but also the poor. Neither have the leaders of democracy been observed to queue at banks like the urban commoner. Thus, it is ironic for political representatives to proclaim that the entire country is with them. It reveals little reality check of the vast ocean of ordinary Indians.

Sadly, the suffering of the poor and the sick could have been averted. For such deeply cross-cutting action, the government should have had ready countermeasures to ensure the poor did not go unfed and the sick received treatment. Reports indicate that daily sellers in Kolkata's vegetable and fish markets were unable to sell since bangali babus do their shopping with ₹500 notes—understandably, given fish prices per kilo. Fish rotted. The sufferer was not the buyer but the seller whose daily earning feeds the family. Such examples abound.

Understood that the government's action had to be kept secret for effective outcome. But news flashes, for example, that ₹3 crore were deposited in old 500s and 1000s by government's political party, or its use of new 2000s, just before the demonetisation announcement, are disturbing. The government's full explanation is warranted. Indeed, the prime minister's advisers should have counselled him to leave behind a national address before being flashed on a Japanese bullet train ostensibly pursuing the luxury Mumbai-Ahmedabad bullet train project. A prior address would have been reassuring and effective rather than exhorting punishment post-event from Goa's shores. Is the team that assured him that it would be just a two-day pain being asked to resign or is absence of accountability being ignored as always?

Finally, further draconian policy could be expected to square the circle. Complementary would be reinstatement of the Bank Cash Transactions Tax that was introduced, and removed, by the previous government despite BCTT's success in diminishing fictitious long-term—therefore untaxable—capital gains by limiting the high velocity of bank transactions that illegally converted black money into white. Whatever occurs ahead, a monitoring cell should be established to minimise adversity, reflecting its gravity, for honest taxpayers and the vulnerable.

Business Standard, 15 November 2016.

60

Ease of Doing Business (EDB) Cross-Country Indicators

As 2016 nears its end, the World Bank has just published the cross-country *Doing Business Database 2017*, the basis for the assessment here. India's ranking has changed from 131 to 130 out of 190 countries. This is not good news in the midst of the challenges of demonetisation and its likely short term dampening of GDP growth that will take time to recover. Unless there are countering improvements such as in EDB, growth will be a mounting challenge in the short to medium run, as is already being talked about in government circles.

Table 60.1 shows EDB rankings for the US, the UK and BRICS since they are trading partners as well as competitors. India lingers at the bottom. While these countries have all worsened a bit—other than, of course, China—India remains last. Further, Table 60.1 reveals the UK and the US as holding 7th and 8th EDB ranks respectively, while Brazil (123rd) and India (130th) are close competitors at the bottom. Thus, there is no need to justify legitimate worries regarding the unlikelihood of success of India's current attempts for Make in India.

The stubbornness of India's low overall EDB ranking leads one to examine India's EDB component indicators (Table 60.2). Amazingly, getting electricity has improved by a whopping 25 ranks, taking India to the 26th rank out of 190, while the next best is for enforcing contracts (by 6 ranks), nevertheless keeping India at the 172nd rank. Disappointingly, there has been no improvement at all in the ease of paying taxes, languishing at 172nd rank. And dealing with construction permits has worsened (by 1 rank), with a present rank of 185th.

Table 60.1

Ease of Doing Business Ranking (of 190 Countries)

Rank	*2017*	*2016*
United Kingdom	7	6
United States	8	7
Russian Federation	40	36
South Africa	74	72
China	78	80
Brazil	123	121
India	130	131

Table 60.2

India: EDB Ranking and Change

Indicators	*2017*	*2016*	*Change*
Ease of Doing Business	130	131	1
Getting Electricity	26	51	25
Enforcing Contracts	172	178	6
Registering Property	138	140	2
Trading Across Borders	143	144	1
Paying Taxes	172	172	0
Dealing with Construction Permits	185	184	-1
Resolving Insolvency	136	135	-1
Getting Credit	44	42	-2
Protecting Minority Investors	13	10	-3
Starting a business	155	151	-4

Since in this jumble of numbers the improvement in getting electricity stands out, it calls for an examination by a fine toothed comb (Table 60.3). Four criteria—number of procedures, days needed for connectivity, cost as per cent of income per capita, reliability of supply—define electricity and an averaging procedure yields its score (the same process is used to derive scores for all indicators).

Table 60.3 shows the electricity scores for the worst and best global performers, together with how India's scores fit in between. It reveals that India is much better than the worst and has actually

Figure 60.1

Cross-Country Changes in Indicators

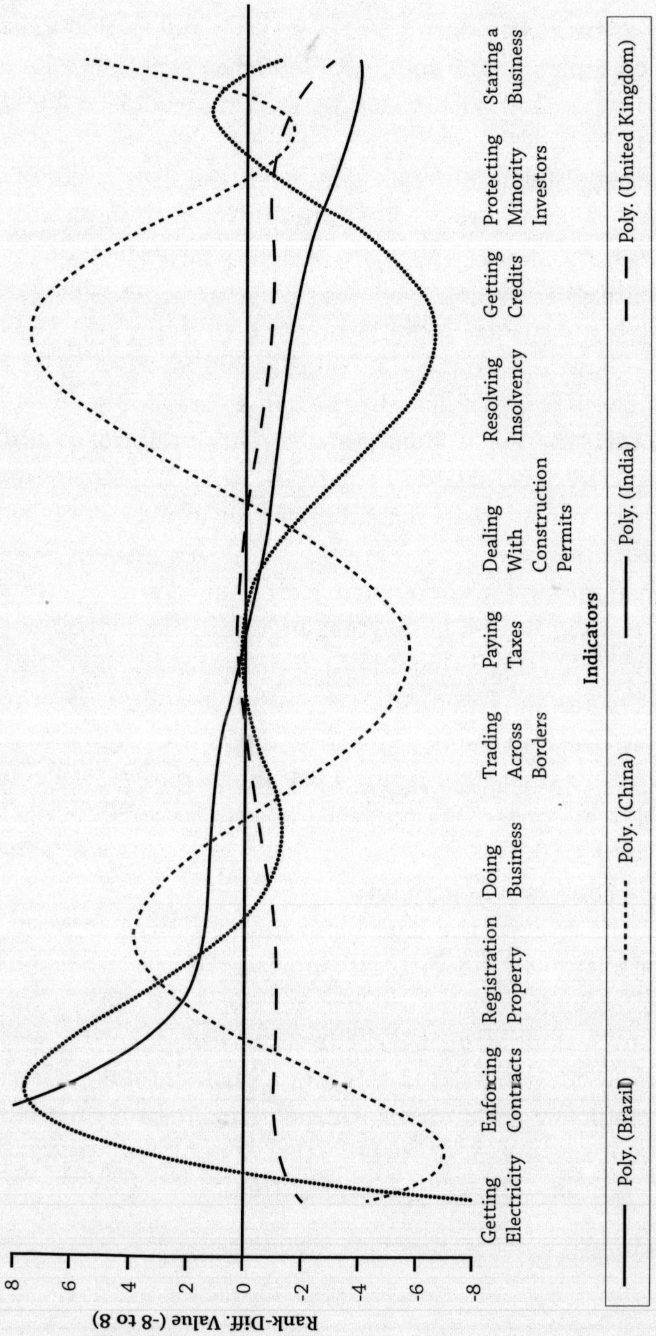

improved significantly during 2016. The flip side is that electricity seems to be explaining much of why India has maintained its overall EDB position at 130. Otherwise its ranking would certainly have worsened.

Accordingly, Table 60.4 calculates what the EDB rankings would have been without the electricity indicator for the sample countries. The procedure removed the score for electricity from the total of 10 EDB indicators and recalculated the score as an average of the remaining 9 indicators. India is revealed to decline to 143rd rank from 130. South Africa, the US, China would improve in their EDB rankings; the UK would remain the same; Brazil and India would worsen; India, the most. Thus the electricity indicator is really the supportive criterion that has kept India at its 130 score—however low it may be considered—for, otherwise, it would have fallen even more, to 143.

This is alarming for government's attempt to attract investment. Government can emphasise start-ups and incentives but, in a globalised world, there remains little incentive to invest in India when, for example, a depreciated pound sterling makes it more attractive to invest in the UK. This is on top of UK's high EDB ranking of 7. Indeed, to elaborate, Figure 60.1 shows how a stable location for EDB should appear to a potential investor: the 2016-17 changes are the least for UK for the 10 component indicators while those for Brazil, China and India vary a lot.

To conclude, even the low EDB rank of India has managed to maintain itself due to the electricity indicator. It is worth emphasising that India's ease of paying taxes has not improved. Other important criteria such as dealing with construction permits, resolving insolvency, getting credit, or starting a business have worsened, a far cry from policy declarations. Unless sharp improvements in EDB are achieved, any dream of manufacturing occupying a significantly higher per cent of GDP will remain just that.

Table 60.3

Getting Electricity Indicator

Indicators	*Best*	*Worst performance*	*India*	
		2017	*2017*	*2016*
Procedures (number)	3	9	5	5
Time (days)	18	248	46	87
Cost (% of income per capita)	0	8,100	133	442
Reliability of supply and transparency of tariffs index (0-8)	8	0	7	7

Table 60.4

EDB Ranking without Electricity

	EDB RANK 2017	
Country	*Overall*	*Excluding Getting Electricity*
Brazil	123	134
China	78	77
India	130	143
Russian Federation	40	49
South Africa	74	72
United Kingdom	7	7
United States	8	5

Business Standard, 14 December 2016.

Supplementary Readings

Below are listed several readings mainly in the field of taxation as well as development issues that the author has written in the form of his own authored volume, or has published as the main editor of a volume, or has published as one of the contributors in a volume edited by another author. It is a short and selective list for the reader who is interested in further readings. For a longer list of the author's writings, please contact the author at *parthoshome@itraf.org*.

Shome, Parthasarathi (ed.) (2016a). *Base Erosion and Profit Shifting (BEPS): The Global Taxation Agenda*. Bangalore: International Tax Research and Analysis Foundation (ITRAF) and New Delhi: Wolters Kluwer.

__________. (ed.) (2016b). *Insights into Evolving Issues of Taxation: Existing and Continuing Challenges*. Bangalore: International Tax Research and Analysis Foundation (ITRAF) and New Delhi: Wolters Kluwer.

__________. (ed.) (2015). *The G20 Development Agenda: An Indian Perspective*. New Delhi: Cambridge University Press.

__________. (2014a). *Taxation Principles and Applications: A Compendium*. New Delhi: Lexis Nexis.

__________. (2014b). *Tax Administration Reform in India: Spirit, Purpose and Empowerment* (6 Volumes). Report of the Tax Administration Reform Commission (TARC) (Chairman: Parthasarathi Shome). Ministry of Finance, New Delhi, available at: *http://finmin. nic.in/the_ministry/dept_revenue/tarc_report.asp*

__________ (ed.) (2014c). *The G20 Macroeconomic Agenda: India and the Emerging Economies*. New Delhi: Cambridge University Press.

__________ (ed.) (2013a). *Indian Tax Administration: A Dialogue*. New Delhi: Orient Blackswan.

__________. (2013b). "Political Economy of Debt Accumulation and Fiscal Adjustment in a Financial Crisis," in Deepak Mohanty (ed.), *Monetary Policy, Sovereign Debt and Financial Stability: The New Trilemma*. New Delhi: Cambridge University Press.

__________. (2012a). *Tax Shastra: Administrative Reforms in India, United Kingdom and Brazil*. New Delhi: Business Standard Books.

__________. (2012b). "Rebalancing and Structural Policies: An Indian Perspective," *Oxford Review of Economic Policy* 28(3): 587-602.

__________. (2011). "Fiscal Stimuli and Consolidation," in Olivier J. Blanchard, David Romer, Michael Spence and Joseph E. Stiglitz (ed.), *In the Wake of the Crisis: Leading Economists Reassess Economic Policy*. International Monetary Fund. Cambridge, Massachusetts: M.I.T Press.

__________. (2002). *India's Fiscal Matters*. New Delhi: Oxford University Press.

__________ (2001). *Tax Policy and Tax Administration for the Tenth Five Year Plan*. Report of the Advisory Group (Chairman: Parthasarathi Shome). New Delhi: Planning Commission, Government of India.

__________(ed.) (1997a). *Fiscal Policy, Public Policy & Governance*. New Delhi: Centax Publications Pvt. Ltd.

__________ (1997b). *India: Tax Policy for the Ninth Five Year Plan* (1997-98 to 2001-02) (Chairman: Parthasarathi Shome). New Delhi: Centax Publications Pvt. Ltd.

__________ (ed.) (1995). *Tax Policy Handbook*. Washington, D.C.: International Monetary Fund.

__________ (ed.) (1986). *Fiscal Issues in South-East Asia: Comparative Studies*. New York and Singapore: Oxford University Press.

Shome, Parthasarathi and Christian Schutte (1993). "Cash-Flow Tax, *Staff Papers* 40(3): 638-62. Washington D.C.: International Monetary Fund

Shome, Parthasarathi, Bernardi,L. and Fraschini, A. (ed.) (2006). *Tax Systems and Tax Reforms in South and East Asia*. London: Routledge.